RACE TO JUSTICE

She Was The Darling Of The Indy 500
Teams... Until She Was Murdered

LARRY SELLS
MARGIE PORTER

WILDBLUE
PRESS

WildBluePress.com

RACE TO JUSTICE published by:
WILDBLUE PRESS
P.O. Box 102440
Denver, Colorado 80250

WILDBLUE PRESS is registered at the U.S. Patent and Trademark Offices.

ISBN 978-1-948239-23-3   Trade Paperback
ISBN 978-1-948239-22-6   eBook

Interior Formatting/Book Cover Design by Elijah Toten
www.totencreative.com

RACE TO JUSTICE

CHAPTER 1

November 15, 1992

The meat locker bite of November winds chafed the flesh of the three rabbit hunters. Dreary skies cast a haunting fog through stark branches. The hunters were having no luck. An army of bunnies could nest beneath the slender trees, camouflaged amongst millions of windswept leaves.

DeMotte, Indiana police officer Kevin Jones, and his two neighbors, Bill Whitis and Terry Ward, kept a keen eye on the landscape that Sunday afternoon. Where there were rabbits, coyotes and wolves also roamed close by.

The rural wooded area, owned by a local woman named Mrs. McFarland, lay a mile from the interstate, one quarter mile west of County Line Road, and along a dirt path. The place was good for hunting but also frequented by daredevils on all-terrain vehicles. It was an illegal dumpsite too, as evidenced by aging appliances and outcast furniture.

Jones, Whitis, and Ward wended their way through naked tree limbs, marking the air with ghostly breaths. Then Jones spied what appeared to be a discarded mannequin about twenty yards away. The men stepped closer. Maybe not a mannequin? It looked so real. Maybe someone drugged or drunk? Possibly. There was a nudist colony a mere mile down the road.

The ivory limbs peeking through the leaves were no passed out nudist. This was a young woman, clearly dead.

None of the men recognized her. There had been no recent reports in the area of a missing woman.

The body was that of a nude, slender white female. She appeared young, twenties or early thirties. Her pale skin wore a crust of fallen leaves and slivers of snow. One arm lay to her side, the other flopped across her abdomen.

Animals had come to sample the corpse, leaving nibble marks in the flesh on both feet, her upper right chest, and her left upper arm. Tan lines showed she had worn both a bikini and a one-piece swimsuit. Knobby knees projected from her slim legs. Her left ankle was adorned with two delicate gold chains: one plain, the other with three joined hearts.

Sexual assault was not likely, as evidenced by a tampon string dangling from her vagina.

Cold weather had slowed decomposition of the corpse. It would be difficult to identify the young woman. Her head and neck had been severed near the collarbone by some sort of serrated blade. It was not with the body.

As a police officer, Jones understood the need to preserve the crime scene. No one in his group touched the body or removed anything lying on or near it.

Officer Jones called for his friend Mr. Whitis "to run to my house and to notify the state police and to tell them what I had there and also there is an officer at the scene." He said, "It was probably a good hundred yards across the field to my house."

The call went out just after three p.m., but afternoon shadows had already begun to wisp through the lonely woods when Indiana state police investigators arrived. They lined up their vehicles along the dirt path and hiked about eighty feet through the woods to the crime scene.

An immediate search of the area turned up neither the victim's head nor a murder weapon. Soil samples were taken, but by five p.m., winter darkness blanketed any attempts to search further. A more thorough investigation would have to wait until the following day. Investigators hoped to identify the woman through the shriveled remnants of her fingerprints.

The leaves covering the body were collected, and then she was wrapped in a sheet and placed inside a body bag. Newton County Coroner Gerald A. Burman took the body to the Tippecanoe County Morgue in West Lafayette for autopsy.

The only potential evidence found was a piece of Styrofoam lying in the dirt beneath the corpse. A red rag hugged the ground fifty feet southeast of the site, and a piece of cloth lay seventy-five feet east. Investigators marked off the area with crime scene tape as darkness smothered the lonely saplings.

Investigators converged on the area the next morning to reexamine the slip of ground where the body had lain and to scour the surrounding area for clues. Indiana State Police Detective Sergeant William F. Krueger met with Detective Sergeant Richard Ludlow. Technicians called to the scene included Sergeant Rick Griswell, Sergeant Dave Kintzele, Gary Ekart, and Ken Buehrle.

The officers examined the area in a four hundred foot radius from the body's dumpsite. They combed an adjacent area containing items of trash for the missing head. The team also searched the sides of the field road and Jasper/Newton County Line Road. They found nothing but a silver and black PPG jacket in a ditch on the west side of County Line Road, about two hundred-fifty feet south of the dirt lane. The jacket did not appear to be evidence, but they collected it.

The young woman was no longer abandoned to the weather and the rats. Was she just another druggie, homeless and friendless? Surely she was someone's daughter, girlfriend, cousin, friend. The missing head could keep her nameless for years.

She would be easier to identify if anyone was actually looking for her.

CHAPTER 2

May 1992

The shock of the drive-by broke the peace of a perfect spring evening in Speedway, Indiana. The softball players stood on the field, open and defenseless. After a grueling and intense day at the Indianapolis Motor Speedway, members of the Marlboro-Penske team had escaped to a local park and challenged some other teams to a pickup game. Eager to unwind, drivers and mechanics were soon involved in the game, whooping and cheering the daring moves of team members and competitors alike.

A rented white cargo van swooped into the tidy small town park. The victims knew their attackers. The aggressors were three women who had tantalized them with a hot meal just hours before. Cynthia Albrecht, the thirty-one-year-old executive chef for Penske's Race Team, grinned with anticipation. Pretty and vivacious with blonde curls that bounced to her shoulders, Cindy exuded energy.

Cindy was joined by her best friends and partners in crime, Sandra Fink and Rebecca Miller. Cindy was the Penske Team's heartbeat, the personification of an enduring folk song. Sandi Fink, blonde and svelte, was their Barbie doll. Playful and stylish, she moved like soft rock. Jazzy little Becky Miller, the bright-eyed brunette, was quick and impromptu, always eager to swing into the next adventure.

As cooks for Penske, the three were acquainted with all the drivers, but they aimed their van toward Penske drivers Rick

Mears and Emerson Fittipladi. Their crew chiefs Richard Buck and Rick Rinaman were also targeted. The assault came as a shock and everyone on the field began ducking and running — and laughing, as the three women pelted them with grapes, orange slices, kiwi, and strawberries.

"They loved it," Becky remembers. "We cleaned out the fruit basket that we stocked every day." Before any player could react, much less throw anything back, the three women sped away, cheering themselves for a successful drive-by fruiting.

"Did you see their faces?"

"We totally shocked them."

"Bet they can't make those moves in a race car."

Cindy, Sandi, and Becky were all married women whispering into their thirties but "acted like teenagers," Sandi says. "We were silly and goofy and bought each other underwear... it was a great time." And they danced with the thrill of being a part of IndyCar racing.

The race circuit was pure adrenaline. It had everything three young women could want: fast cars, excitement, travel. But most of all, the respect of their peers. Among Penske's IndyCar tribe, there was no pecking order. The hospitality team was held in no less esteem than drivers were. "We were family, all of us," Sandi says.

In the IndyCar community, team lines were fluid. If the women needed some tall guys with muscle to upright a tent, they only needed to ask. If Mary-Lin Murphy of Newman/Haas needed to borrow an ingredient, someone would gladly lend it.

Guests to the Penske hospitality tent included the cast of *90210* and George Harrison of Beatles fame. George made his way to the kitchen with his beautiful wife Olivia. Coffee was the hot beverage beneath the tent that day and the charming couple approached the cooks to ask for a cup of tea. Other VIPs included Donald Trump, General Norman Schwarzkopf, and Colonel Oliver North.

Food from the hospitality tent fueled much of the event, as no one had time to exit the track for a meal. No one wanted to leave anyway. The hospitality food could top the fare offered at any restaurant and it was plentiful enough to keep a hungry man hustling—no bologna sandwiches or limp noodle soup for these guys!

The parade of hot meals included Lobster Newburg, grilled blackened salmon with dill sauce, and southwest chicken with Mexican rice. Breakfast could include lox, caviar, omelets, and heart-shaped waffles with fresh fruit.

The Food Network channel had not yet been launched. If it had, Cindy could have starred on the channel as a gourmet chef. Her specialty was leg of lamb with fresh rosemary and mint. She had the talent to create her own sauces and dressings. The stylish Brazilian driver Emerson Fittipaldi liked to eat turkey on whole wheat with olive oil and red onion just before qualifying or racing. Cindy always made it just for him.

The three Penske hostesses were all married to IndyCar mechanics and met each other through their husbands. They traveled to all the races and made friends all over the country, but none of the events could top their hometown race, the Indianapolis 500, which is still the single biggest one-day sporting event in the world.

In 1992, Penske ran a three-car team, about fifty crewmembers. Another two hundred-fifty people, including sponsors, media, and special guests, were served at each meal. The hospitality tent buzzed like a school cafeteria. The service had to be fast, almost choreographed. Guests applauded the food as fabulous. Even on a budget, Cindy could dream up artistic meals which satisfied everyone from executives to famished mechanics.

The entire team embraced the Penske Way. In everything they did, their performance was to be exemplary. They were to be professional at all times. Presentation of the food first class. Most importantly, they were never, ever to run out of food.

Meals were cooked in a fourteen-foot trailer, its appliances and counters wedged in place with mathematical precision. Efficiency demanded the trailer carry all the cookware and service utensils needed to feed a variety of food to hundreds of people.

Penske hospitality was a team of five persons, the three hostesses and two men, working under the direction of Pete Twiddy. A born leader, Pete was the Marlboro side of Marlboro-Penske. In his trademark jeans and flip-flops, he was a bright-eyed and fluid guy on the beach, unhindered by his 6'8" height.

Canadian Glen Smith, tall and rugged, was Pete's right-hand man. He was humorous and ended his sentences with "eh." He was very protective of the women.

Smith and Bob Lawes, a British Adonis in short shorts, shared duties of transportation, setting up, and overseeing hospitality. Pete represented Marlboro while Lawes made sure the interests of the Penske family were respected. Working in sync, the five set up the awning, tables, chairs, and the buffet. "If we were on grass instead of concrete, we might lay down artificial grass to keep mud from guests' shoes," Lawes recalls.

All through the race they cooked, cleaned, and served and delivered food. Then they tore it all down and moved on to the next city on the race circuit. "Sometimes," Lawes recalls, "we'd be cleaning up a Sunday race and hurrying to get to the next race."

Each cook had assigned duties and a designated work area. Cindy created main courses, Sandi usually prepared desserts, while Becky was a sous chef, meaning she chopped tons of vegetables and juggled a myriad of other tasks.

From their trailer, the cooks could not see the race but they were very much a part of the excitement. The energy vibrated all over the Indianapolis Motor Speedway, and it was contagious.

Roger's rule was no alcohol would be served before the checkered flag, but once the race ended, Pete would say, "Make cocktails, girls. Make cocktails." They were also to keep champagne chilled and ready to pour in case a Penske driver won the race.

Becky says, "It was like Christmas every day, but very tiring." Although the race season only runs from April to October, the hospitality people who worked all the races were considered full time because the long hours over those frantic months equaled the hours a normal worker would log during a calendar year.

Bob Lawes says the schedule was nonstop. Sometimes they set out snacks for after the race and started tearing down to be off to the next race site by Tuesday. He recalls one weary morning when they were traveling to the track at five-thirty a.m.; Cindy was riding shotgun, singing cheerily with the radio. Bob, sitting in the back seat, asked who the song artist was. She told him and he said, "Well, why don't you let them sing it?"

Cindy turned, fuming, and smacked at him playfully. Bob says he can remember nothing but good times with Cindy, even though they were chronically exhausted and frequently under pressure.

Of course, they weren't the only team members racing the clock. Sometimes, Becky says, some driver or crewmember, due to car issues or other problems, would have no time to eat. They'd stand across the fence in Gasoline Alley and yell out, "Throw me a banana!" The women responded, flinging the fruit to their starving comrade or passing over a sandwich. The food was delivered with good wishes and the promise of more substantial fare later.

The trailer had no storage space and the women launched into the weekend running a grocery shopping marathon.

"We'd trailer carts through the store," Sandi recalls, "and the bill would be, like, two thousand dollars."

Sandi's well-honed organizational skills enabled her to memorize the layout of all the grocery stores they used, from Pennsylvania to California. Cindy would hand the grocery list over to Sandi and have her organize it in the order of the aisles to save time.

Grocery shopping became an adventure in itself. First of all, the hospitality team was given thousands of dollars in cash to buy food at the beginning of the season. Becky says, "In May, that could be thirty thousand dollars, so we'd hide it in our pants, carry it inside our jackets, just stuff it all over the place, and act all innocent."

Cindy prowled the perishable departments, seeking ideas for tantalizing meals. She selected spices to blend into her own salad dressings. She bought packages of edible flowers and exotic vegetables that looked like they were fighting their way through puberty. Sandi describes Thumbelina baby carrots as "squirrelly-looking, stubby carrots with long strings on them." Cindy was horrified when Becky, while cleaning this alien produce, cut the strings off, but the women claim no one ever ate those carrots anyway.

Becky recalls that Cindy would eat anything, or at least try it. That would have been fine, except Cindy insisted her friends also try calamari, and cheese that smelled like an outhouse, and unpronounceable foods probably designed as torture by the CIA. Becky laughs, remembering, "If I wouldn't try something, she'd shove it in my mouth or just smear it on my face."

The cucumber game was Cindy's invention. When they shopped, she awarded the vegetable to whoever guessed closest to the register total. Becky claims Sandi always won, and usually guessed within ten dollars. "And she'd never guess an ordinary round number. She'd come up with some weird figure, like, $2,071.42, and she'd be maybe just a few dollars off."

The money was never really a game to Cindy. She kept careful watch over Penske's money. It was a matter of honor to her that the receipts and money matched to the penny. Between shopping trips, all the cash, including the loose change, stayed in a separate compartment in her travel bag.

On the way through the store, Sandi and Becky made a game of slipping items into Cindy's cart: adult diapers, feminine hygiene, dog treats, nasal spray... just any unexpected item that might startle her at the register. Now the women claim that when they're shopping, an odd item will simply fall off the shelf in front of them. They say it happens a lot. "And we'll be like, hi, Cindy!"

Whether shopping, working, or just being together, the trio had spontaneous fun. But not everyone was laughing with them.

CHAPTER 3

Sandi Fink's life revolved around racing. She worked with several IndyCar teams as a timer/scorer using the new Data Speed computer technology, one of the only positions open to women in racing. Then, in 1991, her job became obsolete. She says, "Basically, the timing and scoring technology overtook it. They started doing the timing with devices inside the car."

Cindy and Sandi's husbands, Michael Albrecht and Mike Fink, were IndyCar mechanics. Sandi and Mike were an easygoing couple, comfortable socializing together. The Albrechts seemed less in tandem.

If Cindy was sunshine, Michael was thunder. Dark and brooding, he stood ten inches taller than his wife and tried to keep her in his shadow. He had a reputation as a bully. Co-workers dubbed him "Crabby." Mike Fink was also big and powerfully built, but sociable with a quick smile.

Both worked for Dick Simon Racing. Cindy loved racing as much as Sandi did and the women quickly became fast friends, each couple dining at the other's home on occasion. Both were dazzling cooks.

Cindy's cooking skills had earned her a place in IndyCar hospitality, which was becoming the latest cutting edge for teams to showcase hot race cars and even hotter drivers. This was a rare opportunity. Women had only recently been allowed into Gasoline Alley at the Indianapolis Motor Speedway.

Cindy and Sandi were as good a team as Ben & Jerry. Cindy had mastered entrees and spices; Sandi was queen of pastries and desserts. The popularity of the Marlboro-Penske hospitality increased exponentially. Soon, a third person was needed.

When Sandi's good friend Becky Miller came on board, the bond was instant and unbreakable. All three had great culinary skills. They could have been sisters. Becky's husband Kirk also worked for Dick Simon Racing. Dark haired and tan, Kirk lived in work boots but moved as if he wore roller blades.

Sandi and Becky say Cindy was sort of a tomboy when they met her. She had a great personality, but she wore shapeless clothing and her hair looked like it had fallen asleep. They gathered Cindy under their wings. They took her to get her prematurely gray hair highlighted. They encouraged her to wear makeup and they bought her cute clothes to wear instead of her habitual men's t-shirts and jeans.

Along with these confidence builders, Cindy lost weight, about twenty-five pounds. Her newfound attractiveness bothered her husband, but Becky and Sandi cheered Cindy for leaving her shell.

The trio loved buying each other gag gifts, but honed in on Cindy's granny panties. They could not believe she would wear such non-fashionable undergarments and they introduced her to Victoria's Secret. They bought her beautiful lingerie. Becky and Sandi, happy in their own marriages, did not realize Cindy did not wish to entice her husband. They found out later that she saved the lingerie and wore it for Pete Twiddy, who was handsome, enthusiastic, highly motivated, and successful. He also made Cindy feel pretty.

Among the race circuit, Cindy's nickname became Ellie Mae. With her blonde curls flashing in the sunlight, she reminded people of the Clampett daughter from *The Beverly Hillbillies*. She was also like the Ellie Mae actress, Donna

Douglas, in the way she greeted everyone with a dazzling smile. And she loved animals, all animals. She contributed money to wildlife groups.

Don't be late was Roger Penske's primary rule for all employees and Cindy would never risk tardiness unless she had a dire emergency, like she needed to stop and help an injured squirrel. Becky tried to point out that they had hundreds of squirrels but just one job—and a great one at that. Cindy might have listened to Becky if she'd had fur, a tail, and twitching ears.

But Cindy's greatest passion was for people. A couple of scruffy, motorcycle gang types the women referred to as Hutch and Wayne came around at the Toronto race. "They looked like ZZ Topp," Sandi says. In 1991, the women were working and heard a scuffle outside their kitchen window. Hutch and Wayne were hurt and Cindy immediately invited them to come inside the trailer.

Alarmed, Sandi pleaded, "Don't let them in here!"

But Cindy was already bringing out bandages and saying, "You're a human being. You are bleeding. Come here. Here's some water. Let me tape you up."

It turned out the scuffle was a takedown and Hutch and Wayne were undercover cops. "Deep, deep undercover," Sandi says. "No one would have ever known." Because of Cindy's compassion, Hutch and Wayne took all three women out for a meal that night and they all became great friends. Becky and Sandi are still in cahoots with their favorite constables. Hutch and Wayne are now both retired from the Toronto Police Department but still keep in touch.

Marlboro sponsorship had its benefits. "Back in the day, we were allowed to give away cigarettes," Sandi recalls. Cigarettes were on all the tables. The team had cases and cases of free product and could give them away by the carton. The free cigarettes lured a twenty-eight-year-old woman named Susie Harmon.

Tiny, dark haired Susie was sometimes stoned but was a decent girl with many problems. Her boyfriend Lee Kunzman was an older racer. She stayed with him and he looked after her. They all felt sorry for her, but Becky and Sandi cringed when she came around, fearing her presence would dull the shine on the Penske reputation.

"But Cindy was always so nice to her and she'd always give her cigarettes and a plate of food," Sandi says. The pair tried to warn Cindy it wasn't good for the team's image to have Susie seen around their hospitality area, but Cindy always defended her, saying, "Oh, she's a nice girl. She won't stay long after she gets her cigarettes." And she was right!

The Reverend Phil DeRea, a mirthful, barrel-chested, Washington, DC Catholic priest, served as chaplain to the IndyCar circuit. Each Sunday before Mass, Cindy greeted him with a big smile as she served him breakfast. "Say a prayer for me, Father," she would say. "You know I can't be there."

The women worked long hours, often from predawn until after a late cocktail hour. Their work was not completed until every person was served and everything was cleaned up. They also had to prep for the next day and go over the menu to make sure they had everything. Many nights on their way to the hotel, they stopped to pick up more groceries.

Sometimes Cindy would get an after-hours call at home. More people were coming. Add meals. A CEO required a specialty dish. The women had to be flexible to allow for these sudden changes.

The workload could be daunting, but Cindy, Sandi, and Becky were having the time of their lives. Working together in the food trailer, the trio developed a dance routine to Aretha Franklin's song, "Respect." They gyrated in unison, shouting out, "R-E-S-P-E-C-T!" and high-fived each other. Cindy belted out the song in a voice Sandi says sounded like

Karen Carpenter's. It seemed like the more fun they had, the more people wanted to join the crowd at their tent.

One day they were practicing the routine, swishing around each other with oven mitts on their hands. Penske team coordinator Tim Lombardi caught them in the act. Laughter shook him to his toes.

Pete Twiddy often insisted they perform another routine for everyone. They had adapted an old classic, "King of the Road," to poke fun at a media writer who complained they lacked chopped onions for his hot dog. "Hot dogs for sale or rent!" they'd sing. "Buns are just fifty cents. No onions, no pickles today. Go to the concession stand if you want it that way!" The song continued, earning the trio a reputation for sass.

Garth Brooks, who was a rising country singer at the time, recorded Cindy's favorite music. Brooks first gained national recognition at Fan Fair in 1989 as a new artist for Capitol Records. Two years later, in 1991, he was named the Country Music Association's Entertainer of the Year. Cindy adored Brooks' music, but not for its popularity. The young singer performed with an authentic, navel-deep emotion that embraced her. His intensity and air of confidence matched Cindy's.

Brooks sang about rodeo riding, the transforming power of love, and the need for people to cherish each other. Cindy's favorite Brooks' song was "The Dance," a wistful ballad about death and loss and knowing there was nothing that could replace the time you had together with the one you lost.

Cindy attended Brooks' "Shameless" tour and prized the white t-shirt she bought with his face and cowboy hat. "Shameless" was Brooks' hit about loving without reservation and Cindy used to say, "I'd pay five hundred dollars to hear him sing that song." Cindy was so tiny the t-shirt fit her as a sleep shirt.

Brooks' singing career mirrored the blossoming of Cindy's own life. Like him, Cindy found her culinary career surging ahead due to her hard work, persistence, and ability to touch those around her in a meaningful way. For Cindy, hospitality went far beyond food on a plate; it was her best way to connect with people.

"She was one of those people who could light up a room," remembers friend and sometimes co-worker Kim Graham. "Cindy was a delight. She had that ability to make you feel special." Perhaps that was why Cindy felt so connected to the humanity that emanated from Garth Brooks' songs.

The happiness that permeated Cindy's life was not a prize package from heaven. Her habitual smile had not always come easily. She had temporomandibular joint disorder, commonly referred to as TMJ, a misalignment of her jaw. TMJ sufferers endure savage headaches, earaches, and pain in their face, neck, and shoulders. Cindy's parents, who divorced when she was young, could do nothing about it.

On November 1, 1989, Cindy had a Le Fort osteotomy to correct upper and lower jaw deformities. The surgery involves sectioning or repositioning the upper jaw to correct its abnormal position. Her husband Michael claimed he paid thirty to forty thousand dollars for Cindy's facial reconstructive surgery, which utilized titanium and a cadaver jawbone.

Cindy grew up in Hialeah, which is Miami, Florida's version of south Chicago, Harlem, or Watts. It was an impoverished, high-crime area of mostly Cuban residents. Hialeah was the kind of place where people hid their money in the bags of old vacuum cleaners because they expected to be robbed. It was the kind of place where people prayed the explosive noises in the night were just cars backfiring. It was the kind of place where Cindy's alcoholic and dysfunctional parents were nothing unusual.

Housing was crowded and cheap. In Hialeah homes, bugs darted from every crevice. At night, rodents scratched between the too-thin walls, hidden, but leaving evidence of ruin like the dark family secrets which drove Cindy from the house and into an early marriage at seventeen.

The escape was temporary. The marriage lasted barely two years. While Cindy was sleeping one night, her husband came home drunk, attacked her, beating her brutally. The wounds were so savage she had to be hospitalized. Cindy's mother came to the hospital, saw the trauma done to her daughter's body, and said, "Cindy, what did you do to him to make him do this to you?"

"Like it was her fault," Sandi grumbles, "but she was asleep." Cindy never learned what triggered the attack. Possibly the man was just drunk, but Cindy did not stay for round two.

Cindy also disconnected herself from the mother who could not nurture her, and began building her own life. She went to work for Publix Super Markets and rapidly earned a position as a deli manager.

Life in Hialeah diminished multitudes of young women. A tragic number would find themselves trapped between the walls, choiceless, and destined to be beaten down repeatedly.

But the hardship of her early years only made Cindy more feisty. It gave her courage and spunk. Water sports became her passion. Nothing was too challenging for her to try. The faster, the more daring, the more she loved it. It was as if her life craved the world's most thrilling roller coaster. She was determined to find herself a ticket and ride.

Working at the Miami Grand Prix for Provimi Veal, Cindy met Michael Albrecht, a mechanic for the Indy Lights team. He was a handsome man, six feet-five inches tall, with a roguish mustache and a crown of boyish brown curls. They started dating. As a race car mechanic, Michael was powerfully built, with the strength to lift a tire as easily as a basketball. He was also at home on the water.

Cindy had found her prince. He was from Milwaukee but she did not care. She would go anywhere with him. It did not pain her to leave behind the nightmare that was Hialeah.

CHAPTER 4

Cindy moved to Wisconsin and, for a while, worked as Arie Luyendyke Jr.'s nanny. Then she found out Michael was already married. He had a wife named Kathleen and three daughters. But it was too late; Cindy was in love and had moved her entire life to Milwaukee.

Still, she was willing to walk away. Her heart might break, but she would not destroy his marriage. Michael begged her to give him a chance. His marriage was over except for some paperwork, he said. He insisted he loved Cindy and only her. He said it would be all right. She believed him.

Michael divorced his wife and married Cindy. The wedding was at the Mitchell Park Historical Conservatory in Milwaukee, where they made their home. Later, they moved to Indiana to be nearer to the Indianapolis Motor Speedway.

Friends describe a glowing relationship between the two during their first five years of marriage. They seemed to be constantly going places, doing things, always together. When another member of the racing team got married, Michael and Cindy hosted the wedding reception at their home. They invited all their friends to a spectacular dinner party to celebrate Christmas in 1991.

Michael had a broken relationship with his eldest daughter, Noel. "The girl can't even send her dad a birthday card," Cindy fumed. The younger two girls, Missy and Dawn, would come to visit.

When the girls arrived, Cindy dropped everything to do things with them. Michael continued with his work and his life. Nothing took precedence over his career, but the girls were in good hands with Cindy. She made a sincere effort to see they had a good time.

Cindy made a caring connection with everyone she met. One of Roger's rules was *Never run out of food* so the Penske team frequently had food left over. The women packed up the uneaten food and delivered hot meals to workers on other teams, buzzing up to garages on a golf cart with full, steaming trays.

Bob Lawes still chuckles about a day when Cindy neatly aligned metal pans of leftovers on the deck of the golf cart and drove off to serve starving crewmembers. But she misjudged a turn "and all that food slid off onto the ground," Bob says. "She was embarrassed, of course, and just fuming about the wasted food."

On May 15, 1992, during rookie orientation and practice for the Indy 500, Jovy Marcelo came out for warmups. Marcelo had never won an IndyCar race, although he had won races the previous year at Lime Rock Park and Nazareth Speedway, but the twenty-seven-year-old Filipino driver was still little known. At warmup speed, his car snapped around and crashed at the entrance to Turn 1. The young man was killed instantly.

Marcelo was the first driver killed at Indy in ten years. Cindy bought a wreath of flowers to hang on his garage and mourned the racer who had shown so much promise.

In a couple of years on the race circuit, Cindy's career had taken some winning laps. She'd gone from part-time hostess to sous chef to executive chef of a prosperous and winning team. She was well liked and respected. Her job offered her opportunities to meet important people and attend some grand functions.

She was dazzled when the team boarded Roger Penske's private yacht. She loved meeting the crew. Her social life had sped miles past any dreams a Hialeah girl could conjure.

The only thing that put a damper on Cindy's spirit was when her husband Michael stopped attending functions with her. While Cindy's career continued to escalate, his was sinking. He stayed away from the fun, claiming since he was working for a competing team, he could not be associating with Penske team members. Cindy was expected to attend team functions, so she usually went alone, sometimes riding with Mike and Sandi Fink.

If Michael's behavior disappointed Cindy, she did not complain about it. She continued to be the fun and spontaneous young woman who reigned as Miss Popularity among the racing community.

Fruiting became a fun tradition which was endearing to other team members. Sandi recalls the guys yelling, "Here come the girls! Duck!"

One night they had a team dinner, serving steak and lobster in the hospitality area. Roger Penske was there, along with some executives. The celebration morphed into a food fight when some crew guys began throwing cake. Then a banana flew and someone counter-launched a carrot. Roger stepped out of the tent. A couple of the higher-up people wanted Roger to stop the chaos, but he didn't. He knew his people had put in some long, brutal days and needed to blow off steam.

Bob Lawes said Roger was a businessperson to his core, but very fair minded toward his employees. The food fight was acceptable recreation to Roger because the danger of racing magnified the fun times. During the race, the entire team tensed with the knowledge their driver or crewmembers could die suddenly and fiercely.

Cindy, Sandi, and Becky all had husbands working on the other side of the pit wall, where they were often in more danger than the drivers. Fire, a spinning car, or a thrown tire could mangle or kill a man.

The food fight was their joyful sigh of relief that all had gone well for one more day. They took a picture afterward.

Then Becky and Sandi helped clean Cindy up. Seeing herself in such a mess, Cindy's laugh was the joy of heaven. Becky and Sandi plucked banana out of her hair, sprayed her curls, and found her a clean t-shirt. They cleaned her up, literally wiping the smile from her face before she went home. Michael would have a fit if he saw she'd been having so much fun.

No. Michael Albrecht wouldn't like it at all.

CHAPTER 5

Each year, a quarter of a million people pack the seats at the Indianapolis 500-Mile Race. Add to that number the multitudes parked in front of their television sets, and the event generates hiccups of excitement all around the globe.

In 1992, the infield at the Indianapolis Motor Speedway was still open. Four hundred thousand people surged into the 560-acre Speedway to watch a most unusual race. The temperature, hovering around fifty-one degrees, was unexpectedly chilly, but the fans had come to see a spectacle of danger and speed. Adrenaline was hitting on all pistons.

The thrill never got old for Cindy, Sandi, and Becky. They could not see the race from their food service trailer, but they could hear every heartbeat of the event. Cell phones were not yet in common use, so they had to rely on others to tell them if their husbands, working in the pits, came to harm.

In the moments leading up to the start, Roger Penske chauffeured Rick Mears to the starting line in a golf cart. Mears offered the cameras his trademark youthful smile. He had crushed both feet in a September 1984 wreck. Nevertheless, painful walking did not dampen Mears' desire to drive. He was a man with good instincts and sharp eyes. In his youth, he honed his driving skills in desert races. The trick, Mears said, was to "stay on top of it. Drive what you see, not what you know."

Mario Andretti said, "This place, more than any other, will push you to the limit. There comes a time when you… go for it."

Announcers described the race as "a human struggle against all odds" by drivers determined to earn a place in history.

The 76th running of the Indy 500 began in the traditional manner, the crowd falling to silence with the first notes of "The Star Spangled Banner." The American flag waved as four Black Aces flew above the field, paying homage to those who made America free and those who had died in the sport of racing.

Jim Nabors, Gomer Pyle on *The Andy Griffith Show,* sang "Back Home Again in Indiana." The song ended with a balloon launch. Mary Hulman George, chairman of the Indianapolis Motor Speedway and daughter of the late Tony Hulman, who owned the Speedway, yelled into her microphone, the traditional words blasting through the speakers, "Lady and gentlemen, start your engines!"

The crowd and engines roared. Across the wall, the women caught their breaths.

A car not starting was a common problem at the beginning of any 500. Each car had been torn down and reassembled in the previous week. When every engine roared, there was a palpable sigh of relief.

That relief lasted about half a moment. In the first lap, the pace lap, Roberto Guerrero slid out, his cold tires unable to grip the track.

Michael Andretti leapt ahead of Eddie Cheever on that first lap, with Mario Andretti running second. Tom Sneva crashed in the fourth turn, littering the track and forcing the racers into single file. By the 37th lap, the track had become slippery. Michael Andretti continued to lead. His two-way radio failed and he fell back on the old system of communication via hand signals until someone found a thrown switch in the suite.

By lap 48, race announcements were dominated by concern about the debris on the track and questions about whether tires built to withstand heat could perform on a chilly day. "The track is slippery. The guys are going clear down into the grass."

Yes, the track was slippery. But cars weren't the only things sliding off into the grass. Becky and Sandi sat with their good friend, the bright and bubbly Cindy Albrecht, and they could not help worrying about her.

Sandi had been aware of Michael and Cindy's marital problems since October 1991. Michael tried to keep his wife wrenched in close. He wanted Cindy to be working or at home. Period.

Sandi says, "Well, he would fly into rages that scared her, a lot. I mean, she's little compared to him." Sandi had heard that when the couple lived in Milwaukee, "Michael beat the shit out of Cindy."

Not that Cindy would ever admit it, not even to her good friends. Still, it was obvious to them that Cindy's stress levels were zooming from more than the day's race.

"It was usually mental abuse," Sandi says. "He had a violent temper, and with these fights and everything, she just—she was very strong-willed, I think, because of how she grew up and where she grew up, and she would stand her ground, which might not have helped the situation."

Cindy shrugged off their worry and refused to complain. Everything beneath her hood was fine-just-fine, but wasn't that what today's drivers had thought?

On the track, it looked like a one-man race. No one could catch Michael Andretti. Between slide-offs, crashes, and over-heated engines, drivers found themselves off the road. Arie Luyendyke's left rear tire began to vibrate. If his axle gave out... Not yet fifty laps into the race, top drivers were dining on disappointment instead of glory.

Gordon Johncock's engine suffocated from "bad air." Phillipe Gache was not hurt when he wrecked, but another car hit him before he could clear the track. "Debris everywhere," the announcers said. Scott Pruett stalled with an overheated engine. Then somebody hit him. "You see components of the car tearing off and absorbing energy," the speakers boomed. The women flinched.

Stan Fox was almost in a spin himself, trying to avoid the wreck, as an announcer told the crowd, "He was in a drift, trying to get to the left and miss him. You come away really disappointed."

In their trailer on Gasoline Alley, the trio of hostesses shared the anxiety. The race was not supposed to go like this. They cheered that the Penske drivers were still in the race, but they were also on a very treacherous track. Bits of debris could cause anyone to crash.

Michael Andretti still led the remaining cars. Then, on a restart, Emerson Fittipaldi hit the wall. Rick Mears crashed into him. "Both Penske cars out in the same instant," the speakers told the bewildered crowd. Roger Penske had "suffered a tremendous loss in these last few seconds." The announcer described "Penske's two, million-dollar warriors being carted off at the same time."

Another broadcaster rejoined, "There's just nowhere to hide on an oval with a big concrete wall."

A third added, "What an unusual race this has become!" The women agreed, and listened anxiously for news from the track hospital.

By lap 70, Michael Andretti was concerned that he had run over debris on the littered track. Mario Andretti's back end came loose. The race had turned into a demolition derby. The announcers stopped talking about race and speed and commented on dangers, saying, "Once you've gone so far sideways, there's nothing left to do with the steering wheel" and "a crash is a self-fulfilling prophecy because of course it produces the chance for another crash."

A mere hour and twenty minutes after the start, Scott Brayton's motor blew. Jimmy Vasser went into the wall, and Paul Tracey, the third Penske driver, was out of the race.

"It's hard for a driver in a big race like this to have little chance to win but be exposed to all the same dangers," the announcer said. The race favored the experienced drivers. "Guys who can adapt to the situation—and it is changing from lap to lap."

Arie Luyendyke, who had made it to the 130th lap, lost his brakes and went into the wall. "That piece we saw come out has to be a half shaft," the women heard. It sounded like the danger was ratcheting up by the minute.

The race wasn't tragic for everyone. The Canadian Scott Goodyear was having "the best show on an oval of his life."

Then Al Unser Jr. stunned everyone by taking the lead from Michael Andretti. "Where did that come from?" Then Michael took Al. "We're watching a terrific battle for second." Suddenly, everyone focused on the race instead of the wrecks. At 149 laps, Little Al was leading the race.

In the midst of the excitement, Cindy, Sandi, and Becky listened for injury reports. Rick Mears had busted his knees. Jeff Andretti had suffered a concussion and some injuries to his feet and ankles.

An unbelievable turn of events happened when Michael Andretti began to slow down with eleven laps to go. He had dominated the race, leading for 163 laps. "I can't believe it," sputtered Michael's microphone. "The engine quit." From the roar, it was obvious four hundred thousand spectators also could not believe it.

Scott Goodyear began closing in on Little Al Unser, and Unser responded by keeping Goodyear out of his slipstream. "Little Al's making dirty air for Scott Goodyear to run in," the announcer said. Goodyear wasn't backing down. If he could pass, he could win.

The two drivers dared each other through the final lap. No other traffic was involved, just Unser and Goodyear grasping for that checkered flag. In the closest race in Indy history, Little Al beat out his opponent by half a breath.

As Little Al took his swig of milk, emblematic of winning the Indy 500, he told the spectators, "Well, you just don't know what Indy means."

CHAPTER 6

What Indy meant to Michael Albrecht was that he was a loser and it was Cindy's fault. She was the one winning the race to glory while he was left behind to breathe her exhaust and be crippled by the debris of her success.

It wasn't her success anyway. It was his. He was the one who helped her get the job, put in the good words, and did the paperwork. And that famous smile of hers? He paid for that, and it wasn't cheap either. Some houses didn't cost as much as her jawbone.

There were other conflicts too. Sandi recalls that in June, Cindy visited her cute and spunky friend Heidi Dras in Lebanon, Indiana. "She had a couple margaritas with Heidi and her husband" and called Michael for a ride home. "He, of course, was furious, thought something was going on. She just didn't want to drive drunk.

"She went home early the next morning, and he had changed all the locks on the house. He parked his car down at the Kroger in Speedway and walked back to the house." Cindy arrived home while he was parking the car. "It was his intent, from what he said to her, to be in the house when she got home and found... she couldn't get in."

Sometimes Cindy talked about Michael getting angry. Sandi recalls, "And Becky and I asked her several times if he had ever hit her, and she would just clam up. I mean, she would always say no, but it just didn't seem right. She sometimes had bruises on her arms and legs."

That summer, Michael complained to his brother Randy, who lived in Ft. Lauderdale, Florida, that the marriage was not living up to his expectations. Cindy had dinner with a co-worker.

"He was upset, very upset, and a little depressed." Randy sensed Cindy was moving away from Michael and he was chasing her, so he advised his brother to "let go of the situation, and if the person wanted to be with you, they'd come back." Several weeks later, he said, Michael was crying because Cindy was growing more distant from him and staying out more.

Michael's specific complaints were that she was dressing in a more provocative manner and staying out late more. Then he claimed she was using alcohol and cocaine, and Randy said, "By that time, I felt it was more or less over."

A similar situation had happened in the Albrecht family when Michael and Randy's brother Scott was ill and on his deathbed. Scott's wife had an affair, but no threats were made. Randy's parents told the four Albrecht siblings—Randy, Michael, Mark, and April—to say nothing to the wife. "It was a hands-off situation," Randy said.

Michael's personal engine blew at the end of that 1992 Indy 500 race when he got fired from his job as head mechanic for the Dick Simon Race Team.

Michael was an excellent mechanic, earning seventy-five thousand dollars a year at Simon. But he found himself bounced out the door like a used tire and the season wasn't even a third of the way finished. Simon said he couldn't afford to keep even a good full-time mechanic on the payroll, not when he wasn't winning races and couldn't get sponsors.

On the surface, it made sense. The reality was that money or no money, Simon was through with Michael Albrecht. Michael had lost his focus. He was paid to work on cars, not drag his marital woes around the garage like a bad muffler. Michael had become a distraction to the other workers, and he wasn't easy to get along with either.

In the racing world, Michael lived up to his Crabby nickname. At Simon, he habitually called the other mechanics vulgar names and talked down to them. Sandi's husband Mike never had a personal quarrel with Michael; he tried to get along with him as a colleague, but he resented the way Crabby treated the workers under him.

Mike and Sandi Fink had joined the Albrechts in Detroit to celebrate their fifth wedding anniversary "and it was the most miserable meal we've ever had," Sandi recalls. "You couldn't laugh at the table. You just felt like you couldn't have any fun."

During the entire meal, Michael ignored everyone at the table and stared off into the distance, watching television. The only thing that enlivened the evening was the waitress accidentally doused Michael and Al Unser's crew chief Owen Snyder with a dish of rice. It enraged Michael but added levity to the rest of the table.

Becky's husband Kirk resented Michael's habit of performing a "neck muscle test" on some of his co-workers. He never did it to Kirk nor to Sandi's husband, but the two smallest mechanics on the team suffered at Michael's hands and were forced to laugh it off in order to keep their jobs. To perform his muscle test, Michael came up behind his victim, grasped the back of their neck, and clutched their muscles in a painfully tight squeeze, often bringing the man to his knees.

Once Michael had managed to embarrass and humiliate the other man, he was ready to laugh and call it harmless fun. People on the racing circuit agreed that Michael was great at his job but treated people as if they were beneath him.

Kim Graham's husband, Terry Hopkins, hated Michael Albrecht. Terry was strong but rather short. If Michael ever did the muscle test on him personally, he never admitted it to Kim. He did complain about Michael's lack of self-control and his outbreaks of temper.

As far as Michael and Cindy's marriage went, Sandi noted a drastic downhill after the 1992 Indianapolis 500. "It was all fine and dandy until he got fired," she says.

Michael went to work for Euro Motorsports, but he was no longer king of the road. He worked on a day-to-day basis, always needing to be available, never knowing when he might work. His earnings blew a tire. Suddenly, Cindy's star was rising and his was sinking in mud.

Michael resented the fun his wife had. If she went to a Penske function, she might accidentally be paying more attention to someone else than she did to him. "He could have come," Sandi argues. His boss would have allowed it. He just couldn't talk business while he was there. "Crabby used his 'different team' line as an excuse not to be socially engaged."

Sandi and Becky recall a special high-class event at an old theater in downtown Indianapolis, an event sponsored by Philip Morris. Penske team members were expected to be there and they were fed and entertained like royalty.

All the other spouses were there, but Cindy went alone as usual. Michael told her to be home by eleven. The party was still going strong at that hour and Cindy saw it would be rude for her to leave ahead of others, so she called Michael to explain.

"I only heard her end of the phone conversation," Sandi relates, "but it was pretty obvious that he was yelling at her and he basically ordered her home. She left in tears."

Becky, who seems gifted with strong intuition, felt the tension in the marriage before she heard any details. During the Indianapolis 500, the hospitality team had two rented cargo vans and two parking passes. Glen Smith and Bob Lawes used one van. The three women used the other. Becky and Sandi met at Cindy's house each morning and the three rode in together.

Becky lived in Broad Ripple, a half hour drive from Speedway. Obsessed with never being late, Becky's chronically early for everything, so she often arrived at Cindy's house while her friend was still rushing around, trying to get ready.

Michael and Cindy's home, a tidy, red-brick ranch-style house with a nicely finished basement, stood facing a pleasant park on a quiet street. Cindy was an immaculate housekeeper but Becky did not find the home welcoming when Michael was around.

If Becky saw Michael was home, she'd avoid entering the house and simply drive around the park or the neighborhood, waiting. "I was never comfortable in that house when he was there. I sensed something," she recalls, and her lips tighten.

It was like there were two Cindys. The true Cindy had fun and enjoyed life. She worked hard, but also pulled silly pranks. Exuberance filled her like homemade soup. The other Cindy was a timid and tense shadow of herself, a noodle of a woman who tried too hard to shape herself into everything Michael expected her to be.

Sometimes, Becky, in her enthusiasm, would start to mention some fun they'd had recently and Cindy would give her a look and shake her head, letting her know it was not okay to talk about it in front of Michael. "I was never afraid that Mike would do anything to me," Becky says, "I was just concerned about getting her in trouble with Mike."

Trouble with Mike was a ghoul in the mind of Cindy's friends. They never saw overt mistreatment. What they saw was Cindy's anxiety when he was around. He would come up to her at the track and speak quietly but with military sternness. When he did this, they cringed at the menacing look on his face as he towered over her. They could see her embarrassment and sense her fear.

His need to control Cindy escalated. He openly yelled at her. When the women went out, Cindy had to change her clothes before she went home so Michael wouldn't smell cigarette smoke on her. Michael judged his wife harshly for everything she did. Early in their relationship, she had stopped smoking to please him, but had started again and was smoking more and more as the stress of her marriage etched itself bone deep.

One night, after a long day's work, the trio took a break, sitting on the steps of their cooking trailer. Cindy was sipping a drink called an Oklahoma, milk with Kahlua and cola. Michael approached and Becky took the drink from Cindy's hands and began drinking it as if she'd had it the whole time.

Cindy rarely chose to drink alcohol with her friends but when she did, Michael was ready to pounce. He'd rant that she was becoming an alcoholic like her mother. He knew this would hit a nerve.

Becky says, "I don't know if I felt it from her or from him, but every time he'd come around," they would all tense up. "You didn't want to say the wrong thing. Intimidation was his big thing."

Sandi agrees. "He was always trying to get people to bow down to him."

It got to the point, they say, that Michael wouldn't even allow Cindy to go shopping at Kmart for an hour with her friends.

One day at work, Becky and Sandi buzzed off in the golf cart to deliver food to the men working in the garage. When they returned moments later, they found Cindy sitting on the steps with a bandage on her knee. She had stepped down with a tray of vegetable medley and fallen. The cooked vegetables carpeted the floor. Glen Smith swept up the mess with the Shop Vac and put a sign on the machine that read Veg Med.

Cindy acted a little steamed, but of course saw the humor. Still, this was not a story she could go home and share with her husband. The women never saw Crabby laugh.

One day between races, Cindy sat at home, watching television and discussing the next race with Sandi and Becky. Sandi said, "I won't tell you to leave him. I can't make that decision for you, but I will say that if you decide to go, we're here for you." They knew Michael was mentally and emotionally abusive to Cindy, they could see it. Sandi says, "And we'd go, Cindy, he might not be hitting you, but..."

He is abusive, they said. She did not deny it.

She could take money out of their bank account and get her own apartment. They were still discussing possibilities when Michael came home for lunch. Becky says the women became instantly angelic and friendly. *Hi, Mike. Good to see you. We're just here watching our soaps and planning our next race meals.* "Cindy was very into soaps."

Michael barely acknowledged them and went down to the basement.

That night, Cindy called her friends. Michael had set up a tape recorder in the basement. Becky was instantly worried for her friend. *If he heard what we were talking about...* The thought made her shiver involuntarily. She knew from her husband that Michael had a violent temper at work. When she heard about the recorder, her immediate thought was Michael would kill her and Sandi if he heard what they'd said. But Cindy said the recorder was hooked up to the telephone line.

Another boil erupted in the relationship when Michael found greeting cards from another mechanic, Pat Hawes. Cindy insisted the notes were mere signs of friendship. Michael thundered that things were going on behind his back. The women chuckle sadly, remembering Michael's jealous fury. They say Cindy never dated anyone while the marriage was intact, but Michael was intent on believing the worst.

Sandi says, "He was a typical abuser, trying to isolate her and then control her."

Bob Lawes recalls a time when Cindy showed up for work in dark shades. Eventually she took them off to reveal a bruised eye. She insisted the injury was caused by an accident, her own clumsiness. She bumped it. The other workers pretended to believe her.

Lawes recalls another strange instance. He was trying to call Cindy and Michael to meet them for dinner. Cindy was extremely quiet. She told Bob, "I can't come out. I can't leave the house." Bob said it was not the Cindy he knew.

Friends and co-workers repeatedly asked Cindy if Michael was hitting her and she always denied it. Still, it was clear to everyone he was demeaning her or there was some form of emotional abuse going on. One abuse Cindy did confess to was Michael was demanding sexual practices that upset her. For example, he insisted on performing oral sex on her when she was on her menstrual period. This sickened her.

He also liked her dirty and sweaty. During race season, the workday was often twelve to fifteen hours long. After working all that time outside, Cindy went home, ready for a cleansing scrub, but Michael didn't want her to shower. He wanted the two of them to share their sweat and grit. She said she hated that.

Unknown to Cindy, Michael was frequenting strip clubs and he gave gifts to women who pleased him. He awarded one "soiled dove" his silver badge: a serial-numbered, highly-coveted badge which gave the bearer unlimited access to all areas of the Indianapolis Motor Speedway during the month of May, including qualifications and the race itself.

Months later, the fortunate bearer of this prize turned it in to Lieutenant Bill Jones of the Speedway Police Department. It was traced back to Michael Albrecht.

Cindy didn't want to spend her life being run over roughshod, but maybe the marriage could still be redeemed. Michael told her, often in front of others, that he loved her and would do anything to keep her. Cindy agreed to keep living with Michael and see if they could work things out. She moved into a separate bedroom.

CHAPTER 7

By early July, Cindy decided she could not stay in the house with Michael. Her friends helped her find an apartment, an upstairs, one bedroom in Eagle Creek Courts, a newer complex half a mile from the Albrecht home.

Jim and Joanne Delaney, who had been next-door neighbors to the Albrechts for two years, witnessed the move. "Well, our bedroom window looked out over their driveway," Mrs. Delaney explained, "and their back door came out on that, and I just happened to be making the bed, looked out and saw them moving stuff out, and it upset me a little bit, so I sent Jim over to ask what the problem was... And he asked them, and Cindy spoke up and said, 'Jim, I'm moving out. In order for us to be friends, I'm going to have to move out for a little bit.'"

Michael helped Cindy move, chafing his shins and banging his knuckles in the process. He helped her hang artwork. Over the bedroom dresser hung a framed Penske picture. Above her bed hung a picture of an Indian maiden adorned in white buckskin. A warrior stood beside the maiden, one protective arm circling her shoulders.

Cindy decorated her apartment, hanging more race prints and eye-catching art on the walls. Her collection of stuffed bunnies adorned her dresser. She chose bright, ocean-colored towels for her bathroom. Sandi gave her some things and others she bought her herself.

The bedspread, white with big peach-colored flowers, was a big deal to Cindy. She bought it, along with matching shams, from the JCPenney catalog and was very proud of it. It was girlie stuff.

A photograph on the living room wall represented one of Cindy's best pranks. An official team photo was being taken and Cindy sat beside Becky, wearing her Marlboro zip-front jacket. Some moment before the camera flashed, Cindy tugged the jacket to the crown of her head and zipped it, cinching the opening closed. Becky never realized what Cindy had done. No one did until the photo was printed and there was Cindy, with a small thatch of hair protruding from her collar, looking like a headless figure beside her friend.

Cindy exploded in laughter when she saw the result of her prank. She had the photograph blown up to an 8"x10" and framed it. She displayed the photo proudly. She had made a home for herself and embroidered her personality into it.

Sandi says, "Some of our best times were recorded on film that month of May. We had no way of knowing five months later how haunting these pictures would truly be."

Michael would keep the house. Cindy would keep her red Nissan pickup truck and take custody of the cats, Billy and Willy. Keeping things amicable, she gave Michael a key to the apartment so he could tend to the cats when she was out of town.

In August, Cindy filed for a divorce, retaining Jack L. Bailey as her attorney. She went to her boss, Pete Twiddy, before word spread.

Pete was at work at the Speedway when "she came up to me and she said, 'Before you hear it from somebody else, I'm splitting up with my husband.' And I was utterly shocked." He believed she told him personally "because in the circuit, it's a close-knit family, everybody sort of knows everybody's business, there's not really a whole lot of secrets out there. Rumors start easily and can grow, so she wanted me to hear it from her first... basically, she was telling me not to worry about it."

1992 had been a big year for the Penske-Marlboro hospitality team. Before that, Marlboro's hospitality program was strictly for the press and Penske's was mostly for VIPs. A collaboration was suggested by Roger Penske in 1991. Each team brought top performers. Pete brought Glen Smith, who was his driver at the time, and Penske brought his top man, Bob Lawes. "And Roger had a staff known around the circuit as being probably the best cooking staff," Pete said.

The result was the most dynamic hospitality team on the race circuit.

Pete Twiddy first met Cindy around 1988 or 1989 when she was a sous chef working part time with Lori Wetzel for Penske. By 1992, Lori had gone back to the NASCAR program. Cindy was promoted to head chef.

His first impression of Cindy, long before they dated, was that she was "amazing." He had a background in catering, "so I had sort of an idea of how I liked to see things done."

Lori Wetzel had her own systems, so there was a certain degree of head bumping, but when Cindy moved up to her position, "she took my advice and she was constantly trying to improve everything," he recalls. "She improved the attitude of everyone who worked around there, she improved the menus. She just worked her butt off and was always constantly trying to do better."

Her will to excel was contagious. Team morale improved immediately. "She'd do little parties for those guys. She knew everybody's birthday." Rather than bolt the minute the day was done, Cindy offered more of herself when she sensed the need.

Tim Lombardi was the team coordinator, Pete explained. "And that's who I would liaison with to go over bills. They would collect all the bills and everything and then they would submit them to me. I would give my approval and then they could be sent to Phillip Morris to be paid."

As a sports marketing consultant for Philip Morris, Pete says his task was to "help negotiate and implement the contracts for Philip Morris at racetracks and with the race team that they sponsor, and personal service contracts. I take care of all the operations at tracks, hospitality, signage, hotel reservations, you name it."

As liaison between Philip Morris and Penske Racing, he oversaw the look of the cars and the uniforms. He attended every race. He also arranged hotel accommodations for Phillip Morris VIPs, staff members, and their guests.

Working in conjunction with Glen Smith, he oversaw delivery of the cooking trailer set up on Tuesday of race week: the awning, the flooring, the tables, chairs, and grill. The cooks shopped at each race and he reviewed the menus with them, letting them know how many diners and which VIPs to expect.

It was also his responsibility to see that everything was operational. He checked power, cable feeds, and telephone lines. Cindy coming to him about the divorce right away told Pete she was operational. She would not let her responsibilities to the team slide because of her personal problems.

With the divorce pending, Michael's moods seesawed. He would cry how he would do anything to maintain his marriage and keep Cindy happy, and then turn on her, pouncing with teeth bared.

Sandi and Becky witnessed, but seldom heard, arguments between the two of them. Becky said it seemed every time Michael came to their trailer, when he left, Cindy would be upset. They did hear Michael pleading with her to talk to him and not sign the divorce papers. Sandi also heard Michael trying to coerce Cindy to sign some insurance papers.

One day, Michael arrived, bringing Cindy a letter he had written to her. It made her cry. Sandi read part of it and

Cindy told Becky that Michael had said his daughters hated her and she would never see them again. "It really hurt her because she loved those girls," Sandi said. It was never clear whether Michael's daughters truly felt that way or he was just using them to whip his wife.

A call from Michael during the Toronto race sparked another thunderstorm. Michael had gone through Cindy's dresser drawers and found an envelope from a divorce attorney. He went ballistic. The fight was huge, even over the phone. Sandi and Becky urged Cindy to get her locks changed.

She did. Michael could no longer be trusted having access to her life.

Sandi says, "We never thought she should have given him a key in the first place." But Michael did not give up on keeping Cindy's private life open to his inspection. "I know he tried to get into her apartment one time while we were gone. He tried to get the key from Heidi. I don't think she gave it to him."

After Cindy started dating Pete Twiddy, Michael made snarky comments. *He's this* and *he's that*, the sort of things girls whisper behind their hands in middle school. "He makes a lot of money, so that intimidated Mike," Sandi says. "I think it was more comments along the line that she wasn't worthy of being with him because she was nothing."

During the races, Pete's job as a promoter allowed him no time to notice Michael Albrecht. "I'm out there watching what's going on... When the car's on the track, I'm in the pits. As soon as the car is off the track, I'm over to the sales trailer; I'm over to the hospitality trailer; I'm overseeing a promoter. I'm all over the place."

CHAPTER 8

The relationship between Cindy Albrecht and Pete Twiddy was strictly professional. She was his cook. At the end of July, the Murphs, Pete and Mary-Lin Murphy, hosted an annual bash at their Skeleton Lake home in the beautiful and pristine District of Muskoka, north of Toronto. The Murphs handled cooking and hospitality for Mario Andretti's Newman/Haas Racing Team and offered this weekend break to other hospitality workers.

Pete Murphy described the gathering as "a mid-season relaxer for those in the business." He reminisces about the fun Cindy had. "This was her first time. She had a riot… it's a great way to remember her, always with a big smile and having fun in the water."

That weekend was magical. IndyCar's finest hospitality people were there to enjoy the aurora lights and the huge barbecue pit in the center of the deck. Cindy's cheerful chatter and sense of humor added to the celebration. "Cindy did a spoof of a person with Tourette's," Pete Twiddy recalls. "We all laughed so hard—she thought she wet her pants. Cindy could hang with anyone; she could do anything.

"I actually had brought a gal out to the Toronto race myself. Things didn't work out real well," Pete says. He sent her home and went up to Skeleton Lake. "And I can't explain how it happened, but at the end of the night, all of a sudden, I looked at her and she looked at me and there was something there."

Maybe it was the firelight. "That was the first time I even looked at her in any way except as an employee. Beforehand, she was just my chef, the coolest, neatest chef in the whole world."

Cindy was looking right back. Pete had mesmerizing blue-green eyes and dark, wavy hair. Canadian crewmember Glen Smith told Pete, "You've got the greatest thing that ever walked the earth right here. It's Cindy."

Glen was right. Even with the weighted cloak of Michael's anger pressing down on her, Cindy glowed with vitality. Pete thought it was weird there was squabbling and then, all of a sudden, in July, everything was fine and Michael did not seem to be mad. Yet everyone sensed Michael's anger was a jack in the box, waiting for any microscopic movement to flick the spring.

That spring snapped the next day when Cindy had her accident. "And he was upset from that point on," Pete says.

The accident happened when Cindy wanted to go out on the lake on a wet bike, an extreme water sport ride like a motorcycle. Glen Smith told her if she got in trouble to hit the gas.

Pete looked at him and said, "What are you telling her that for?" He told her, "No, just back off and let it come back in the water and then try again.

"Well... she was listening to Glen, and she takes off, and she wasn't but forty yards, fifty yards off the dock and... just all of a sudden I heard the engine go up, I... saw her feet flying over the front and she actually came over the front, and the big ski on the front hit her right—and it was a sound I'll never forget. And I actually thought she was dead, because it was... a bone-crushing sound."

Pete raced onto the dock and swam out to get her. "I was trying to swim her back because I had lifeguard experience. I could see she had knocked out all her teeth, but this girl was just tough. And she wasn't crying. And I think that was when something in my heart just changed. Completely just how I felt for her. Just overnight it changed."

They took her to someone in Canada who tried to put something fake over the roots. "And when she came back, she went and saw somebody, and she was telling me it was going to cost a whole lot of money and this kind of thing to redo it. And she was at the race in a lot of pain... whatever they had put... over the top of her teeth, it was like they never had taken care of the roots. So, she still was experiencing a lot of pain."

Doctor Jack Miller was a race car driver and a dentist with an office in Broad Ripple, Indiana. He came by and told Cindy that when she came back to Indy, he would take care of her.

Pete and Cindy began secretly dating in August. Pete did not believe Michael knew about the relationship "because Cindy kept complaining about all the rumors running around the circuit that she was dating all these men, and she was laughing at it, saying, I don't know what—you know, he's telling people that I'm going out with all these people and, you know, had the wrong guy completely."

Cindy told Pete very little about Michael. Like the rest of the team, Pete wondered if Albrecht was practicing his muscle test and other tortures at home. Cindy never told anyone Michael was violent or had even threatened violence.

Pete says, "She told me that, as she put it, he mindfucked her all the time, but there was never anything of a physical nature. She told me she really didn't want to talk about it. She just said, you know, he didn't treat her right, and it was a situation that, you know, it was in the past and she was moving on. The only thing that she did reiterate to me," he adds, "was that she found she was underneath his thumb, and that she couldn't... she had to hide certain things... she felt like she was being treated like a child."

Sandi says that Michael's levels of being upset gyrated from July to October. Cindy never seemed to know how to respond to him. "She didn't really have a good read on everything at that point. She—you know, she just kept saying, it's going to be over soon, it doesn't really matter."

In September, he tried to get her to sign over the deed to the house but she told him to wait until the divorce was final.

After the October 4 Nazareth race, Cindy informed Michael she was dating Pete Twiddy. His response was "it was pretty much common knowledge."

CHAPTER 9

Cindy left for the last race of the season at Leguna Seca near Monterey, California, on Monday, October 12. While those final engines cooled, Cindy, Sandi, and Becky scoured every counter and utensil to a race car shine and closed the trailer. Cindy said goodbye to her friends in her traditional manner, hugging them, kissing their faces, and saying, "Love you! Mean it!" Her face beamed. She literally bounced with happiness and hope.

After the race, Pete and Cindy flew to Albuquerque to attend a Halloween party hosted by Al Unser Jr. and his wife Shelley. Glen Smith and the Murphs were also there. Cindy was excited about the party and dressed as Morticia from *The Addams Family,* wearing long black hair, bright red nails, and a svelte gown over her trim figure.

Everyone was still celebrating Al Jr.'s seasonal victory, especially his daring half-hair win of the Indy 500. Team Marlboro had a guitar painted like Little Al's car and presented it to the ecstatic driver via Pete and the band 38 Special.

Shelley Unser delighted in the sparkle of romance that cocooned Pete and Cindy. She says, "Wow! I remember how in love Pete was. That night was magical; they had a blast. He finally found the one. I was just so happy for them. They truly seemed so in love."

All her life, Cindy had publicly bubbled while holding in a silent pain and that night was no different. Cindy exhibited a strange, silent strength in Albuquerque that Pete only recognized in hindsight. She seemed to be struggling to reveal something to him in the car, saying, "Would you love me no matter what?" He tried to reassure her he would, but she would say no more about what was on her mind.

They dressed and attended the party, and then Cindy asked to go back to the hotel. She said she just wanted to be with Pete. "It was not like her to want to go back to the hotel," Pete said.

The strangeness continued the next day when he drove her to the airport and she asked Pete to drop her at the curb at the airport. "She wouldn't let me walk her to the gate. It was like she sensed something," Pete said. It made Pete anxious. She would not let him go with her from Albuquerque to Indianapolis. "If I'd gone with her, it wouldn't have happened," he said.

Those final conversations felt surreal and reminded Pete of his childhood dreams that someone he loved was in peril and he was driving sideways into an airport. "There were extremely deep spiritual things that went on that to this day I can't explain," Pete says.

On Sunday, October 25, Cindy flew to San Francisco and then to Indianapolis. Pete Twiddy flew home to Naples, Florida.

Arriving home, Cindy found her house in order. She called Heidi Dras, the good friend who had taken care of her cats. Cindy told Heidi that she had opened the sliding glass door onto her balcony to allow Billy and Willy to look out through the screen door. She was tired. The chore of unpacking her bags could wait until morning.

With Michael out of the picture, other relationships were healing. Cindy's mother had stopped drinking and Cindy was rebuilding their connection. Michael was not pleased. Sandi says, "He would go through her mail and if she got any letters from her family, he'd take them and not let her see them." In spite of his efforts, Cindy had reconnected with both her parents and planned to spend time with them.

She bought two necklaces, each half a heart. She wore one and gave the other to her mother. On the night she arrived home from Leguna Seca, her mother, Pat Woodward, called from Ft. Lauderdale around nine-thirty.

Cindy told her mom that she had arrived home ten minutes earlier. In good spirits, she chatted about her upcoming move to Florida. Her mom asked, "Are you wearing your necklace, Cindy?" She was, and her mother replied, "I'm wearing mine too."

Cindy's divorce from Michael would be final on Monday, October 26. Her trip home would be a short one. She planned to see that the divorce was final and sign a quit claim deed, giving Michael the house. Then she would pack up and move to Florida to be with Pete. Sandi says, "They were both so in love. They planned to spend the rest of their lives together."

Another great opportunity awaited Cindy in Florida as well. Roger Penske had hired her as the chef on his private yacht. She was thrilled that she would be part of the staff on the beautiful boat.

While Cindy and Pete had gone to Albuquerque, Becky and Sandi spent time with their husbands in San Francisco. They visited friends who raced in the America's Cup, and all went out on a sailboat. "We just had a great time," Sandi says.

Cindy called Sandi, leaving a message to let her know she'd gotten home safely. "She said, 'It's your birthday, call me, and blah, blah, blah' and I almost didn't call her. We'd just flown across the country and I was beat, but I did call her back." She reached Cindy before ten p.m.

Cindy merely wanted to wish her friend a happy birthday. It was a pleasant day for late October, temperatures in the high fifties with almost no wind and a gentle fog. Cindy said the patio door was open a little so the cats could look out and get some air.

The conversation was short, about fifteen minutes. Cindy had started her menstrual period during the layover in Kansas City. She was exhausted beyond endurance. She was waiting for Pete to call when he arrived in Florida and then she wanted to sleep. The friends said goodbye and hung up their phones.

Cindy lounged peacefully on her sofa with a pillow and afghan. For the first time in her life, Cynthia Albrecht was in the driver's seat of a first-class vehicle with a steering wheel tooled to fit her hands. The path behind her was falling to dust while the road ahead was paved with pure joy.

CHAPTER 10

Pete Twiddy exited his plane in Florida and called Cindy on his cell phone at 10:44 p.m. He got no answer. He left a message, asking her to call him, saying he would wait up. By one a.m., when he still had not reached her, he assumed she was asleep. He called Monday morning and left more messages.

"Hey, where are you? I tried calling you last night, and I didn't hear from you. I'm starting to get worried. Give me a buzz, baby."

"Okay, now I'm starting to get worried and I don't like this. Please call me. I'm worried something might be wrong."

4:40 p.m.: "I'm starting to call up the world to find out where you are and what happened."

Pete called again at six-thirty and several more times that evening. His messages revved like an engine with nowhere to go. Cindy's tape was a continual cycle of messages from her lover, Pete's voice building in intensity with each unanswered call.

11:30 p.m.: "I'm starting to freak out now. I just don't know what to do. I hope I hear from you."

An hour later, he phoned again, then again. "It's me for the hundredth time. I hope we're going to laugh about this later."

His final message was "I know something has happened to you or you would have called. I love you, Cindy."

Cindy did not call him back. Pete called Sandi Fink, worried.

"She's fine," Sandi assured him. She told Pete that during their Sunday night conversation, Cindy had said she was super tired and she had a bunch of errands to run on Monday. There was the divorce to take care of and she might have gone to get her teeth fixed. It was normal to have a lot to do at home at the end of the race season.

The three women were supposed to get together on Monday and go over receipts from Leguna Seca. Cindy would turn these in to Penske along with a check for the remaining cash, about twenty-four hundred dollars. "She never called so she must have got busy. We'll see her tomorrow." Sandi says, "So the rest of the day, I called, Pete called, we never heard from her." Then she learned that on Monday morning, Cindy failed to meet with her attorney and complete the divorce from her husband.

Urged by Pete, Becky and Sandi drove to Cindy's apartment Tuesday morning, bearing gifts of coffee and donuts. It was a clear day with just a bite of autumn, a good day to be out visiting friends. They could go over receipts and call Pete back to ease his mind.

They found Cindy's red Nissan pickup truck parked in front of the apartment building. Sandi swept a hand across the hood. It was cold and covered with dew. "That bitch! She's home. She's just not answering her phone," Sandi muttered.

They entered the red brick apartment building through the big white door that guarded four apartments, two upstairs and two down. Upstairs, they rapped on the door of Apartment D, ready to blast Cindy with some good-natured teasing.

No one answered and no sound came from the apartment. Strange. There were endless possibilities, of course. Cindy could be in the shower or sleeping in, but the fact she didn't answer the phone or the door worried them.

They circled the building and climbed up fifteen wood-and-metal steps to Cindy's balcony.

"Right away we knew something was wrong," Sandi says. "The patio screen was completely off." Although the patio door was shut, no lights, no music, no sound came from Cindy's apartment. The friends stepped to the closed patio door and peeked in. What they saw alarmed them.

Cindy's purse and keys lay in plain sight on the dining table. They saw the two cats, but no sign of Cindy. "There was cat poop and cat throw up on the floor," Becky noticed. Cindy was a meticulous housekeeper, and her cats never left a mess. Plus, her cigarettes lay abandoned. "She wasn't going nowhere without her cigarettes," says Becky.

Sandi nudged the door with a finger. It slid open. "Cindy?" they called hopefully.

No answer. There was no doubt someone had been in the apartment. "Then we realized he might still be in there, so we went back down to my car where I had an umbrella and some mace. If he was in there, we were gonna blind him and poke him," Becky says.

Hoping to arrive in time to effect a rescue, Sandi and Becky mounted the back stairs again. This time, Sandi slid the door open with two fingers. "It was like we already knew it was a crime scene and we shouldn't touch anything," Sandi remembers. "So we were careful to touch nothing."

With their first step into the apartment, it was like dusk had fallen and choked the world with fog. Fear was palpable. "It was surreal," says Sandi. They clutched hands. "Cindy? Cindy, are you here?" Their voices shook. "Cindy." The word was a prayer.

No lights were on. The apartment was a vow of silence with no movement except the occasional anxious wisp of a hungry cat. Becky says, "We were instantly freaked out and scared." They could already feel that nothing was ever going to be the same again.

It did not look like the scene of a robbery. Cindy's purse perched on the table beside Pete's oversized Marlboro Tag Heuer watch that he gave her. Her keys lay there too, along with a check made out to Heidi Dras for taking care of the cats.

Cindy's travel bag lay on the living room floor. Penske's cash would be inside it, but neither woman touched the bag.

Trying to be rational, Sandi thought, "Okay, let's see if she's made coffee." No. The unused coffee pot was still in the dishwasher.

Cindy's bags waited in her bedroom, still not unpacked. This too was worrisome because Cindy maintained an orderly life and would certainly have put things away by Tuesday. She had kicked off her sneakers. Her clothes lay in a layered pile by the dresser: jeans, t-shirt, socks, bra, and panties. It looked like she'd stood there and undressed.

In the bathroom, the white shower curtain was closed, two bright blue towels hanging mutely over the rod. A single drip of water would have shattered the stillness. Becky shrank back. She told Sandi she could not open it; she could not look. Sandi agreed to open the shower curtain if Becky would look in the closet.

Becky scooted from the bathroom and flung herself into the bedroom. She peeked inside Cindy's closet and beneath her bed, breathing a sigh of relief when she saw nothing. The bathtub was empty too.

Becky said, "I think he's got her."

They both knew she meant Michael Albrecht.

They gazed around the apartment again. The cats were litter box trained and did not usually make a mess. If they did, Cindy cleaned it up right away. They were hungry, anxious, and neglected. Too many things were weird.

They had been prepared to see Cindy move away. They were prepared to launch their friend into a new and ecstatic life on the beach. They weren't prepared to find her gone.

CHAPTER 11

Sandi decided to call Michael and see if they could learn anything. First, they tried his job at Euro Motorsports and found out he wasn't working there anymore. The receptionist said he'd be in later that day to pick up his check. Sandi thanked the woman and dialed Michael at home.

"We did not tell him we were standing in Cindy's apartment," says Becky. They made it sound like a cheerful social call. "Hi! How are you?" They were expecting to meet with Cindy on Monday and here it was, Tuesday, and she hadn't shown up and wasn't answering her phone and they just wondered if he'd heard from her.

Michael told them that Cindy was in Albuquerque and probably wouldn't be home for another week. "We knew that was a lie," says Sandi. "There's no way he thought she was in Albuquerque. He knew exactly when she was coming home."

He knew the divorce was to be finalized on Monday the 26th because they had been heard arguing about it at the race. Michael had claimed the date was the 24th and Cindy told him that it had to be Monday because you could not get divorced on a Saturday.

They called Pete Twiddy and told him that they were in Cindy's apartment, she was not there, and something was wrong. Pete urged them to call the police and said he'd be on the next plane to Indianapolis.

Sandi's next call was to the Speedway Police Department. She explained that her friend appeared to have been missing for a couple of days. She asked them to send someone out, anyone but Steve Turner, who was best buddies with Michael Albrecht and the last person they wanted to investigate Cindy's disappearance.

Some reports claim that when Sandi called the police department she asked for Steve. She shakes her head. "That could not possibly be true." She describes Steve as a weekend warrior, a sometime mechanic who was a wannabe on the race circuit.

The first officer on the scene was Patrolman Dane Morgan from the Speedway Police Department. He arrived about nine-thirty a.m. and summoned Detective Steve Turner.

Turner did not enter the apartment with the attitude of a law enforcement professional investigating a crime. He took a cursory stroll through Cindy's home and noted that the neatness and order did not suggest any type of struggle. His demeanor was condescending. He responded to the concerns of the two women as if they'd merely been startled by a mouse.

He went through the apartment, touching every cabinet and door, using the excuse that he was looking for food for the hungry cats. Becky started to step out to smoke and he told her not to bother. "There's an ashtray right there," he told her. He sniggered at the idea that the apartment could be a crime scene.

Turner did ask if anything was missing and the women mentioned that the Penske cash was always carried inside a zippered bag in Cindy's travel bag. Turner asked Sandi to check for the money. It was gone, including the loose change. Turner tried to imply Cindy had taken off with the money. Her friends knew better. She would never have touched the Penske money, not even if she planned to put it back the next day. She was always able, on a moment's notice, to account for every cent of it.

The cash stash was a company secret. The only people who knew where that money was carried were the three women, their bosses, Glen Smith and Pete Twiddy, and Michael Albrecht.

Plus, forty dollars in Cindy's purse was untouched. Why would a robber take loose change and leave behind cash?

Steve brushed off their worries, saying Cindy was probably nearby. "He told us, 'She's just hooked up with some guy here in the apartment building,'" Becky says. "But we knew that wasn't right. She's in love with Pete. She's tired as hell. And she's on her period. We didn't say that but we were thinking it."

Turner called Michael to tell him Cindy was missing. He reported that Michael broke down and cried, saying he did not know where Cindy was. The officers locked the apartment. When Turner offered to go talk to Michael Albrecht, Morgan let him go but signaled to the two women to stay behind so they could talk.

Officer Morgan appeared to take the crime more seriously than Turner did. He took their statements and learned that Michael and Turner were close friends. He called for a search of the wooded area behind Cindy's apartment building.

Because of that friendship and the fact Michael was a potential suspect, Lieutenant Detective William "Bill" Jones took over the case on Wednesday, October 28. Intelligent, resourceful, and persistent, Lieutenant Jones was precisely the person the case needed. Jones was not a tall man, but he was every inch the professional. His salt and pepper hair and eyeglasses reflected a sharp mind. He remembered people and what they said. He always wore a suit, but had the soul of an NFL player determined to tackle bad guys and vindicate their victims.

When Pete Twiddy's flight arrived in Indianapolis, he went straight to the Speedway Police Department. He, Sandi, and Becky met with Steve Turner. Turner was no longer on the case, but he interviewed them. Pete, not knowing Turner, told him he was there because he was Cindy's boyfriend. Turner responded that she had many boyfriends. "Where'd you hear that?" Pete asked. "Because I'm the only one going out with her."

Turner blustered, "Oh yeah, that's what you think." Pete wanted to know if Michael had been brought in for questioning. Turner ignored the question. He said that Cindy might be out with one of her friends on a binge.

"What are you talking about?" Pete demanded.

Turner replied, "She's been doing drugs."

"Hey, man, that girl's been working with me all year; there is no way. I don't believe it for a second."

Turner told Pete he should get on a plane and go back home. Turner pegged Pete as very hostile concerning Michael Albrecht. He was not alone in that hostility. The trio all thought Michael was involved in Cindy's disappearance. Turner ignored their suspicions. He gave them the bum's rush, telling them to go home. Later, he falsely accused Pete of being intoxicated.

Pete went to see Speedway Police Chief Jeffrey Dine and explained what had just happened with Turner. Chief Dine assured Pete that Turner would no longer be running the investigation into Cindy's disappearance.

The three left the police department feeling certain that officers would not make a serious search for Cindy. Had they known Lt. Bill Jones, they might have felt differently, but they decided to launch their own search.

CHAPTER 12

Behind Cindy's apartment building was a wooded area with a gully, but residents could take a path across to the back lot of a Marsh Supermarket. Cars could park back there unnoticed. The women suspected that Cindy had been taken out that way.

To begin the investigation, Det. Steve Turner met with Lt. Bill Jones and together they returned to the apartment. The two photographed the interior of the dwelling, took fingerprints from the sliding glass door, then resealed the apartment. They also requested local and long-distance telephone records for both Michael and Cindy's phones.

It was later learned that Michael's calling card had been used to place a long-distance call to William Filter of Milwaukee. The call had come from a payphone at the entrance of the Lafayette Square shopping mall.

Officers also interviewed Cindy's seatmates on the flight home, Peter Munson and Scott Renecke. They could only say what everyone else knew, that Cindy was a pleasant conversationalist. If she was worried about anything, she didn't tell them.

The Hendricks County Search and Rescue Team brought in bloodhounds on October 30. The dogs sniffed Cindy's shirt and underwear from a paper bag. The dogs found nothing in their search. Officers sent the clothing to the crime lab.

Cindy's property, taken as evidence, included: eleven magazines from the coffee table, three drains from the kitchen, bathtub, and bathroom sink, an Apex computer, Legend I, a Packard Bell keyboard, and a Panasonic KX-P1124 printer.

The initial investigation and search of the wooded area had turned up nothing, and Cindy's friends struggled to decide what to do next. They expected the process would emulate television. They would report Cindy as missing to the proper authorities and somebody would go out and find her. Otherwise, they did not know who to contact or what questions to ask.

Sandi says, "Nothing had prepared us for this. It was a rude awakening to the justice system."

On October 30, the *Indianapolis Star* newspaper published a photograph of Cindy, along with an article describing the events of her disappearance and asking for information. No one responded.

Just days before, Shelley Unser had celebrated the glowing romance between Pete and Cindy. Could her young life have gone so quickly from flames to ashes? She says, "I just remember hearing so many conspiracy theories, including that her Halloween costume was lying on her bed in Indy."

Pete Twiddy found there was little he could do. Cindy seemed to have dissolved with the dew. No one knew where to start looking for her.

Michael's former boss at Euro Motorsports, Antonio Ferrari, had recently returned from Italy. A slim man of medium height, Ferrari was quiet and thoughtful. But after reading in the newspaper about Cindy's disappearance, he felt the need to speak up and came forward with some significant information. Michael had told him in confidence that he wanted something to happen to Cindy. That report became part of the police department's confidential investigation. Cindy's friends heard none of this information. They felt ignored.

Word went out to the racing community. Cindy was missing. Since the racing season was over, people were able to drop their lives and come to Indiana. Sandi and Mike Fink's large, open ranch-style house became the comm center. During the search for Cindy, thirteen people lived there. Others came during the day but went home at night.

Among those who camped out at Sandi's house were Pete Twiddy and Glen Smith with his wife Dee Dee. New Yorker Susan "Sukie" Bradshaw and Kevin Diamond worked in public relations for Philip Morris as press liaisons. They stayed to help and so did Pete and Mary-Lin Murphy, Eric Stewart, and the Newman/Haas team. Mike Andrus from Dick Simon lived nearby and was constantly there helping.

They slept in shifts, working around the clock, questioning people, analyzing evidence line by line, and when the rain pounded like a dribbling basketball, they were out in it, searching, because Cindy had to be somewhere they hadn't thought of yet.

Sandi and Becky were freaked out and furious as days passed and nothing was heard from Cindy, but now they had reinforcements. Roger Penske offered, "Whatever you need, I'll help you."

In those pre-cell phone days, there were a couple of early versions of a portable phone, what the women called a bag phone, but for the most part, communication was dependent on the landline telephone. Stress moved between them like electricity. They took turns falling apart, saying to each other, "You can break down today because I feel okay. Tomorrow I'll go nuts."

They remember it all like it was yesterday. They remember the clothes they were wearing, the food that was brought over. All of it.

The racing community partnered into teams and went out searching all day, every day. They walked cornfields and creek beds, slogged through woods and wandered lost trails.

Everyone was looking for Cindy except Michael. He showed no concern at all. Becky's sister, Karen Welch, who lived in the Meadow Wood Park area on Hollister, was also a neighbor to the Albrechts. She was driving to the grocery store to get supplies, sandwiches and such, to take to Sandi's house. Karen called and said, "I don't know how concerned Mike is, he's out in the driveway right now washing his car."

Becky and Sandi seethed minutes later as they sat parked across the street from Michael's house, taking photos of him playing basketball with his buddies and cleaning his car. Becky says, "Number one, why are you cleaning your car when your wife is missing, and second—" Sandi's voice blends with hers, "Why are you cleaning your car?"

The girls were pleased when word came from Det. Steve Turner that Michael had been questioned by police on the 28th. He agreed to take a lie detector test, which was scheduled for the 29th at two-thirty p.m.

Michael never took the test. Instead, he fled. While everyone they knew was searching for Cindy, Michael left for a Florida vacation. He claimed the trip was planned. He said his daughter, Noel, was flying into Ft. Lauderdale and there would be no one to meet her. He failed to mention he had a brother and other family members living there.

Several days later, Cindy's friends received a phone call saying that Det. Steve Turner had been taken off the case. The news didn't relieve them much. Becky says, "He was still there. It wasn't like he didn't have any opportunity to read the reports. We knew he was feeding information about the investigation to Mike." More than twenty years later, neither Sandi nor Becky can say Steve Turner's name without making a face.

The sky sprung a leak on Friday, October 30. By Sunday, it was an ice bucket downpour, swirling the landscape into sludge. Day after day, in the cold November rain, teams were out looking for Cindy, searching woods, ditches, and drainpipes.

Frustrated with the drizzle of investigative information, Pete felt gut punched. Just because the police weren't finding Cindy didn't mean he couldn't. He got a referral from B.J. Flowers, a narcotics detective retired from the Indianapolis Police Department and affiliated with the Newman/Haas racing team as a security consultant. Flowers put Pete in touch with Don Campbell.

Don Campbell, of Campbell & Associates Private Investigations, was a former detective, a grizzled, tough-as-nails retired veteran of the Homicide Branch of the Indianapolis Police Department. Don not only looked like a boxer, he could throw a mean right hook. Just ask the idiots who tried to resist arrest while he was still on the force. Don also had a reputation among the police force because he had been successful in resolving a number of unsolved homicides.

Campbell began the initial meeting with a warning. "Wherever this investigation leads, I will go, even to you, kid! Most people that hire me to find killers *are* the killers. And right now, you are the number one suspect."

Pete replied, "Bring it on!"

"Let's see some money," demanded Campbell. Pete pulled five thousand in cash from his pocket and slammed it on the table. Pete blinked; the money was gone. They had just hired an investigator.

Sandi says the investigator actually cost ten thousand dollars. Pete and Mary-Lin Murphy loaned the group the additional funds.

CHAPTER 13

Campbell sat down that Sunday with Pete, Sandi, and Becky. Then he set to work immediately, following leads and seeking witnesses. He interviewed neighbors in the other three apartments of Cindy's building. Had they seen or heard anything suspicious from Apartment D on the night Cindy disappeared?

Downstairs neighbor Mark Good said he was up watching football. He was certain that no one opened the front door and no one climbed the stairs that night. He would have heard them.

However, the next evening, on Monday, October 26, around 5:15 p.m., he heard a man and woman come in the door and go up the stairs to Cindy's apartment. Good never saw their faces but through his door view, he definitely saw two pairs of legs, a man's and a woman's, climbing the stairs. He heard their voices but could not discern their words. The couple unlocked Apartment D, went inside, and stayed five to ten minutes. Then they left, probably in a vehicle.

The interview with Good turned suspicious eyes on Heidi Dras, the woman who had taken care of the cats while Cindy was in California. The police department had allowed Heidi to keep her key to the apartment even after Cindy was reported missing.

Mark Good also mentioned that he saw Cindy's truck, at times, parked in front of the apartment building while she was in California.

Another resident, Connie Galbraith, who was moving into the upstairs Apartment C, confirmed this story. She said the movers complained because they had to shuffle around Cindy's truck, and she and her boyfriend parked on opposite sides of it.

Indianapolis International Airport long-term parking had a system of recording daily the license plate numbers of patrons. Their records indicate that Cindy's red Nissan arrived on October 12, 1992, and left October 15. It was in the lot when Cindy arrived home on October 25.

The third resident of the apartment building was William Joyce Jr. in Apartment A. He stated that he had left on Monday to visit his parents in Brazil, Indiana, and had just returned. He told Campbell that he had seen Cindy but had never spoken to her. He neither saw nor heard anything unusual on the night of October 25.

However, Campbell noted, "He states a few days to a week before October 25, 1992, that he had seen a black Chevrolet Impala or Caprice four-door, parked in front of 6140 Nalon Court several times, driven by a white male with longish type hair. The subject would back the vehicle into a parking place and stay in the car. Mr. Joyce saw the subject parked there several times. He states the vehicle had a badly bent antenna or was using a coat hanger for one. He did not obtain a license number."

On Monday, November 2, Campbell met with Speedway Police Chief Jeffery Dine, Assistant Chief Phil Smith, and Lieutenant Bill Jones and Sergeant Joel Rush. Campbell and Pete Twiddy agreed that Campbell should offer his experience and expertise to the Speedway police if they were willing to accept it.

Campbell began rearranging pieces of a jigsaw puzzle of stories that didn't seem to connect.

Michael's story was that he was in Milwaukee the weekend of the 25th. He stayed with his parents and his ex-wife Kathleen. At the time of the abduction, he was out drinking with his old friend, Bill Filter, a self-employed painter. The two bought a six pack of beer at Filter's dad's bar and hung out at a park, just talking, and drove around from early evening until one a.m., when Michael returned to his ex-wife's house.

Kathleen's version of the story was that she overheard Michael calling Filter on the afternoons of Saturday the 24th and Sunday the 25th. She said he left on Sunday between five and six p.m. and returned around two a.m.

Kathleen wanted to renew her relationship with Michael. The girls wanted that too. Although Michael was intimate with his ex, he insisted he still wanted Cindy.

The next morning, sometime between eight and nine a.m., Michael arrived at Filter's worksite and visited for about an hour.

Sandi found the story illogical. Two grown men hanging out at a park when they could be sitting comfortably in a bar? Who does that? Certainly not two men in their thirties. Michael had been saying that he'd do anything to get Cindy back, but he was already hooked back up with his ex?

None of it made sense to her.

On November 5, the temperature tumbled, mixing snow with the rain. The search for Cindy continued. No one left and no one gave up. Cindy's photograph was plastered all over Speedway and published repeatedly in *The Indianapolis Star.*

There were still more questions than answers for the amateur detectives. They wanted to contact everyone, ask everything, but they felt like they were under a gag order. Becky says that Speedway Lt. Bill Jones warned them, "If this goes to trial and you have said this or this or this, you could jeopardize the trial."

Their jobs were also threatened. Marlboro did not want any publicity that linked their name to any crime, especially a possible murder. Sandi and Becky would be fired from their jobs if they spoke to the media. Public relations person Susan "Sukie" Bradshaw was the appointed spokesperson.

Someone, somewhere, had to have some answers. In desperation, Becky and Sandi consulted psychics. Their advice was both vague and conflicting. One said Cindy had already suffered a terrible death. Another suggested a search around the Milwaukee garden where Michael and Cindy had married. Still others said to look near water. This suggestion seemed to be the least help since it seemed that enough water was falling from the sky to churn Indiana back into its native swampland.

One psychic, whom they had heard on the Bob & Tom radio show, refused to do a reading for them. "She said it was too dark and she wanted nothing to do with it," Becky says.

Sandi adds, "She said, 'Your friend is dead but it's worse than you can imagine.'"

Becky remembers the moment Cindy's death became a reality to her. She had just left the Finks' house and Kirk was waiting for her at home. "I was driving home one night after Joel Rush showed us pictures (of Cindy's apartment) and her bed looked very neat, so it was obvious that no one had slept in that bed.

"So, I'm driving to Broad Ripple that night—I mean, I will never forget this because it was on Kessler Boulevard and it hit me—out of the blue, it hit me—her bedspread was not on the fucking bed! I lost it. That told me. Why would you take her bedspread unless she was wrapped in it? Until then, I had been able to fool myself a little bit, thinking maybe she's being held somewhere, maybe being tortured or something... I mean, there's all kinds of things."

Sandi says, "That spongy blanket was there but the comforter was not. Yeah. That was tough."

CHAPTER 14

Cindy could not have simply disappeared. Pete Twiddy had been in Speedway almost a week, searching for the woman he loved. Maybe if she had just talked to him more. Maybe if he had just…

In Leguna Seca, Cindy had seemed very worried about something. Scared. And Pete said, "Something's wrong." She never told him what worried her. She kept starting to, and then she would stop and she would not tell him. He didn't force her. He loved Cindy and he was determined to treat her with respect.

They were making the morning drive to the track and Cindy kept insisting nothing was wrong but she asked Pete, "Do you really love me? Would you love me no matter what?" He'd said yes. He wanted to know what she was so worried about. She tried to make light of it but said she was a little worried about Michael.

He asked her, "Well, do I have to worry about something? I mean, am I going to get cheap-shotted walking down through pit row one day or something like that?"

No. She told him not to worry about it. The divorce would be over soon and then she could put it all behind her. She did not want to cocoon herself in thoughts of a past with Michael. She wanted to stretch her wings and fly in the sunshine with Pete. Everything would be all right, she assured him. Soon.

She should be in Florida with him now. Instead, she was... It made him crazy to think where she might be.

He tried to keep tabs on what the police department was doing. Did they have any suspects? Turn up any leads? Know of places to search that had not come up on the radar yet? He was anxious for any word but the police told him nothing. Then he was kicked out. Steve Turner told him to leave. Steve Turner, who was Michael Albrecht's good buddy... bet good ol' Michael was getting all the details he wanted.

The Speedway Police Department issued a missing persons alert to all police agencies in the nation. Lieutenant Jones and Sergeant Joel Rush pursued every possible lead. Eleven Speedway police officers conducted an extensive search around Cindy's apartment. Interviewed, her neighbors had no information to offer.

Theories raced circles and blew smoke, but Cynthia Albrecht's newspaper photo elicited no real answers. The young woman could not be found, so no one could prove anything had happened to her. While others continued to search, trudging through trenches, Don Campbell focused on digging up clues.

Jones and Rush assured Becky and Sandi that progress was being made on the case, but they didn't see any proof. More importantly, they didn't see Cindy. Every person searching believed Michael was responsible, but Michael had not been arrested.

Lt. Jones obtained the passenger list for the flight Cindy came home on. No names raised suspicion and Cindy's seatmates did not appear to be involved. Forensics experts from the crime lab meticulously examined the contents of Cindy's apartment and truck. They found no clues.

Campbell asked the investigators if Michael Albrecht was a suspect in his wife's disappearance. Had they checked out his alibi?

The police gave Campbell limited information. Yes, Michael was still a suspect and they would be checking out his alibi that day. In person or by telephone? They would not say. They did tell Campbell that no physical evidence was found in either Cindy's home or her truck. There were no signs of forced entry and no signs of violence or trauma. Indiana state police processed the residence with laser print equipment.

The Milwaukee FBI was contacted. Special Agent Daniel Craft went in person to interview Kathleen Albrecht. During that interview, he obtained additional telephone numbers for Michael's alibi in Milwaukee. He interviewed these people by telephone.

Craft also spoke with Michael's parents, Gwen and Gerold Albrecht. They told Craft that Michael left their home on Sunday, October 25, around four to four-thirty p.m. to have dinner with Kathleen. Gerold Albrecht knew about the pending divorce. He said that he cared deeply for Cindy and was quite upset she was missing.

After his investigation, Special Agent Craft told Speedway's Chief Dine that Michael's alibi had been checked out and verified from noon on Saturday, October 24, until Monday, October 26.

Now it sounded as if there were no leads.

Lt. Jones now says that a shell was clamped over all out-going information from the investigation because "everybody was a suspect." Michael, Pete, Sandi, Becky, their husbands... everyone was under the magnifying glass and he wasn't giving out information to anyone.

The day after Campbell's visit, Jones went to Florida to interview Michael.

Campbell learned through a confidential source that Michael had recently tried to hire a hit on Cindy and had tried to coerce her to change the beneficiary on a life insurance policy to him. Campbell also traveled to Ft. Lauderdale where Michael Albrecht was staying with his brother Randy. He was there vacationing with his daughter Noel.

Michael and Noel had been staying with Randy since the Thursday after Cindy's disappearance. Campbell arrived at Randy's house at nine-thirty p.m. and noted a red GMC and a black Chevy pickup in the driveway. Michael's white BMW was parked behind the house. The lights inside the house were on and the blinds were drawn.

Michael answered the door wearing shorts and a t-shirt. When Campbell introduced himself, Michael appeared visibly shaken. He did agree to the interview on the assumption that Campbell wanted a profile on Cindy. Campbell noted a small, quarter-to-half-inch nick on the left side of Michael's neck but did not question him about it.

In Campbell's professional opinion, Michael looked scared. His heart appeared to be beating fast. Campbell's gut instinct and decades of experience as a homicide detective told him Michael had killed Cindy. He also knew he was a long way from proving it. And Cindy had not yet been found.

Michael described Cindy as a careless woman who left her doors unlocked. He told Campbell his wife was not well endowed and often went braless at home, sitting around the front room in scanty clothing. It bothered him that Cindy watched television in total darkness. He added that she would have chased the cats if they got out.

Michael did not appear interested in learning who was responsible for Cindy's disappearance. He did not suggest any theories nor make any speculations. He made sure Campbell knew he had an alibi for the 25th and 26th. Campbell said, "in all probability, Heidi, whether she was aware of it or not, was supposed to verify that Cindy was missing on Monday the 26th."

Campbell said that Michael seemed to feign sadness at Cindy's disappearance and showed surprise at the news of the missing Penske money. He stated that the police had told him nothing was missing.

Michael's alibi was a litany of whom he had been with and when. He had taken a friend to Milwaukee to get parts for his BMW at the Little Car Shop on Saturday. All weekend he had been with friends or family, sleeping with his ex-wife Kathleen, and making the rounds of the bars with his old pal, Bill Filter.

He helped his dad winterize the swimming pool and watched the Green Bay Packers/Chicago Bears game. He had dinner with Bill Filter and his girlfriend, and then was out drinking all night with Filter.

Nope. He had been in Wisconsin, hundreds of miles from his wife all weekend. End of story.

Campbell wasn't so sure that was how the story ended. There were plenty of questions he still needed to ask.

Michael was in Milwaukee when Cindy disappeared? Campbell and Sandi agreed to conduct their own investigation. Sandi knew her way around Milwaukee. She was acquainted with some of Michael's family and friends. She agreed to fly with Campbell to Wisconsin to help him locate people and check out Michael's alibi.

They spoke to each person on the list and noted some discrepancies in the times given by Michael. He claimed that he and Bill Filter were at two bars on Sunday night. Bartenders insisted they were there, but on Saturday night. Since Michael was with Filter, Kathleen Albrecht could not account for her ex-husband's whereabouts from about five-thirty p.m. until two a.m.

In his report to Pete Twiddy on November 16, Campbell said, "The reason we now feel that Mike is the number one suspect: He gave conflicting times and dates when establishing alibis, using Bill as a cover for Kathy and Kathy as a cover for Bill. Bill and his girlfriend, Eunice, as a cover from Kathy."

Further suspicions were aroused, Campbell said, because Michael flew home from Leguna Seca and immediately went to Milwaukee on October 18. Earlier that day, Becky had heard a conversation between Mike and Cindy. "He did not want the divorce," she said. "He was still asking her not to file the final papers and to please consider talking with him." Since he was still married to Cindy when she disappeared, he could collect her fifty thousand dollar life insurance policy.

Michael's alibi, Campbell said, was shaky. "We know he wanted to be free on Sunday, October 25, from seven until one for whatever reason. Then there is the withdrawal of the unexplained money."

On Monday, October 26, the day after Cindy disappeared, Michael and his dad went to the First Wisconsin Bank in Milwaukee to withdraw five thousand dollars. Michael told Kathy he'd been saving the cash all summer and hiding it from Cindy. He said he didn't even know she was missing until the next day. Then he said he assumed she was in Florida.

Campbell wondered how Michael managed to save that much money in one summer when he was only working part time for daily wages.

Other investigators too thought the timelines were shifting like Scrabble board letters. The initial report read that Kathleen said Michael left her home at six p.m. and returned at two a.m. In William Krueger's Indiana State Police Supplemental Case Report dated December 15, 1992, he stated that on December 2, he and Jones traveled together from Speedway to Milwaukee to continue the investigation.

His report read, in part:

It was noted that Lieutenant Jones was able to travel from Speedway, IN, to the State Police Post at Lowell in one hour and 50 minutes. The subsequent trip to Milwaukee, from the Lowell State Police Post to the West Allis suburb of Milwaukee involved traveling up I-65, across the Indiana Toll Road, to the Illinois Sky Way, to I-94 through downtown Chicago during the noon hour time period. I-94 was then taken into Milwaukee and then Interstate 894 to South 60th Street to West Allis. The travel time for this leg of the trip was 2 hours and 22 minutes for a total time from Speedway to West Allis of four hours and 12 minutes. This was done at a reasonable travel speed and with heavy traffic through the Chicago area.

The investigators also noted that Michael Albrecht claimed problems with his BMW but never purchased any car parts on October 24, 1992, at the Little Car Shop.

After a phone call with Campbell, FBI Special Agent Daniel Craft re-interviewed Filter. Bill Filter griped that the private investigator was obnoxious. He further complained that Campbell badgered him, trying to get him to change his story.

Special Agent Craft appeared sympathetic in order to draw more information from Filter, who tried to assure Craft that he was telling the truth. He explained that on Sunday, October 25, he had finished a big job and received a large check. He went to his father's bar, arriving in time to catch the second half of the Packers/Bears football game. He became very intoxicated.

He believed Michael picked him up at home around nine or ten p.m. They drank at Filter's bar, and then went bar hopping and cruising. They sat in the car and drank a few beers. Then Michael dropped him off at home between two and three a.m.

Craft issued a warning to Filter, telling him that Cindy was missing and feared dead. Michael Albrecht was a suspect in the case and Filter was providing him an alibi for a very crucial time period. He warned Filter not to get involved in a cover up. "If Cindy Albrecht was killed and if Michael

Albrecht was responsible, then you providing him an alibi could be used against you."

Filter said he fully understood the consequences of lying about something so important and emphatically maintained that Michael and he spent that entire Sunday evening together. Neither of them went to Indianapolis that night.

He thought that Michael would have confided in him if he'd done something to Cindy. He said, "I told him to move on with his life. That in one year he would laugh about it and wonder why he ever felt so bad."

CHAPTER 15

Lieutenant Jones asked Michael if he had ever attempted to find someone to do something "dramatic" to Cindy, perhaps during the course of a robbery? Michael was quick to deny he had ever considered such an idea.

He told Jones that he and Cindy each had a fifty thousand dollar Prudential life insurance policy. He had recently changed the beneficiary on his own policy from Cindy to his children, but he continued to pay the premiums on Cindy's policy. On October 28, the day after he heard Cindy was missing, he sent in another regular premium payment. Michael was the sole beneficiary of the policy.

What Michael did not know was that Cindy had obtained her own life insurance policy through John Alden Life Insurance on July 13, after moving into her apartment. She had initially named him as beneficiary, but changed it to her father after discovering Michael snooped through her apartment.

It was time to talk to Bill Filter again. Campbell perceived him to be the weak link in a phony alibi scheme. On November 9, Campbell made a recorded call to Filter.

Campbell advised Filter that he was calling "to narrow this down again." He said, "I want you to go over what you told me last week and make sure I didn't misunderstand you." Then he asked, "When you guys parted on Saturday, what did he tell you about Sunday? That's where it's getting crucial."

Filter stammered through his story again. Michael called him, he didn't know where from, on Sunday night at ten-thirty. He wasn't sure what time Michael picked him up because he was already in bed and may have dozed while he was waiting. It could have been midnight or later. He believed Michael took him home around one or two a.m.

Had Filter talked to Michael since he last spoke to him in Milwaukee on November 5? Filter said, "I thought, maybe, this thing was all dropped."

"No, it isn't. It's heating up. You know he's put you right in the limelight by using you as an alibi. And I would foresee several interviews from me, the police, and the FBI. If everything you are saying is the gospel truth, then stick to it. But, Bill, you've been around the block. I know you guys were good friends, but don't get involved to the point of going to jail for the man," Campbell warned. His efforts brought no new light to the case.

Roger Penske offered a reward for information that would lead to the whereabouts of his friend and treasured employee. No one responded.

Sandi, Becky, and Pete Twiddy were fuming. It was obvious to them that Michael had done something to Cindy. Why wasn't he being arrested? Why was he in Florida playing on the beach while the woman he claimed to adore was missing?

Police told them that the case was under investigation but they could get no other information. So they plastered Speedway with posters, collected information from every person who would speak to them, and raised questions of their own.

Why hadn't Detective Steve Turner treated Cindy's apartment as a crime scene? He'd gone through the apartment touching items. He allowed smoking in the apartment and requested that Sandi and Becky touch items as well. He specifically told Sandi and Becky as late as Tuesday afternoon that he refused to consider foul play, and he totally refused to consider Michael as a suspect in Cindy's disappearance.

Two days after Turner was supposedly removed from the case, Lt. Jones asked him to obtain Cindy's dental records. Dentist Jack Miller said Turner intimidated him into giving up the dental records immediately without a subpoena. Dr. Miller had meant to be helpful but was angry Turner treated him so rudely.

Other issues that had Cindy's friends pacing the floor were what they saw as delays in the investigation. The police did not interview Cindy's apartment building neighbors until she'd been missing a full week. Most importantly, they did not verify Michael's alibi until November 3. It seemed that Cindy disappeared and for ten days, and no one questioned her husband's whereabouts.

When they were not out wading through mud or talking to people, the tribe gathered at Sandi's house. They discussed, debated, tried to puzzle out an answer. If it was a robbery, why would valuables be left behind? If Michael was still in love with Cindy and eager to do anything to win her back, why did he keep going up to Milwaukee to sleep with his ex? Why wasn't he making any effort to help find her?

Michael climbed into his BMW on October 29, hours before he was scheduled to take a polygraph test. He never notified Lt. Jones that he would not be there. He simply beat a hasty retreat to Florida. Didn't that spell suspicious in capital letters?

When Becky and Sandi were finally allowed to go through Cindy's clothing, it was immediately obvious what was missing. She had not left with a bathing suit, as if going on vacation. She had not dressed stylishly for a meeting with anyone. She was wearing her Garth Brooks t-shirt, the one she bought when she attended Brooks' "Shameless" tour. Since she wore the white shirt as a sleep shirt, she would be wearing nothing else. They were looking for a woman in a big, white Garth Brooks shirt and they were looking for a bedspread. If they could find any of those items, preferably Cindy, alive and well… Not likely, but no one was giving up hope.

Sandi says, "At that point, we just wanted the truth."

The truth from Cindy's own lips would have been most welcome.

CHAPTER 16

Becky and Sandi knew that Cindy had a secret. Just before the final race, she tried to tell them. She kept insisting her secret was big. They would have to give her their most solemn promise that they would never leak one word.

Even though they promised, she kept saying, "No, really. You can't believe what will happen if one word of this gets out." They promised again. She just kept repeating the secret was huge and finally they reached the grocery store and she got out of the vehicle. They realized she wasn't going to tell them.

They decided to give her some space. She would tell them when she was ready. Looking back, they thought it was the job offer from Roger Penske to work on his yacht. That could be the big secret because of course Michael would not like it.

Then Don Campbell discovered some unusual details on some car titles, odometer readings, and VINs that didn't quite jive. Michael often rebuilt cars, especially BMWs. It was starting to look like some of his cars might be stolen.

Sandi's mother-in-law, who worked at the title office, procured more documents for them, more evidence the vehicles Michael claimed he purchased as parts didn't start out that way. The proof was not absolute, probably not enough for a warrant, not yet. The women wondered if Steve Turner was involved in the scheme.

Lt. Bill Jones says absolutely not. "Steve Turner was a lot of things but he wasn't a thief. He was a stand-up guy and I have a lot of respect for him." Jones relates that the day they got the call about Cindy; Turner came to him and offered to take himself off the case. "He said he knew the missing woman, the husband, the friends, everyone involved, and it wouldn't be ethical for him to be a part of the investigation."

The home Michael had shared with Cindy was never searched. There was no probable cause, no hard information that would lead investigators to believe Cindy was being held in the home or had been there since she moved out.

On Monday, November 16, Sandi received a phone call at six-thirty a.m. A former sister-in-law, Wendy Nish, had just heard a report on the radio. Hunters in northern Indiana had found a body. "But I'm sure it's not her," Wendy said.

Becky made the call to Newton County.

The body had been found about a mile off the interstate in a wooded area. There could be multiple explanations for the appearance of a body there. However, it just happened that the spot was about halfway between Speedway, Indiana, and Milwaukee, Wisconsin.

Becky reached dispatch in Newton County and explained her situation. "Our friend is missing. We've been looking for her." An officer took the call and asked Becky to describe her friend. White female. Age thirty-one. Brown hair highlighted blonde. Wearing a big Garth Brooks t-shirt. Thin. Long, skinny legs. Might be wrapped in a flowered bedspread. Five feet, seven inches, 123 pounds. An appendectomy scar on her abdomen. Small scars on her right knee from arthroscopic surgery. Extensive dental work including screws in her jaw.

With each descriptor, Becky could hear the person on the other end of the line take in a breath. She couldn't help thinking that her description matched the body.

The body. Not Cindy. No. If she were describing Cindy she would say, *great smile, agile, energetic, vivacious, and full of kindness. Loving. Caring.* No. The words that described Cindy could not be used to describe a body.

The officer on the other end of the line asked Becky where her missing persons report had been filed. He would get back to her.

Pete Twiddy's recall of the event was, "I got a phone call, I don't remember what day, from one of my friends at Newman/Haas who said that they were driving to work and they had hit an AM station on their radio and they heard somebody say something about a body that they found in Newton County.

"I called Chief Dine up and said, 'do you know about this body?' And he didn't know anything about it. I said there's this body up in Newton County and I need you to check on it.

"He called me back later and said, 'well, we don't think so but we're just going to double check.' I said okay. Then they called me back again, or actually I don't think he talked to me the first time, he talked to Sandra and he asked if anybody knew scars or anything like that that Cindy had on her body. I sort of heard out of the corner of my ear and Sandra was saying, no, I don't know of any scars. And I said, 'I do.' She said, 'what scars?' And I said, 'well, I know that she had an arthroscopic scar on her knee because I had one too and we sort of joked about that we both had this scar on our knee.' I knew she had an appendectomy scar, which Sandra evidently didn't know about. When I told that to Chief Dine, you know, this is where they are and I could tell in his voice that that had to be her body, because he said, 'I'll get back to you.' I knew then that that had to be her. About two days after that, they confirmed. I wanted to see the body, but they wouldn't let me."

CHAPTER 17

The process of examining the crime scene and identifying the body was meticulous and slow. Cindy's friends paced and cried and waited for news. They believed the hunters had found Cindy's body, but prayed they had not. Cindy, dead and tossed out like trash? It was too horrible to think about.

The scant crime scene evidence included a silver and black PPG jacket in a ditch along the dirt lane. It was collected but no one in the investigation realized that PPG had sponsored the IndyCar series at one time. Decades after the murder, Sandi recognized the significance. It could have been Michael's jacket.

No investigator would say anything until they had gathered the facts. The body fit many of Becky's descriptions. The appendix and knee scars were there. The t-shirt and bedspread were not. The positioning of the body implied a sex crime, but this seemed unlikely with the string of a tampon dangling from her vagina. No weapon or other clues were found.

The body would not be easily identified. The pathologist, Dr. Albert Kaltenthaler, removed the seventh cervical vertebrae to preserve the saw marks on it. He severed the woman's hands to keep them for evidence.

Cynthia Albrecht had never committed a crime. Her fingerprints were nowhere on file. Due to decomposition and dehydration of the body, her fingertips had to be injected with saline solution to plump them up enough to get prints. These were compared to prints taken from her apartment.

During the autopsy, the body was examined for trace evidence. None was found. Nothing was found either on the hands or beneath the fingernails. A quantity of maggots were scraped from the left shoulder blade and sent to entomologist Neal Haskel. The tampon was extracted. Pubic hair and a blood standard were obtained. Dr. Kaltenthaler utilized a rape kit on the victim. Noted were an appendectomy scar and scars above and below her right knee.

Neal Haskel took the maggots harvested from the body. He would attempt to pin down an approximate time that the body had been dumped at the site, utilizing evidence from the maggots and climatological data.

Toxicologist Daniel Conn received specimens from Dr. Kaltenthaler for study. He tested for drugs and looked for evidence of any anesthetic that would cause the victim to black out.

The victim had never given birth to a child. The neck laceration appeared to have been inflicted with a sharp instrument with a jagged portion at the rear, like a deer hunter's knife. The saw marks were on the seventh cervical vertebrae, which is at the top of the rib cage. Her larynx and trachea were missing due to an irregular tear in the body cavity. That wound could have been caused by the chewing of some animal. The blood in the cavity was thinned, possibly because it had frozen or maybe because of rain collecting in the gap. There was also a diagonal cut across the upper right portion of the woman's chest, adjacent to the neck area.

The cause of death was listed as "traumatic separation of head and neck from body." The manner of death: homicide.

On November 17, Indiana State Police Detective William Krueger logged details into the FBI's National Crime Information Center and received numerous responses. He also was alerted to a missing persons case in Speedway, Indiana. He contacted Lt. Bill Jones of the Speedway Police

Department, who indicated that he and some other officers would be en route to the state police post at Lowell.

Krueger instructed Jones to bring any items from Cindy's apartment that might help identify the body, including, if possible, hair found in the bathroom sink or shower drains.

When Jones got the call that a body, possibly Cynthia Albrecht's, had been found, Becky filled him in on more details. Cindy had just started her period on the flight home from San Francisco. She would be wearing a tampon. She might still be wearing her Morticia fingernails from the Unsers' party. Jones hurried to make the hundred-ten-mile trip. Steve Turner gathered Cindy's dental records and arrived ahead of him.

Lt. Bill Jones, Sgt. Joel Rush, and Chief Jeff Dine met with Krueger at two p.m. They brought items from Cindy's apartment as requested and gave them to technician Sgt. Rick Grisel. The officers collectively discussed Cindy's case. There were similarities but they needed to be cautious in declaring a positive identity.

They discussed the numerous contacts made with Pete Twiddy, Cindy's boyfriend in Florida, and the fact that he had hired a private investigative firm to look into Cindy's disappearance. They also discussed the interviews with Michael Albrecht and the investigation into his whereabouts in Milwaukee at the time of the abduction. The officers all went to examine the site where the body had been found.

On November 18, Krueger traveled to Speedway to pick up a sealed cardboard box containing Cindy's bedding, personal clothing, and hairs retrieved from the apartment. The Speedway Police Department also had Cindy's luggage, and Krueger was able to collect seven pairs of underwear that possibly contained pubic hair. Also in the luggage and Cindy's purse were three wrapped tampons, which Krueger wanted to try to match to the one the victim had been wearing at the time of her death.

Technician Mike Smilko arrived from the Indianapolis-Marion County Forensic Services Agency and began to examine the luggage and purse for fingerprints. Then Smilko, Rush, Krueger, and Jones went to Cindy's apartment to seek fingerprints from personal items to compare to the corpse.

At the apartment, they discovered that the high embankment through the woods and across the ravine behind the apartment offered a clear view into the apartment if the curtains were opened. From that perspective, one could see if a person entered the bathroom, to take a shower, for instance. The officers also noted scratches in the area of the locking mechanism on the patio door.

On November 19, Lt. Jones contacted Krueger to let him know that the fingerprints from Cindy's apartment were a positive match to those taken from the body. The State Police Laboratory at Lowell also confirmed that pubic hairs taken from the body were a positive match to Cindy Albrecht.

Cindy's body had just been found when Michael and his buddy Willie Hernandez arrived in Indianapolis to pack up the house. The Speedway Police Department picked Michael up for questioning. Hernandez was stuck at the house with a U-Haul truck, wondering what he was supposed to do. If he went outside, he found himself surrounded by reporters. He packed up the contents of the house and filled the U-Haul. He later said that he found nothing inculpatory in nature in the house: no weapon, no bloodstain, and no sign of Cindy.

The next day, Lt. Jones and Sgt. Rush met with Michael Albrecht at the Speedway Police Department. Accompanied by his attorney William Van Barteau, Michael said he wanted to cooperate fully with the investigation, but would not take a polygraph test.

CHAPTER 18

Michael asked to clear up a discrepancy in his previous statement. He said he was at The Rodeo and Filter's Place bars on Saturday night, not Sunday. Bill Filter had been with him in Indianapolis during the month of May and before the Nazareth, Pennsylvania, race.

Michael said he had discussed events with his ex-wife Kathy, and had to remind her that he left her home around nine-thirty that night, as that was the evening he met his daughter's boyfriend. He told officers that he left Kathy's house, stopped at a Super America gas station, and then met Bill Filter around ten p.m. They drank beer, drove around, and picked up a six pack at Filter's father's bar.

They saw no one there Michael knew. Then the pair drove out toward the lakefront and the airport. They were in Michael's vehicle because Filter's had clutch problems.

At one a.m., Michael said he dropped Filter off at home and then returned to Kathy's house. He awakened her at one-thirty a.m. because there was a problem with his key. He spent the night in his ex-wife's bed and saw his family off to work and school on Monday morning.

Bill Filter had invited Michael to see a house he was refinishing. Michael drove to the residence at eight a.m. and visited with Filter for half an hour. Afterward, he went to the bank with his father to withdraw five thousand dollars in cash.

He drove back to Indianapolis, stopping at the Kenosha exit on I-94 and Highway 50 for gas. He took the 294 around Chicago to I-80, then to I-65 South to Indianapolis. He arrived home at five p.m. or later, and purchased gas at the Shell station on Crawfordsville Road. He could not recall whether he had used cash or a credit card for the purchase.

Michael described Cindy as having emotional problems, which he attributed to her previous husband, who beat her. He claimed she had a drug problem when they met in 1985 but the problem had worked out and they married six months after meeting. Recently, he said, Cindy had reverted to smoking cigarettes and marijuana. At times, she stayed out all night with her friends. He tried to discourage this.

Marriage to Cindy, according to Michael, had been "great," particularly from 1990 to 1992. Then the marriage began to crumble. He told the officers that Cindy had told him he was "sometimes not a nice person" and "sometimes not fun." He felt left out when she went to parties without him. He had found cards from another man and marijuana in a dresser drawer. He also found contraceptives she'd bought when they were not sleeping together. He described their fights as screaming and yelling but no physical confrontation.

Her move into her own apartment was an amicable breakup. He did not think it was permanent, just that she was into the party crowd and he was not. It would work out. They split their assets, leaving each with about five thousand dollars. A month later, Cindy was broke and could not explain why, so Michael agreed to buy her BMW from her.

Michael said Cindy told him her relationship with Pete Twiddy was "not serious."

The divorce, Michael said, was to have been final on October 23, 1992. His attorney verified the marriage was officially over at that point. All that was lacking was for Cindy to sign the final papers and the judge to stamp them.

Michael claimed that he forgot to show up for his polygraph test. He was in a hurry to get to Ft. Lauderdale and meet his daughter, Noel.

Michael denied harming Cindy and pointed his finger at Antonio Ferrari, his former boss at Euro Motorsports. He claimed that Cindy had misappropriated funds while working for Ferrari and that "he was extremely angry and wanted to get even with her for doing so."

In his deposition, Michael's brother Randy also raised suspicion about Ferrari, saying, "Apparently, from what Mike told me, that he had affiliations with the Mafia, and they didn't mess around even with small sums of money; they would find a way to get even with her."

Randy said, "He seemed legitimately concerned. However, the Mafia doesn't exist in the nineties as it did in the sixties, fifties, forties, so I was a little skeptical with respect to the situation."

Michael gave Randy's wife Mary Jo a sealed letter expressing his fear of Antonio Ferrari, saying he suspected he might be the next person to be hurt or to disappear. Michael blamed everyone he could think of. He said Pete Twiddy might be having problems with Cindy going out on him. It could be a drug related killing.

The officers collected blood, hair, pubic hair, and fingerprints from Michael. At that time, it was noted that Michael had released Cindy's body to her family with the stipulation that she be cremated. He contributed no money toward her funeral or cremation expenses. Becky and Sandi say that Roger Penske paid those costs and took no credit for having done so.

Michael offered a brief statement to the press:

One: I did not kill my wife, Cindy. Two: I had nothing to do with the disappearance or death of Cindy, directly or indirectly. Three: I have no knowledge of any events leading up to her death or disappearance that I have not shared with the police. Four: I will continue to cooperate with police until her killer is found and convicted. And last, I ask that anyone who has any information about Cindy's disappearance or death come forward and tell the police and help them find the person or persons who did this to her.

Who did this to her? Obviously not Michael—or so he claimed.

Within a day or two, Michael's life in Speedway became miserable. He could not leave his house nor walk through a store without people pointing him out. Randy said, "Oh, he said it was living hell, press was haunting him, everybody knew who he was, he was in the local news. He said he had to leave."

Michael had said nothing about remaining in Indiana. If law enforcement wanted his cooperation, they would have to go to Florida to get it. Michael and Hernandez cleared out the house and put it up for sale. Before they drove south to Florida though, they traveled to Milwaukee to see Michael's family and friends. He wanted to say goodbye to his parents "in case anything happened."

Steve Turner told the Indiana state police on December 1, 1992, both he and Michael had been fired by Dick Simon. He also related that Michael had taken boxing lessons in Chicago in his late teens. After Cindy's disappearance, Turner took the cats to Michael's house. He said he implored Michael to take the polygraph test.

Lt. Jones had Sandi and Becky re-interviewed. Becky said, "Bill Jones believed us to some extent because in December, Turner suddenly retired."

Officers also questioned Pete Twiddy. Pete described final days with Cindy in Albuquerque and his growing concern when she failed to answer his phone calls. He said Cindy had been beaten in previous relationships but she claimed Michael never hit her, although other members of the Penske team insisted that he did.

Pete confessed he called Michael while he was in Florida and said, among other things, "Your alibi sucks." After taking Pete's statement, officers collected hair standards, a blood sample, and fingerprints from him.

On the drive home, Krueger measured the distance from Cindy's apartment to the site where her body was dumped. Traveling I-465 to I-65 to State Road 10, the distance was 100.5 miles.

Cindy's friends felt like they'd taken a fast curve and crashed into a concrete wall. Their souls were so bruised they wanted to limp away, maybe crawl into a pit. They couldn't do that. Not yet. The same vigor they had thrown into the search for Cindy turned another direction. They needed to have a memorial service; not for the body that had been found, but for the vivacious and lively person Cindy had been.

Arrangements for the memorial service were not made public but the message passed with record speed. The vivacious blonde's tragedy united members of all teams. Police stood among the mourners, discreetly watching to see if Michael would show up. Sandi said, "Of course he did not."

Cindy's friends and family filled the St. Christopher Catholic Church in Speedway on November 24, 1992, the day before Thanksgiving. Thirty days after Cindy's disappearance, everyone stopped to grieve. Father Phil DeRae, the cheerful priest Cindy liked so much, flew in from Washington, DC, to officiate.

Roger Penske, whose team was based in Reading, Pennsylvania, chartered a bus for his team members to travel to Indianapolis for Cindy's funeral. Standing among the mourners were Rick and Chris Mears, Emerson and Theresa Fittipaldi, Arie and Mika Luyendyk, Roger and Kathy Penske, and the Bettenhausen family.

Practically the entire racing community, members of racing teams from all over the country, converged on the city of Speedway to pay their final respects, share memories, and collectively embrace their loss.

The church, crowded as it was, fell to stone silence when "The Dance" by Garth Brooks played. The words of the song with its haunting melody echoed their loss.

Details of the investigation were still concealed from Cindy's loved ones. Sandi believed she had been strangled "because there was not one drop of blood in that apartment." No one believed the murder was a sex crime or a drug killing.

Cindy's autopsy revealed she had, at the time of her death, zero percent blood alcohol content. There were absolutely no traces of drugs in her body. The sample was received on November 17, 1992, and the results reported December 10. Michael had lied about Cindy's drug use, her friends said bitterly. What else had he lied about?

In accordance with Michael's wishes, Cindy was cremated, her body delivered to the Central Indiana Crematory on December 16, 1992, where it was reduced to a pile of bone fragments and ash. She was disposed of without her trademark smile and golden curls. She left this world robbed of the hands which had done a thousand acts of kindness.

Sandi was listed as the informant for the death certificate. Wilson-St. Pierre Funeral Home was in charge of the cremation. John F. Worland was the funeral director. The certificate was signed by Gerald A. Burman, coroner of Newton County.

The ashes, given to Cindy's parents, would find their home in Florida. Becky and Sandi chose their own way to memorialize their friend. They had a tombstone made for her. Sandi states, "It just says *Cindy*, but not 'Albrecht' because that's Michael's name, and *RESPECT*."

CHAPTER 19

Days, then weeks ticked past with no news of an arrest. Becky and Sandi kept checking in with Lt. Bill Jones, always hoping for news. There was none. The investigation appeared to be stagnant water and it was choking them to death. The wait evolved to months, then years. "It was like we were screaming and no one was hearing us," Becky said.

December arrived and so did the holidays, but Cindy's mother, Pat, a frail, withered woman, could not wish anyone a happy or merry anything. She wrote to Sandi and Becky: "Cyn doesn't seem to be with me now. She is not at rest or peace and I am bitter and bleeding. Of course I've sat and stared at your cards, sweet caring words, and said, 'I've got to write.' And I haven't. The daily showering, eating, tending to the apt., bills, get done—and I try not to think. Or remember—but aah God—it's hard."

Pat fretted, "My heart's child isn't at peace or at rest yet; and I can't let her go until she is." She begged for information and said, "It's been raining practically all of this month—grey skies. Even the skies weep for my lost girl."

On April 25, six months after Cindy's death, there were still no answers. Pat wrote, "I don't know what I've been waiting for—a light beaming down from the skies—a roll of thunder—a personal message from God—but since I haven't heard from anyone since January—of *course* not the police—I wanted to ask you if there's anything new?

Anything at all? Has anyone found my darling's beautiful head?—Jesus! I nearly go mad thinking of that!"

In May, the girls sent Pat flowers for Mother's Day. Pat sent a card, thanking them. She said her grief was "a natural & normal process—just hard, hard, hard."

Life continued without Cindy. Another racing season began and Sandi took the lead, cooking, and being a gracious host for Team Penske. After that year, the two women wandered away from the work they had loved. They got busy with their own lives and had children. Yet their friendship remained sealed and it was still a three-way friendship. Silence from the police department was discouraging, but they were determined to have justice for Cindy.

After her death, they began to see the world more through Cindy's eyes. They were more aware of the hurts others suffered, more determined to be kind.

Nine months after Cindy's death, Susan Harmon, the young woman Cindy had befriended, fled the scene of an accident causing property damage. She was arrested. At the Marion County lockup, she met a man, twenty-seven-year-old Jeffery Robinette, who was in on a cocaine charge.

Six days later, on July 19, 1993, the pair spent the day boating with some of Susie's friends. That night, Susie refused to have sex with Robinette. He flew into a rage and assaulted Susie with a butcher knife. She tried to escape and managed a frantic call to 911, but he stabbed her twelve times. An unofficial report said he cut her breasts off. When officers arrived, twenty-nine-year-old Susie was breathing her last, and Robinette was fleeing out the back door.

Robinette was caught, arrested, and charged with murder. He was sentenced to sixty years for the murder plus eleven years on other, unrelated charges that had been pending. He went to prison, leaving behind a wife and two young children.

Reading the reports, Cindy's soul sisters realized Susie's life had been a litany of horrors. Perhaps the girl's attraction to the hospitality tent was not just cigarettes. Perhaps the young woman had been starved for a morsel of kindness.

The National Coalition Against Domestic Violence reports that, on average, there are twenty instances of domestic violence every minute.

The National Criminal Justice Reference Center says one in three women will be a victim of this crime in her lifetime.

Safe Horizon's data shows that, although most instances of domestic violence are never reported, one in three homicide victims are killed by their partner.

If the reader has never been a victim of domestic violence, statistics say he or she has a friend or a family member who has been.

Women know they are vulnerable.

Kim Graham had worked hospitality with Cindy, Sandi, and Becky at some of the races. She never saw a specific outbreak of temper from Michael Albrecht, but her ex-husband Terry Hopkins detested the man. Terry, a mechanic, worked with Albrecht, and resented Michael's inability to control his temper.

Tall, slender, and well-dressed, Kim was a booking agent for US Airways. She booked travel for businesses including IndyCar teams, so she was able to travel to races and be with her husband. She helped with hospitality at Laguna Seca and rebooked Cindy's flight so she could attend the Unsers' party.

There was a shadow of melancholy over the weekend because Sandi and Becky were making plans to get together with Cindy one last time before she moved away. Everyone would miss Cindy. Then she was murdered.

"Once she disappeared, everybody knew," Kim says. No one on the race circuit doubted Michael was her killer. Still, the investigation dragged like a road under construction. "Michael was a beast," she says, "and it looked like he'd gotten away with it."

Kim's own marriage was spinning down. Her husband had given up drinking for the sake of his soon-to-be-born child. Now that child was a two-year-old daughter and Kim was pregnant with her son. Terry was coming in late or missing for long periods of time. It was obvious he was drinking again. When he drank, he became violent. Once the baby was born, Kim filed for a divorce.

Now a single parent to a toddler and an infant, Kim struggled to juggle work and parenting. When her son was six months old and her daughter two and a half, she had to fly to Champagne, Illinois. She got back late and had to leave early the next morning. The babysitter offered to keep the children overnight.

Kim had never spent the night without her children but it seemed the best solution. She called Terry and explained that the kids were fine. Exhausted, she went to bed. At 3:15 a.m., Terry phoned her, saying he was worried about the kids. She reassured him they were fine and tried to sleep.

An hour later, her security alarm went off. Terry had sliced the screen porch and broken in. "He was a powder keg," she says. She tried to speak calmly in an effort to diffuse his behavior. She struggled to keep an even tone of voice, even while he beat her. Because he was a mechanic with trademark powerful arms, each punch was a sledgehammer blow. She was defenseless against him. He jerked her around by her hair, ripped her clothes, and tried to rape her. "Ugly behavior," she says.

Then the phone rang. "I have to answer the phone, Terry. That's the alarm company. If I don't answer, they'll send the police." He held her by the throat while she spoke on the phone. She told the ADT dispatcher that everything was fine but she did not give her password.

Now if she could only survive until the police arrived. Her ex continued beating her. He tugged her into the bathroom, breaking every item in sight. Gripping her hair, he arched her neck back, forcing her face up so she could see the pulp of her features in the mirror. He said, "You think Cindy Albrecht was bad, wait until you see what I do to you. Cindy is nothing compared to what I'm going to do to you."

Then she heard the police car pull up. "If I don't go out and tell them everything's okay, they'll come in." She prayed she sounded reasonable. Seeing the car, he let her put her clothes on. Then they went outdoors but he had a vise grip on her.

The police officer would have a gun. He would be trained. He'd know what to do. Holding her ripped clothes together, Kim, with Terry firmly attached, approached the car.

It was empty. There was no officer.

Terry immediately began pulling her back toward the house but she spied another police car a couple of houses down. She convinced Terry to walk over, each step for her a lion's roar of pain from the beating she had taken.

The second car was also unmanned.

Terry force-marched her back to the house and flung her back through the front door. He tugged her through the kitchen toward the garage. "I'm going to take you to the garage and blow your head off."

Fighting him every inch, she found herself dragged like a puppy. Then she saw a light out back and heard a police radio. Once again, she convinced him she needed to speak to the police, to make sure they knew everything was okay.

When they met the officer at the back door, Terry told him, "She asked me over."

"You're gonna have to leave," the officer replied.

Kim didn't wait for an answer. She squeezed by the officer and bolted.

When they received the alarm, the police were half a mile away, but the alarm company had somehow tied Kim's alarm to a neighbor's address, so they had been looking for the wrong house.

"Terry was arrested, but he thought he'd get by with it," Kim says. She had enough sense to insist that the police officers take pictures. They photographed her bruises, her torn flesh, the bite marks, her ripped anus. They found Terry's gun in a toolbox in the garage. The gun he was going to blow her head off with. "God only gives you what you can handle," she says. At least her children had been safe.

At Terry's trial, the jurors saw the photographs and were fearful for Kim. She was terrified too. A year later, Terry called for a reduction in sentence hearing. The judge wanted to hear from Kim. She would have to face Terry in court again. Still terrified he would get out and come after her, Kim told the judge her ex was a danger to her and to her children. "I'm praying you don't let him come home."

He never got out because she went to every hearing. Sentenced to twenty-six years, he served thirteen. Then he was deported back to England where it was reported he committed five violent crimes.

Kim refused to badmouth Terry to his children. She allowed them to go with their paternal grandparents to visit their dad. Nevertheless, it frightened her to realize he has a new, young wife and a child. With courage and determination, she has continued to live her life, but she is still aware that Michael's years of getting away with murder almost led to her own brutal death.

"Once he got away with it for so long, my ex decided he could get by with it too," Kim says.

Michael getting away with it gouged Becky and Sandi like shards of glass in their throats. They were furious Michael was living the good life in Florida when Cindy would never smile again. Free to spend Cindy's fifty thousand dollars of life insurance money, he found a new wife.

The pair decided to give him as little peace as possible. Michael wasn't the only one who could hide behind a payphone. From their vast circle of friends, Becky and Sandi drafted people to call Michael and remind him he was a murderer.

They found a friend whose voice was exactly like Cindy's. She called him up and began yelling, "Where's my head? Where's my head?" When he received these calls, Michael would bellow and slam down the phone. When he moved from Randy's house, he got a pager instead of a phone.

Sandi had a network of friends in Ft. Lauderdale too because she had lived there. It did not take them long to spot Michael's car and follow him. They learned he was working at a BMW dealership, doing the kind of work he loved.

Not for long, if Cindy's friends could help it. Sandi called the dealership. She said she was from the Marion County, Indiana, prosecutor's office. "He is a suspect in his wife's murder and we're trying to keep an eye on him. Can you confirm his employment?"

If they had their way, Michael would not go a single day without being reminded he was a lowlife killer. They sent him packages. One was a Halloween skull that sang "Dead Men Tell No Tales." Another was Michael in a Box, a four-inch cube that looked like a small wooden crate. With the press of a button, the box jiggled, moving across the table while a voice from inside pleaded, "Let me out of here! Let me out of here!"

The ruses were elaborate and involved a number of people who took a certain satisfaction in letting Cindy's killer know they were not forgetting his crime. The women would find an appropriate "reminder" and package it up, wearing gloves. They would send it to a friend somewhere who would repackage and mail it. Sometimes racing team truck drivers would mail the packages from odd places. They wanted Michael to feel that people all over the country were aware of his guilt.

CHAPTER 20

Five years. Cindy's killing had gone unresolved for five years.

When the investigation floundered, Pete Twiddy felt like he was slogging through quicksand. "I went to the police and pleaded with them to make me a suspect," he says, because he felt that they were doing nothing.

He says Steve Turner broke out in a sweat every time he walked into the Speedway police station. "There was a point when I believed they were all in on it—a cover-up." He felt saturated in "rage and helplessness."

Asked for DNA samples, Pete complied willingly. "Some stooge stuck me three or four times to take blood," he recalls. Officers also wanted a sample of pubic hair. Pete defiantly reached into his pants, pulled out a handful of hair, and "didn't even flinch." He said, "Look, I got nothing to hide."

He was suspicious that Michael had fled to Florida, "the hardest state to extradite a wanted criminal from."

Roger Penske, he says, demonstrated true friendship in sending his head of security, John McGinley. "Roger came to me and seemed worried because I'd been dating Cindy," and maybe the Penske security was "Roger's way of keeping an eye on me."

Roger had also loved Cindy and "gave her his cashmere jacket," Pete says. "I kept that jacket for the longest time because it smelled like her." Pete describes Penske as the only man he knows who will make people feel valued "and reject publicity."

The years that plodded between the murder and the trial were a twilight zone. The need for closure haunted Pete. "To this day I thank my boss—I don't know how I kept my job—but I'd do everything I could to make justice happen."

Rick Mears tried to help him through it, saying, "You have to move on and you have to let this go. We're all moving on."

Pete thought he was bringing people down. Nobody was ever going to take the case. He got a tattoo of a velociraptor coming out of his leg. "It was the meanest, orneriest animal that ever lived on this earth. It was anger coming out of me."

Sandi and Becky's anger kept them focused. They were driven to keep speaking up. They had to be Cindy's voice. They had discovered that when a murder is committed, the victim has been silenced physically and legally. Forever.

A killer, once accused, has many rights, including the right to have an attorney defend him. The victim is at the mercy of the prosecutor. Often, only the most promising and winnable cases end up in court because attorneys are conscious of their success rates. A case with a poor chance of conviction often means that the victim, along with friends and family, will never see justice.

The reality is that more crimes are committed than can be prosecuted. Multitudes of crimes are plea bargained because there is no time on the docket for the court to hear all the cases. Other grievances are simply laid aside. It looked like Cindy's murder would lie in the dust.

Pete and the women were not giving up. They were going to see to it that Lt. Bill Jones and the Speedway Police Department never gave up either.

Jones was frustrated too. The case wasn't going to get any better and the Marion County prosecutor's office appeared to be content to let sleeping bones lie. When the Albrecht case was discussed by prosecutors at all, the question was where it should be tried: in Marion County where she was abducted or in Newton County where she was found? No prosecutor wanted to run with such a high-profile case, not without a confession or some major, not yet found evidence.

The only thing that seemed to have changed since the Albrecht murder was a tweak in politics. Scott C. Newman was elected Marion County prosecutor in 1994. The change in leadership was almost immediately evident. Newman was aggressive about putting away lawbreakers.

Deputy Prosecutor Larry Sells had been with the prosecutor's office since 1991. Under Newman, Larry and his fellow deputy prosecutor John Commons focused on murder. Commons, a former Marine captain, was iron tough and sharp enough to back anyone down. His courtroom style was quick, ferocious, and brilliant.

Lt. Jones had found no new breaks in the Albrecht case. With nothing but circumstantial evidence, it looked hopeless. Then Jones read that Larry and Commons had won a conviction in a case with much leaner evidence. He contacted Newman's office and was told that he could present his case to the two deputy prosecutors. Although they were in the midst of trying fourteen homicide cases in a single year, they took time to hear what Jones had to say.

"I just assumed it was not much of a case until I heard from Bill Jones," Larry says. "Bill Jones' investigation of this case was thorough. He had every statement, every bit of evidence, and background on everyone involved." The Speedway lieutenant had enough depositions and reports to fill several Bankers Boxes. He also had crime scene photos, autopsy records, and maps.

"Then I was aghast that Albrecht was walking around a free man," Larry said. "Let's get this son of a bitch!"

The investigators had established motive. They had ruled out other suspects. Witnesses would testify that Michael tried to hire someone to harm Cindy. Michael Albrecht had slain Cindy for no better reasons than money and his own ego.

1996 and 1997 were hectic years for Larry and Commons. They were constantly investigating, preparing, presenting cases. They would walk out of the courtroom and mindlessly eat a sandwich while studying depositions, arrest reports, and investigators' notes. The work continued until the stars of the sky faded with weariness, and then attorneys and investigators would snatch sleep as they slid into morning.

For Larry Sells, each day of every trial had to be as energetic as his first and as vital as his last. Coffee and splashes of cold water kept him alert enough to close the net around the next villain who sought to flee justice. While he was trying those fourteen cases in 1997, Cindy Albrecht's barbaric murder was never far from his mind.

Between and sometimes even during the task of presenting other cases, he took time to review the voluminous law enforcement investigative files on the Albrecht case. The more he read, the more determined he was to bring Cindy's killer to justice.

Before a prosecuting attorney can go to court and prove his case, he has to demonstrate he can prove it. The paperwork, evidence, and statements that must be collected and presented require hundreds of hours of work. Witnesses must be found, interviewed, and subpoenaed if they are to testify.

Building the case was a Taj Mahal of labor, but Larry was in his element.

His wife Melanie describes her husband as a calm, laidback guy, devoted to his family and considerate of others. He is also predictable, she says, "like at nine p.m., his switch turns off." His face stretches into dinosaur yawns and "he can't even talk," she says. He may turn into a pumpkin when the clock strikes nine, "but at five a.m., he's up and busy and moving around in the kitchen."

That, she says, is Larry at home. Larry the attorney is a complete dichotomy. When working on a case, he can function at full speed all night long, writing out his final arguments in longhand, or producing "Little Drummer Boy" clacks on the keyboard with his two-finger typing skills.

Before joining the prosecutor's office, Larry worked as a small-town lawyer. Crimes were usually petty, court presentations routine. "He was not happy," Melanie says. "Prosecution is his niche. To me, it's what he was born to do."

Larry delved into Lt. Jones' records. He talked to the people who had known Cindy, especially Sandi, Becky, and Pete. Larry was impressed with the fortitude shown by Cindy's friends. He says, "They kept pushing the detectives and the prosecutor's office. Their involvement helped motivate me to work harder on the case."

Their long-term pleas for justice reminded him on a daily basis why he had chosen prosecution. He had passed up other choices. The long and lean attorney, sometimes mistaken for Thomas Magnum from *Magnum P.I.*, had been a model and had taken acting lessons. He had also had a chance at a career in baseball. He chose law.

Larry had worked as a defense attorney, but he resented people juggling their way through the system, escaping conviction when they shouldn't have. "But having done that helped me in prosecution because I always knew what the defense was up to. I knew what I'd do in their place," he says. He was determined to know the case better than the defense attorneys did.

One of the weapons Larry planned to use against the defense was a statement made shortly after the murder by a man named A.J. Mobley.

On November 23, 1992, fifty-one-year-old A.J. Mobley of Columbus, Indiana, offered a voluntary statement concerning Cindy's murder. Lt. Jones and Sgt. Rush took his statement. A self-employed designer who did engineering work, Mobley was known around Gasoline Alley as Dr. Turbo. He was the inventor of the wastegate, which had become a part of every Indy 500 winning car since 1968.

Mobley had been in Indianapolis in mid-May 1992 to sell Dick Simon some of his wheel nut assemblies. There, he met Michael Albrecht "and he said some things that, that kind of astounded me at the time." Mobley thought the man was just venting but "he seemed too serious and too determined about it and so I started questioning."

Mobley and Albrecht were looking over wheel nuts and sockets when Michael was summoned to the phone; he had a call from his wife. He returned and told Mobley, "I'm gonna kill that no good bitch." He was having trouble with his divorce and she wouldn't leave him alone, Michael complained.

The conversation began to ping pong between racing and Michael's grievance. Mobley said Michael told him he could kill his wife and get away with it, that he was smart enough to not get caught. He said Michael told him specifically that no one would find the body "up in northern Indiana" in a place "where I been when I was a teenager a few times." Nobody would figure it out because "I'm gonna cut off her head. I'm gonna take her head with me. I'm gonna take her head and put it about a hundred miles away from the body."

Mobley argued that killers got found. Michael would never get away with it. Why not just go through with the divorce? Was his wife embarrassing him? Running around with other men? He says Michael replied, "Naw, she ain't runnin' around with anybody that I know of." His complaint, Mobley said, was "she waits on other guys hand and foot and sucks up to other guys, and at home she, she won't treat me nice."

That was her job, Mobley pointed out. It would be senseless for his wife to be angry at Michael for doing his job, wouldn't it? Mobley said Michael became more and more insistent that he was going to kill his wife. Mobley said he mentioned the conversation to another employee, Eldon Rasmussen.

Michael's plan included an alibi. "He definitely said that they would help him provide an alibi." Lt. Jones wanted to know, had he named this alibi? Mobley said no, just someone north of Indianapolis. Michael had said, "I'll shoot her or I'll knock her in the head or I'll choke her to death." He'd even mentioned spraying automotive solvent into her mouth, using the volatile substance to kill her. Mobley said Michael was specific in saying that there would be no marks on the body.

Mobley denied hearing the details he related on the news. He had never known Cindy's name and did not realize Michael had actually done the crime until the body was found. Jones asked why it took him so long to come forward. Mobley said other people would come forward or a lie detector test would reveal the truth. He was also afraid that if he spoke up, Michael would kill his family.

Michael also made specific remarks about his wife's head, Mobley claimed, saying, "I think I'll bury it in my parents' yard. It would make good compost. No, I think I'll bury it in her parents' yard. It would be right under their noses. They would never think of looking there."

In a previous interview, Mobley had told Krueger that he was a graduate of Purdue University. He altered that statement. He had taken engineering classes sponsored by IUPUI but had not taken the history or English classes needed for a degree.

Larry studied Mobley's statement and discussed it with Jones. He would have to pass this gem of information over to the defense, of course, but that would not hurt his case any. Mobley was a notorious liar with a fake degree. Let the defense spend time with his testimony. Larry would never put him on the stand.

CHAPTER 21

Michael's brother Randy had hoped to disconnect himself from the investigation, but he worked for the sheriff's department in Broward County, Florida, and was ordered by his superiors to give Indiana law enforcement his deposition and assist in the investigation.

Present at Randy's deposition were Larry Sells and John Commons, along with Michael's attorneys, Drew Findling and Richard Kammen. During the interview, Findling consistently referred to Cindy's murder as "the incident." Larry knew better. He wasn't taking Michael down for an "incident." He was taking him down for murder.

In the summer of 1992, Randy related, Michael called, saying he and Cindy were becoming increasingly distant. Michael often cried during these conversations and asked Randy for advice. Randy counseled him to let go.

Michael kept calling, crying, depressed, lost; he did not know what to do. He was hurt and angry.

Michael alerted Randy to the potential for violence almost two months before Cindy disappeared. Randy received a strange call from Michael in September of 1992, in which Michael said little except that he needed Randy to call him back on a payphone. Randy complied.

When they reconnected, Michael said Cindy was coming to visit her mother in Ft. Lauderdale. Did Randy know anyone who could "rough her up" while she was there? Maybe he could find a Cuban who would do the job cheaply.

Stunned, Randy replied, "Let me think about it for a couple of days." Randy mentioned the call to his friend, Willie Hernandez. Hernandez, who was Cuban and lived in Hialeah, thought the idea was bizarre.

When Michael made a second call, the two brothers once again moved to payphones.

Larry asked, "So even at that early stage, perhaps a month and a half or two months before her disappearance, Michael's already concerned about phones being tapped?"

Yes, he was, Randy replied.

"Do you know why he would have had any concern at that point about either his phone being tapped or yours?" Larry prodded. "Who would have been tapping his phone, did he say?"

Randy answered, "He indicated it might be law enforcement."

"Did you know that sometime about that same period that Michael Albrecht and Antonio Ferrari had a phone conversation that was taped and monitored by law enforcement, in which Michael Albrecht and Antonio Ferrari discussed the fact that Michael Albrecht had asked Antonio Ferrari to do something to Cynthia?"

"No," Randy replied, "I didn't know that."

When Michael repeated his request to have something done to Cindy, Randy told Michael he should "leave that situation alone."

Michael eventually realized Randy was not going to help him exact revenge on Cindy.

Later, after Cindy went missing, Michael told his brother, "Some of the things I tell you may hurt you." When he said that, Randy shut the conversation down. He refused to hear more for fear he would have to take police action against his brother.

In other conversations, Michael asked Randy where he could go and not be extradited. He also mentioned that he owed money to a Wisconsin connection. Then he went with

Randy and Willie Hernandez to look at boats. Randy said, "Mike's plan was to buy a boat. If the authorities came looking for him, he would evade arrest by boating out past the three-mile limit from shore into international waters."

Speaking up for his brother, Randy stated that Michael was being harassed by investigators. A Ft. Lauderdale detective, whom he could not name, had been in attack mode.

In addition, individuals had called Randy's house. "We were getting some death threats on the phone because my voice on the phone sounds very similar to Mike's, and Mike stayed with us for a while… the person on the other side said, 'I'll kill you' and hung up the phone. Then there was heavy breathing and what have you. I believe we eventually ended up changing our phone number, so it was pretty annoying."

Randy knew that marriages could turn ugly. He was trained in domestic violence work. The officer's task in those situations is to de-escalate the conflict, separate the warring parties, and take statements. The officer, Randy said, must speak calmly. "Resolve to come up with some type of decision and act accordingly." His experience was that once diffused, the conflict settled. People got emotional sometimes and threatened to kill over a traffic ticket. Threats were common in domestic disputes.

Randy kept hoping that was the situation with Michael and Cindy. He wanted Michael to be uninvolved. The murder had punctured a dynamic brotherly bond. Scott, Mike, and Randy Albrecht had discussed teaming up to perform. Randy said, "We had connections working together in music. We wrote—co-wrote songs and performed them, and ended up publishing some of our material. So it would have been a lucrative situation." At one point, they were poised to sign a national contract.

Randy and his brothers were all big men. He described six-foot tall Scott as "the dwarf of the litter." Asked about Michael's infamous neck muscle test, Randy told investigators that the grip evolved from childhood nights of watching wrestling on television.

He said the test hurt. The idea was to grasp the victim from the back and "a lot of pressure was applied to the, like, side and upper part of the shoulders, and could probably actually put you to sleep under certain circumstances." He never saw anyone pass out when Michael used the hold.

Near the end of Michael's stay with Randy, the brothers agreed not to talk about the case for fear of wiretaps or parabolic microphones. Michael had developed a fear of electronic listening devices. But one phone call would come back to haunt him.

CHAPTER 22

Antonio Ferrari owned Euro Motorsports, a low-budget Indy Racing League (IRL) team. Michael had previously worked for him. After Dick Simon fired Michael at the end of the Indianapolis 500, Ferrari hired him on a part-time, hourly basis.

Ferrari saw that Michael was hurting and needed a friend. He tried to offer advice and remind Michael there were plenty of women in the world. Michael wanted more than kind words. He believed that because Ferrari was Italian, he had connections to the Mafia. Maybe for a certain amount of money, his Cindy problem could be permanently disposed of?

Ferrari pretended he would make some calls, but he did not take Michael seriously. A little time would fix things.

Ferrari placated Michael's rage with the pretense that his clothing supplier, John Carlos Incasa, was a crime connection. He led Michael to believe something could happen at the Nazareth, Pennsylvania, race, while they were close to New York. When Cindy emerged from that race alive and well, Ferrari offered the excuse that Incasa never called him back.

During the investigation, Jones and Krueger had Ferrari call Michael in Florida and they recorded the call.

Albrecht: "This is 761-8145. I'm sorry I'm not here to be able to take your call, but if you leave a message at the beep."

Ferrari: "Good morning, this is Antonio Ferrari calling for Michael Albrecht. I get his numbers from Steve and am calling on Friday, December 4, 11:30 is the times. If Mike is in these numbers, Michael Albrecht. Mike, please call me back in Indianapolis in my home numbers. I will be here today most of the day or tomorrow morning. I'm leaving for Italy on Sunday. Thank you."

Michael returned the call. Ferrari said he had just returned from Italy and seen the big story. They both agreed that it was incredible.

Ferrari: "You know I was not here, but the few times I was here was something that, you know, I been interview from police, a lot of things."

Albrecht: "Yeah, everybody has, not just you."

Ferrari: "But, you know, it's something that really I can't imagine happening this way, it's so crude way, you know."

Albrecht: "Yeah, I do."

Ferrari: "But you are so down... I asked to Steve Andres again, some, you know, know where you are because I'm leaving again Sunday. I said I want to talk with Mike, I've not talked to him in longs times."

Michael told Antonio he was at a payphone. He gave Antonio the number and asked him to call back. Antonio did.

Albrecht: "When they spoke to me, you know, I didn't even mention your name. I basically told them that, you know, I worked and that is how it is."

Ferrari: "Yeah, but you know that the team has been, you know, you are worked for us. So basically, I was interview a couple of times. Just I was interview also in terms of financially, you know."

Albrecht: "Yeah."

Ferrari: "So I said. yeah, with Mike, I paid him per diem and I give him some money and they wanted to know more detail about it, you know."

Albrecht: "Yeah."

Ferrari: "And they asked all kind of stories. But that was something I told (indiscernible), I have no spend a long times here. So, you can understand that I was not one hundred percent in this case. I learned more from magazine, from other people."

Albrecht: "Yeah."

Ferrari: "Then, Mike, but I know that, what is you feeling, you know, the stories, you know, what do you think about? Because it's ridiculous. It's incredible."

Albrecht: "Well, for one thing, they know I was in Milwaukee and they've been up there and they've talked to the people up there five or ten times already."

Ferrari: "Sure, sure."

Albrecht: "They keep talking to them and talking to them, so they obviously don't think that I did it, okay? It's impossible. I had nothing to do with it."

Ferrari: "But I got to thinks, you know—what do you think, who can be in all those stories? So lurid."

Albrecht: "I personally think that the people who are pointing fingers, I've heard they think Sandi and Mike Fink are involved. That's my personal feeling. I mean, I don't have any way to prove it, but that's my feeling. Because Sandi knew that she was not on really great terms with Cindy. Cindy told me that Sandi was useless and was only in it for the beer and the gear."

Ferrari: "Sure, sure."

Albrecht: "And they had another girl that they liked better, and I think Sandi knew this and she was probably going to be replaced and they would be in shit for money if that happened. Plus, if anything happened to Cindy, Sandi was going to be the first one (indiscernible)."

Ferrari: "God."

Albrecht: "And her husband Mike. You know what I think of Mike Fink."

Ferrari: "Oh yeah, exactly. But, you know, I also heard that it was something regarding drug and stolen car."

Albrecht: "Yeah, they tried to say something about a stolen car."

Ferrari: "Oh yeah."

Albrecht: "That's what they said. But I mean, it's not stolen. I mean, I've had the thing for a fucking year and a half. If it was stolen, they would have found that out when I registered it."

Ferrari: "Sure, sure. Plus, Mike, you know, I don't thinks that is the problem, you get enough money from—"

Albrecht: "Yeah, exactly. I mean—"

Ferrari: "And, Mike, you know what has been asked to me has been if you have any life insurance."

Albrecht: "Yeah, I took out life insurance, but fuck, it was taken about four years ago. It's not something that I just took out, you know."

Ferrari: "Okay. I said, he no have it because he was not official working for me."

Albrecht: "No, that's right."

Ferrari: "Exactly. So I answer it this way."

Albrecht: "I mean, you know, like I said, Antonio, I never mentioned, you know, your name other than the fact that I worked there. I mean, you know, I tried to keep everybody out of it."

Ferrari: "Exactly. Hey, Mike, but you know what, I was scared is that when, is basically, we have all this personal conversation, maybe somebody heard what you was telling me and all this situation and maybe can report. I was scared to, just as I wait, basically, long times before I tried to reach you because I was scared maybe you talk to somebody, and telling that, you know, we was talking, you was asking me opinion. For example, I was scared that you was looking for Nazareth for my friend John Carlos."

Albrecht: "No, it's not a problem. I never spoke to anybody concerning anything that you and I talked about. That was just between you and me. And anything else that comes up is just bullshit."

Ferrari: "No, no, I know because—"

Albrecht: "You know what it is, Antonio, you go out in the shop and you make a joke. You say, you know women, you can't live with them but you can't shoot them. And the next fucking thing you know, the cops come in there and they say, oh well, you know, you made this joke so maybe you were serious."

Ferrari: "No, no."

Albrecht: "I mean, that's all there was to it. I never—"

Ferrari: "Hey, Mike, what you decide to do right now? You are in Florida with your brothers there?"

Albrecht: "Well, I've got a BMW to work on down here, I'm doing that. I'm looking around for work right now because I can't just sit here and do nothing."

Ferrari: "Exactly."

Albrecht: "But I really don't know. I want to see what the fuck happens with the deal because I really have no idea what the hell's going on. I mean, you know, I was just as scared as you when the police came around and asked me all the same questions. They said, yeah, you know, we heard that you wanted to have her killed and all this other shit, and I said it's a bunch of bullshit. And I don't know who the fuck is telling you this shit, but if I said something, it was probably when I was pissed off and maybe I said something, look, you know she's a bitch or whatever or maybe I made a joke about it."

Ferrari: "They show me many of those letters that you also show me. I said I know that Mike has some letters, but I don't remember exactly which one, you know, I did other things. And they asked me when I see you and everything. But I thinks the same interview has been done to a lot of other people."

Albrecht: "Oh yeah, they've interviewed everybody. They went up to Milwaukee and they interviewed my whole family, a couple of my friends. They went down to Phoenix and interviewed John. They've been every place. They're not picking on you or anybody else—"

Ferrari: "No, no, I know."

Albrecht: "They've talked to everybody on the team up here. I never fucking talked to anybody about what you and I talked about at all, she's dead, that was basically just personal and I was asking for your advice and that was it. And I told them I worked for you and that's it. They never asked me how much money or anything like that."

Ferrari: "No, Mike, that's not a problem. But, Mike, you don't have any other feeling, you know, I thinks you are pretty, anyway, down on these stories because when it was so mad, so angry, you know."

Albrecht: "Yeah."

Ferrari: "But is very, very, here is very heavy, it gets to you, you know. Everybody think about you."

Albrecht: "I know everything is headed against me. That's the only reason I left, Antonio. First of all, being in the same house where I was living wasn't no good because everything was a bad memory. So I figured the best thing to do was to get out of that, so I did. And I came back down here because this way I don't have to put up with all the fucking hundred phone calls every fucking day. Stopping by the fucking house. I don't really want to talk about that shit (indiscernible). And I done enough crying and, you know, being bummed about her already. I mean, I really don't need it."

Ferrari: "Hey, Mike, I want to tell you if you need anythings, I leaving again Sunday. I would be back next week. We have press conference in Italy with the CART. But call me. You have my numbers now. So we have an office now in my house that is the new numbers, so call me anytime you needs, okay?"

Albrecht: "All right."

Ferrari: "See you after the stories, because if everything's fine, you may want to go back to racing, still remain an open door."

Albrecht: "I appreciate that. Just like I said, man, there's no problem. I didn't involve anybody else. I didn't tell them what I talked about with Andy or with you or anybody else. It's not their fucking business. I was just crying on somebody's shoulder."

Ferrari: "Sure, sure. Hey, Mike, be strong, okay?"

Albrecht: "Yeah, I'll try to."

Ferrari: "Bye bye."

Albrecht: "Thank you."

Larry listened intently to the recorded conversation and made careful notes of what was said. More important to his case, however, was what was not said.

CHAPTER 23

On June 4, 1997, Michael was living in Georgia with his new wife, Denise. Cindy's goon squad might have driven him out of IndyCar, but she was long dead and he was still doing work he loved, tweaking the mechanical systems of BMWs. He was no longer being harassed by phone calls. He had no reason to think about his ex at all. He was doing all right, just living his life.

It could have all gone smoothly for him except for a bit of paperwork. On that day, all the documentation was finally completed. The State of Indiana was charging Michael Albrecht with murder. The Marion County prosecutor's office presented the State of Georgia with an affidavit for Michael's arrest.

Two days later, on June 6, at his place of employment, Michael was arrested. Handcuffed like a criminal, he was brought before a Georgia State Superior Court judge. Charged with murder, he was detained without bond.

Held in the county jail outside Atlanta, Georgia, Michael called his old friend, Bill Filter, and talked about sports. "But that was pretty much, I think, superficial. He wanted to make sure that my nerves were hanging in there," Filter said later.

On June 9, prosecuting attorneys for the State of Indiana presented and obtained an Order of Requisition for the apprehension of the defendant, Michael Albrecht, and the return of the defendant to the State of Indiana.

Michael filed a Writ of Habeas Corpus on July 2. He hoped to convince a judge that he was held illegally. The State of Indiana did not agree. Larry Sells and Lt. Jones flew to Georgia when the matter went before the Honorable Edward Wheeler. After hearing arguments, Judge Wheeler did not release the prisoner.

Both sides paced for five and a half weeks, awaiting the Court's decision. Finally, another hearing was held on August 11.

At 11:33 a.m., Judge Wheeler rendered his decision. "A Court considering a Writ of Habeas Corpus filed by a person facing extradition is limited to four readily verifiable facts: whether the extradition documents on their face are in order; whether the petitioner has been charged with a crime in the demanding state; whether the petitioner is the person named in the request for extradition; and whether or not the petitioner is a fugitive from justice.

"Accordingly, the Court denies the Petitioner's Petition for Writ of Habeas Corpus and orders that Michael Albrecht be remanded to the DeKalb County Sheriff's custody to be extradited to the State of Indiana. So ordered this eleventh day of August 1997."

Lt. Jones and the Indiana officers with him immediately obtained a copy of the Order and picked up Michael from his cell.

Between eleven-thirty and eleven-forty-five a.m., Michael's counsel received a message from Judge Wheeler's office that the defendant's petition had been denied. Michael's attorneys made plans to visit Michael to review the Order and discuss his right to file a notice of appeal.

While they planned their strategy, Michael was being handcuffed and transported to the airport.

Michael's counsel was unable to contact the local prosecuting attorney until five p.m. Then they were unable to find Michael. At five-thirty p.m., the local prosecuting attorney called Michael's attorneys to report that their defendant had already arrived in Indianapolis.

The murder suspect's arrival in Indiana was big news. Broadcasts of the event illuminated all local television channels. ABC broadcaster Derrik Thomas gave the camera a full view of Michael trudging through the airport, vainly trying to conceal his handcuffs in the folds of his sweatshirt. Lt. Jones, almost a foot shorter than Michael, looked like David leading Goliath. Michael, surrounded by law enforcement, was not going anywhere.

Michael looked at no one and answered no questions until he spied Pete Twiddy amidst the crowd. Then he yelled out in anger, but Jones did not let him pause, not for half a step. Pete had flown from Florida to see the event. "I never said a word. But I positioned myself so that he would see me coming off the plane," he says. He had been waiting a long time to see Michael in chains.

Larry told the viewing audience, "He killed her and we're gonna prove it!"

The Marion County prosecutor's office had filed charges against Michael Albrecht in June 1997. Now that Michael had been unsuccessful in fighting extradition from Georgia, where he had lived the previous two months, his attorney, Susan Brooks, claimed, "Under Georgia law, the Defense is allowed to present evidence at an extradition hearing. The judge did not allow that in this case." She said an Atlanta attorney was handling the appeal.

"It's a moot point," Larry declared. "He's here. We brought him back on a lawful order. Regardless of what the Georgia courts do, the court here has jurisdiction. He's here and here he'll remain."

Brooks also filed a motion to release Michael on bail. She said, "If the Defense shows the evidence against Albrecht is weak, a judge may set bail and allow his release pending trial."

Within seventy-two hours, Michael had an initial appearance before Judge Jane Mangus-Stinson. Susan Brooks appeared on Michael's behalf. Michael claimed that the extradition documents were not on their face in order and that he was not a fugitive from the State of Indiana. His argument was not persuasive. He continued to be held without bond.

Atlanta defense attorney Drew Findling claimed that Michael's extradition from Georgia violated his rights. Findling said, "Either Indiana voluntarily brings him back to Georgia, or we would seek Federal Habeas relief to get him removed."

Judge Mangus-Stinson replied, "I don't intend to move to Georgia. I don't see myself as being on the Georgia Court of Appeals." She scheduled a September 5 hearing to begin the presentation of evidence in the matter. A preliminary trial date was set for October 20.

The following week, Lt. Jones went to the jail and attempted to speak with Michael. Incensed, Michael's attorneys charged that Jones did not advise Michael of his Miranda rights, particularly the right to keep silent and to have an attorney present.

On September 4, 1997, Jones again attempted to speak to Michael without his attorneys, even though he was, according to the defense, "still aware of the fact that the defendant was fully represented by counsel."

The defense filed a Request for Restraint, arguing "Detective Lieutenant William Jones's conduct in twice visiting the Defendant in an effort to obtain incriminating statements and/or confessions, knowing that Defendant is represented by counsel, and failing to advise Defendant of his right not to speak to the officer, is inexcusable. That such conduct warrants not only a reprimand but an order forbidding that any such future conduct take place."

One small window had been slammed on the prosecution's fingers, but Larry had his strategies. He planned to dominate the courtroom from day one.

Larry Sells cut his courtroom teeth practicing with the best attorneys he could find. He also paid his dues as a defense attorney, but weeded out the cases he would not represent. "I never defended a child molester," he says.

Larry decided that his knowledge of defensive schemes would be better used in prosecution. Now he had a chance to put away a killer. He could bring some closure to the lacerated hearts of Cindy's family and friends.

He felt very good about that. He poured more coffee and stayed focused. The clock was ticking.

CHAPTER 24

Lieutenant Jones' vigorous investigation revealed that by late October of 1992, Michael was obsessed with getting even with Cindy. He renewed ties with his old Milwaukee friend Bill Filter. During the 1992 Indy 500 race, Filter stayed in Michael's house, along with Michael's roommate John Weland.

Filter's time with Michael was sporadic that May. They managed a few drinks, some small conversations, and dinner at Hooters. In September and October, the two buddies seemed to do a lot of catching up, generating about thirty phone calls.

That fall, Michael realized that neither his brother, Randy, nor his employer, Antonio Ferrari, were going to help him. But Bill Filter? Now there was a friend. They'd shared a long history and established trust.

Michael invited Filter back to Speedway in October for a little show and tell. Michael showed his friend the wooded area behind the apartment, the steps leading up to Cindy's balcony on the second floor, and the sliding glass door. He showed Filter a path through the woods leading to the poorly lit backside of the Marsh Supermarket, just a moment's drive to the interstate.

Filter could help him kill Cindy. She could be strangled. No blood. No mess. When Michael suggested they could remove her head, Filter told Michael he was crazy and went back to Milwaukee.

A couple of weeks later, Michael was back in Milwaukee, demanding that Filter help him. Timing was crucial. The divorce would be final October 26 and Cindy had to be killed before then. Filter refused to help kill Cindy, but he did agree to be an alibi if necessary.

So how involved was Filter? Did he assist in the murder? Could he have? Larry intended to find out. He obtained a number of documents including a copy of Bill Filter's medical records from the Veterans Administration Hospital.

Since February 4, 1986, when he was thirty-three years old, William Filter had been treated at the VA Hospital for chronic lower back pain and acne. He complained of muscle spasms and weakness in his right leg. He claimed he had difficulty driving more than twenty minutes due to leg stiffness and loss of feeling. The VA awarded him a monthly compensation of $185 for being thirty percent disabled: twenty percent for back pain and ten percent for acne rosacea.

This did not sound like a man who could creep up a flight of stairs in the dark, break into an apartment, and overpower and kill a woman. It certainly did not sound like a man who could carry one hundred-twenty pounds of dead weight silently down stairs and across a lawn. It did not sound like he could tote more than half his own body weight through dark woods treading an uneven path.

No, Bill Filter was no killer. Nevertheless, he was the weak link in Michael Albrecht's alibi. The question was: would Filter be willing to serve prison time for Michael?

Jones contacted Filter and advised him to seek legal counsel. He told Filter that he had until nine-thirty a.m. Monday morning to contact the Marion County prosecutor's office or there would be a warrant issued for his arrest.

Filter hired attorney Pat Knight, who advised him to come forward with the truth. Knight drove Filter to Indianapolis the next morning in time to meet the nine-thirty a.m. deadline.

If he cooperated, Knight was confident that he could keep Filter out of prison.

On August 15, 1997, Cindy's friends discovered an encouraging headline in the *Indianapolis Star*. Murder Suspect's Pal Charged With Concocting Phony Alibi. The article stated that Bill Filter, now aged 44, "faces a criminal charge for allegedly helping a suspect in a 1992 slaying by providing a phony alibi to police."

The charge would be a felony count of assisting a criminal. Filter had claimed that he was out drinking beer with Michael Albrecht on the night that his estranged wife was abducted, killed, and beheaded. Larry told news reporters, "We're not alleging that he was an accessory to the murder or was involved in the murder. We're just alleging the (phony) alibi."

On Wednesday, September 3, 1997, Filter confessed. He had lied about drinking with Michael Albrecht on the night of the murder. He said Michael could not collect life insurance on Cindy after the divorce was final.

"Filter broke down and cried when he changed his story," Jones said. "I think it finally got to him. He had been carrying it around inside himself for a long time and couldn't deal with it any longer."

Having confessed, Filter gave a formal statement in the presence of Larry Sells, Lt. Bill Jones, and his attorney Pat Knight. As soon as he had been sworn in, Larry wanted to know why he had lied to law enforcement about Cindy's murder for more than five years.

"Well, Mike was a friend of mine, a real close friend of mine at one time," Filter explained. "Umm, I really didn't believe he would do such a thing. Umm, as far as murder, Cindy... and I just thought he needed some help."

Looking at specifics in the case, Larry dug for clarification from Filter. "Now, there were three calls made by you to the Albrecht telephone number here in Indianapolis. Ah, right around and shortly after Cynthia Albrecht's disappearance.

One was October the 25, 1992, about 11:54 a.m., and the next one was October 25, 1992, about 2:07 p.m. Each of those calls lasted only a minute."

"What we used to do is, there was a code. I would call up and say 'Indy' and then he'd know to call me at Dad's bar and he would go to a payphone," Filter explained.

"And then another call October 26, 1992, about 4:43 p.m. that lasted about two minutes," Larry noted. "You know why those specific calls were made?"

"I... not at this point. Umm, except, I think we were talking about an alibi." Filter said, "He was going to use me as an alibi. Then he said, 'no, I don't need you,' and then, he came back later and said, 'yes, I do need you.'"

"Where was he on October 25, the day she disappeared, at 11:54 a.m.?" Larry wanted to know.

It turned out that not even Filter was sure. He said, "You see, now I was thinking he was in Milwaukee, but there's a good chance he didn't come up here. Ah, I think this was all part of his plan to say that he was up here." Filter said he saw Michael on the evening of Saturday, October 24, around five to seven p.m. and did not see him again until Monday morning, October 26.

Larry repeated his question. "When was the next time, after Saturday evening, on October 24, 1992, that you actually saw Michael Albrecht?"

"I saw him Sunday, in the morning," Filter replied. "He talked to me about doing it, he couldn't get anybody to kill her, so he was going to do it himself and he asked me if I'd be his alibi." Shaken, Filter said he couldn't do it. "And I call him back and says, I don't think I can. He says that's okay, I have something lined up already, you don't have to worry about it… and then, umm, he said he was going to go down and do it. Umm, and get her out of there. He even talked about wrapping her up in her bedspread."

As for the timing, Filter stated, "He was trying to set up a time frame with me because she was out of town and she wasn't going to get back until this one certain day and it was the day before the divorce and had to be done before the divorce was final so the insurance policy would still be in effect."

"It was important to him that she be killed before their divorce became final?" Larry confirmed.

"Right."

"And he knew that that would not take place until Monday, October the 26th, 1992?"

"That's what it sounded like to me," Filter responded. "I mean, he had it down pretty well where it had to be done that night or everything was going to be screwed up."

Filter told his girlfriend, Eunice Beckendorf, that he had been out with Michael and she believed him. "I says, you didn't hear me leave. I tried whispering goodbye and this and that. I told her that we had a good time and that we went out riding."

Filter said he never told her the truth; he never told anyone the truth until he confided in his attorney Pat Knight.

"Did he ever tell you how he killed her?" Larry asked.

Filter said, "No, he called me up later when they had found the body and he said they found this body with the head missing, and ah, I said, wow. He had kind of talked about her head had to be missing and I put a little doubt in my mind. I asked him, 'well, did you do it?' He said no."

"You asked him if he did what?"

"If he killed her and decapitated her? And he says, no, he did not. So, ah, he says when he got rid of the body, it had a head on it. So I have no clue as to the head situation at all." Hadn't he said before that the head would have to be removed? He had, Filter agreed.

"He never admitted to you that he in fact severed the head from her body?"

"No," Filter insisted. "I guess he was at the police station when he heard it and he cried. But that's, you know, basically, it sounded like it was just a show."

Kathleen Albrecht's statement was that Michael spent the evening at her house and had returned in the hours after midnight and remained with her, having sex that night. "And I assume that could not have happened," Larry said to Filter. "Was it your understanding that he had just arrived back in Milwaukee when you saw him Monday morning?"

Filter could not vouch for the time of Michael's arrival. "He looked pretty tired and he said he was driving all night." He felt obligated to help Michael because he had loaned him money at various times and helped him find work when he needed it.

Once he had lied to law enforcement, Filter could not go back on what he had said without getting himself in trouble. "Mike made it sound pretty good as far as, you know, nobody's going to find out anything if everybody sticks to their story… and I was still with the understanding that Mike didn't do it… He had the body in the car and everything, but I had asked him later, did you do it? And he goes no, I was just screwing around with you. So I kinda believed him."

Michael loved Cindy, Filter stated, "and he didn't want anyone else to have her if he couldn't." Plus, he had an opportunity to work for Penske but wasn't able to take it because Penske had a policy against hiring members of the same family for his team. "I guess it helped fuel the fire because he purposely did not go with Roger Penske so she could keep her job."

That day, Filter faced charges of assisting a criminal, a class C felony. On the recommendation of Deputy Prosecutor Larry Sells, his bond was reduced from one hundred thousand dollars to nothing. Magistrate Ted Robinette agreed.

The defense attacked this decision at Bill Filter's bail hearing on October 17, 1997.

Present for the prosecution was Larry Sells. Challenging him was Michael Albrecht with his wolf pack of defense attorneys: Susan W. Brooks, Drew Findling, Richard Kammen, and Elizabeth Rankin.

Findling first addressed Filter's hundred thousand dollar bond. "Did you ever see the actual petition for the hundred thousand dollar bond, the document asking for the hundred thousand dollar bond?" He pointed out that Filter had not come to Indianapolis packing a change of clothes and his toothbrush. He had not expected to be detained.

Also, Filter's statement indicated that two weeks before the murder, Michael Albrecht had been talking about killing his wife, yet Filter called no law enforcement nor made any move to report that he suspected that Cindy was in danger. Challenged, Filter argued that he "felt like our friendship was strong enough that I could talk him out of doing anything stupid."

Filter reconfirmed that he and Michael met on Saturday, talked on the phone on Sunday, and did not see each other again until Monday morning. With these statements, Bill Filter became the prosecution's paramount witness against Michael Albrecht.

CHAPTER 25

In December 1997, defense attorney Rick Kammen made an early offensive pretrial move. He invoked the separation of witness principal in an attempt to eliminate the testimony of key State witnesses, including Pete Twiddy, Rebecca Miller, Sandra Fink, and Heidi Dras.

Kammen's motion charged that the witnesses' common knowledge of Don Campbell's investigation tainted their testimony. Kammen said Don Campbell had investigated "the disappearance and death" of Cindy. In fact, Campbell's investigation ended when Cindy's body was found. At that point, it became a homicide investigation.

Campbell's report included interviews with witnesses. The defense insisted these records were biased against their client.

Additionally, Campbell had recorded two interviews with Michael Albrecht, "at least one of which was accomplished under false pretenses. The defendant was under the impression that Campbell just wanted to get a profile on Cynthia when Campbell interviewed him the second time."

Campbell's "time and event chart," which compared the interviews of Michael and his two alibi witnesses, Kathleen Albrecht and Bill Filter, was also a source of contention.

Defense attorneys also wanted the Court to disqualify a taped conversation between Michael and Pete Twiddy, and a quote from Jennifer Morgan, who said that Michael told her he was going through a nasty divorce.

The private investigator had also made allegations against Michael. For instance, "that he learned from a confidential source in the police department that Michael Albrecht attempted to put a hit on Cynthia and that he tried to get her to change her life insurance policy so that he would be the beneficiary."

Then there was that little nick in Michael's neck. Campbell had had the gall to mention that shortly before her death, Cindy had worn long fake fingernails to a Halloween party. According to Campbell, Cynthia "possibly fought her attacker and left such a mark on his neck with such fingernails."

Campbell's professional observation that Michael had a rapid heartbeat and seemed scared was also objectionable, as was his comment that Michael did not respond as an innocent person would, asking the "normal questions" and expressing concern about his missing wife.

Campbell's report, with all its biased information, Kammen concluded, had to be excluded in order for his client to receive a fair trial. Additionally, none of the people who had read the report should be allowed to testify against Michael. "Such witnesses have been forever tainted by their knowledge of what other State's witnesses have stated and thus cannot possibly testify at the trial of this case without having been influenced by such knowledge."

The normal recourse—cross-examination of the witnesses in front of the jury to show their testimony had been tainted—was not acceptable in this case, because it would make the jury aware of all those statements the defense objected to.

Prosecutors could have lobbed the ball back, listing defense witnesses who might have gotten together to collaborate on their stories. Instead, they ridiculed the lack of logic in Kammen's motion.

"The State fails to see anything egregious about the conduct of friends of a loved one so savagely and brutally murdered by the defendant," Larry responded. "Are witnesses and loved ones of a murdered victim required to seclude themselves, to take a vow of silence for time immemorial to satisfy the convoluted and misguided logic of defense counsel?"

Larry Sells and John Commons told the Court that "the State has advised all witnesses of the Court's separation of witnesses order and its meaning. And we will report any violations to the Court."

In a note to himself, Larry wrote: *Michael Albrecht is not entitled to a perfect trial of his choosing. Only a fair trial.*

On February 26, 1998, the defense filed a motion to block more evidence. The jury shouldn't hear Michael's statements either, at least not from Lt. Bill Jones. In a move to keep Jones from testifying, the defense wanted Michael's interviews with the Speedway Police Department suppressed. Police had questioned Michael in 1992 on October 28, November 4, and November 20.

When Lt. Jones and Sgt. Joel Rush questioned Michael about leads to Cindy's whereabouts on October 28, Michael was not under arrest. Jones said, "Every time I take somebody into the interview room, because it's a fairly small room, I always tell people that, number one, they're not under arrest; they're free to leave at any time, and actually show them that the door is unlocked."

Michael had agreed to meet Jones on the twentieth but went to Florida instead. When Jones arrived in Ft. Lauderdale, he contacted local police and went to Randy's house with Detective Dave Nickerson of the Ft. Lauderdale Police Department. He said he made the trip to interview Michael personally because he considered him a suspect in Cindy's disappearance. Out of courtesy to local police, Jones read Michael Albrecht his Miranda rights.

Drew Findling asked why Jones did not suggest that Michael call his attorney, William Van Barteau. "Did you ever say to him, in light of the fact that you have a pending divorce, maybe before you start answering these questions, want to consult with your attorney?"

The option of contacting an attorney was covered in the Miranda warnings, Jones replied.

Larry questioned Jones. On either of the two dates he interviewed Michael Albrecht, "did he [Albrecht] appear to be under the influence of any intoxicants?" Jones said he did not. "Did it appear to you on either of those two dates he had any difficulty in understanding anything what you two were discussing? Did he tell you at any time during any of those two conversations or those two interview dates that he did not wish to speak to you?"

"No."

The Court ruled was that there was nothing illegal about using Michael's own recorded words against him in court.

The pretrial fight continued. The defense filed a motion for a continuance and bail. They saw no reason why Michael should languish in jail while they prepared their case.

Bail? The man had already had more than five years of freedom he did not deserve. Now he wanted to complain that he should not "languish in jail"? Reading the petition, Larry clenched his fists. Photos of Cindy's body framed his sleep, and if it were within his power, Michael Albrecht would never take another free step in this lifetime.

On March 20, Larry responded. "In the multiple fragmented hearings that have occurred to date on the issue of bail, the defense has taken great pains to avoid asking State's witnesses any questions the answers to which might incriminate the defendant. The focus of the bail hearings has been rather a 'fishing expedition' by the defense... Wherefore, the State prays the Court deny defendant's premature request for bail."

Michael returned to his cell.

See you in court.

The Albrecht trial would be a tiger fight. Each of his defense attorneys—Richard Kammen, Drew Findling,

Elizabeth Rankin, and Susan Brooks—had their reputation, but Kammen was the opposing tiger.

Larry viewed Kammen as an attorney with an abrasive voice who asked biting questions. In truth, he was a powerful opponent. He appeared to have an advantage, having been lifelong friends with Judge Mangus-Stinson. He was listed annually in Best Lawyers in America, a recognition he received for more than thirty years. Newscaster Derrik Thomas described Kammen as "an extremely smart lawyer" who'd served as a faculty member of the National Criminal Defense College since 1982, and was a highly requested speaker on issues of criminal defense.

Larry and Commons had their scoreboard of convictions, but Kammen's winning record placed the prosecution in the minor leagues. Larry was certain that Michael was guilty, but proving it would not be an easy victory. Each side sharpened their teeth.

The trial opened on June 8, 1998. Immaculately attired in his suit and tie, Larry drove twenty sweltering minutes through chaotic traffic to the Marion County Courthouse. His window was down. The air conditioning in his pickup truck didn't work. He had driven that truck through three transmissions. "He always made sure my maintenance, oil changes, and such were done right on schedule," says Larry's wife Melanie, "but he let his vehicle go."

Larry's mind was not on the Indiana summer heat. He was pumped, going into this first day of the fight with a determination to win. No one, with the exception of Lt. Bill Jones, knew the case better than he did.

He contemplated what strategies the defense might try. If he brought A.J. Mobley to the stand, the defense would use that testimony to discredit his case. Mobley had revealed his secrets days after the body was found. Moreover, he had offered no information beyond what he could have gleaned from news reports.

Larry listed Mobley as a witness, knowing that the defense team would put a lot of time and effort into dissecting his statements. Since they didn't know the case as well as he did, he could toss out other, similar false clues to keep his opponents up late at night.

In the courtroom, he chose the left side table, the one nearest the jury box. He wanted to be certain that the jurors could see him at all times. More importantly, he wanted them to have to look past him to see the defendant.

Once witnesses began to testify, Larry was careful to ensure that each person named and pointed out the defendant, Michael Albrecht. "You have to identify the defendant as the person about whom you are talking," Larry notes. He cited a case where that did not happen and the criminal walked because "no one identified the defendant as the person committing the crime."

Larry says, "I was coming off a bunch of wins and I felt like I knew what it took to try and win a murder case." He had known from the beginning that Filter "would fold like a cheap tent." Without Filter's agreement, Michael's alibi was a used tissue.

Rick Kammen would not be foolish enough to put Michael on the stand. If he did, the State would have an easy win. If Michael testified, all his statements with their inconsistencies would come into play. It would be a game of balloons and darts.

One strategy Larry used and slid beneath the nose of the defense was arresting Bill Filter. No one ever questioned that arrest, but Indiana had no jurisdiction in Wisconsin. Larry had to get Filter to come to Indianapolis. He had to charge Filter before the five year statute of limitations was up. He did not like the man and did not want to do him any favors, but what it came down to was "go after a liar or go after a killer?"

CHAPTER 26

Larry stood before the jury to deliver his opening statement. Adrenaline sparked through his body, but his demeanor was laidback. He gazed at the jury with eyes some claimed were bluer than Paul Newman's. His 6'3" height helped him keep the jury's attention, but he always wore eye-catching neckties, drawing his audience's focus to his face. His voice was calm, conversational.

"This morning as I drove south on Georgetown Road toward 16th Street, I looked to the left at the Indianapolis Motor Speedway. What an awesome, immense structure! Today, the racetrack is a sleeping giant. But every May, it awakens with a roar, the roar of powerful, high-performance engines propelling sleek, colorful race cars around the IMS' two-and-one-half-mile oval track. And the roar of two hundred and fifty thousand frenzied fans screaming their tribute to the fearless drivers they came to see.

"Everyone knows about the Indianapolis 500-Mile Race, even those who are not normally racing enthusiasts. Millions of people around the world watch the race on television or listen to it on the radio. The attention of everyone turns to Indianapolis during the month of May, anxiously awaiting the 500, 'the greatest spectacle in racing.'

"Racing legends are made there. Drivers are worshipped by fans hoping to get close to their heroes. Race car drivers risk their lives pursuing speed, fame, and fortune. The most skilled and fortunate win. The less fortunate lose the race and sometimes their lives."

Yes. They were seeing that image, hearing the roar of the engines and the crowd. He had their full attention. He continued.

"Cindy Albrecht was part of that world. She was thrilled to be part of championship auto racing. She loved it, and she loved working for the Marlboro-Penske Racing Team, the best racing team in the IndyCar Racing League. Cindy was head chef for team owner Roger Penske and Marlboro. Cindy was constantly upbeat, happy, glad to be alive. When she walked into a room full of people, she lit it up with her smile and enthusiasm.

"Cindy and her staff catered to the rich and famous while working for Marlboro-Penske. In May of 1992 at the 500, and at other races, Hollywood stars, celebrities, rich corporate sponsors visited Marlboro-Penske hospitality, and it was Cindy's responsibility to make sure they were comfortable and well fed. She did that with a zest."

Larry moved slightly, using his space, making sure twelve pairs of eyes followed him. He spoke to the jury now as friends, confidants.

"She rubbed shoulders with the racing fraternity as well: the Andrettis, the Unsers, A.J. Foyt, Emerson Fittipaldi, Rick Mears. Mears and Fittipaldi were driving for Marlboro-Penske in 1992. Al Unser Jr. later joined the team.

"Cindy's husband Michael was a chief mechanic on one of the cars in Dick Simon's Racing Team. Simon's team was not as successful as Marlboro-Penske. But as a chief mechanic, Michael was respected in the racing community and commanded a salary of nearly seventy-five thousand dollars in 1992.

"Al Unser Jr. won the 1992 Indianapolis 500. Michael Albrecht lost. His team lost the race. He lost his job. And he lost his wife Cindy."

Larry allowed a brief pause to let that sink in.

"A great deal of animosity developed between them in the spring of 1992. A.J. Mobley, an eccentric inventor, witnessed that animosity. Mobley stopped by the Simon Racing Team garage before the 500-Mile Race to attempt to sell a race car part he had invented. He encountered chief mechanic Michael Albrecht working on a car and struck up a conversation. Michael Albrecht received a phone call from his wife Cindy. Albrecht returned from the call very angry. He told Mobley, 'I'm going to kill that no good bitch.'

"Mobley told him, 'You're not serious; you can't get away with that!'

Larry dropped his voice to a low growl. "Albrecht replied, 'Oh yes, I can; I'll get away with it. I'll take her to northern Indiana. I'll cut her head off. I'll get somebody to help me, someone who will give me an alibi. I think I know someone who might.'"

In the silent courtroom, Larry could see the jury following his story, syllable by syllable, and worrying about the details that would come later.

"Mobley did not report that conversation to law enforcement authorities until after Cindy's body was found. He later told police detectives that he thought Albrecht was just upset and blowing off steam."

Larry described the breakup of the marriage. Michael lost his job with Simon Racing in part because he let his wounded ego interfere with his work. He blamed Cindy for that. He tried to block her friendships. "He tried to prevent her from doing those things her job required. He tried to stifle her very existence."

People couldn't help glancing over at the hulking form of Michael, hunched over the defense table, but Larry's next words pulled their attention back to him and the tale of woe that had brought them together that day.

"Michael Albrecht also became increasingly perverted in his sexual practices. Even though Michael Albrecht and Cindy separated in June, they continued to live in the same house for a while, sleeping in different rooms, but that did not work out." Cindy moved out.

Near the end of the summer, he called his brother Randy, a Broward County sheriff's deputy in Ft. Lauderdale, Florida. "Michael told him that he and Cindy were becoming increasingly distant. He told Randy that Cindy cost him his job, and that now she was divorcing him. 'I want to get her for destroying my life.'"

Larry saw some unconscious tightening of lips. He raised the tension a notch.

"Michael told Randy that Cindy would be visiting her mother in Fort Lauderdale in early September. He asked Randy, his brother and a law enforcement officer, if he could find someone, perhaps a Cuban, to rough Cindy up while she was there.

"Randy put Michael off. Michael eventually realized that Randy was not going to help him exact revenge on Cindy. He turned to Antonio Ferrari. Ferrari owned Euro Motorsports, a low-budget IRL team that Michael had previously worked for. After the 500, Ferrari decided to employ Michael on a part-time, daily basis because Michael was an excellent mechanic.

"Ferrari soon became aware of Michael's domestic problems. Michael began to trust and confide in Ferrari. In late September, early October, he asked Ferrari if he could find somebody in the Italian community, in the Mafia, to do something permanent to Cindy. Michael said he could pay for the crime with the money from Cindy's fifty thousand dollar life insurance policy. Ferrari put him off, just as Randy had.

"By late October, Michael became increasingly obsessed about getting Cindy. He had renewed ties with Bill Filter, an old friend in Milwaukee. He believed that Bill Filter would help him get Cindy.

"Michael invited Filter to Indianapolis in October. He took Filter to the apartment complex where Cindy lived.

Showed him the wooded area behind the apartment, the steps leading up to Cindy's balcony on the second floor, and the sliding glass door. He showed Filter a path through the woods leading to the back of the Marsh Supermarket, right by Crawfordsville Road, then Interstate 465, providing a quick getaway.

"Michael asked Filter to help him kill Cindy. He told Filter that Cindy could be strangled. And because of extensive dental work and reconstructive surgery to her jaw, her head would have to be cut off so she could not be immediately identified when her body was found."

After all the months of preparation, it was still hard for Larry to not blanch at the idea of Cindy's head being an unwanted object, a macabre trophy. His listeners appeared unsettled by the idea too.

"Filter told Michael he was crazy and went back to Milwaukee. A couple of weeks later, Albrecht visited Filter in Milwaukee and demanded that Filter help him. Said that the timing was crucial. The divorce would be final October 26 and that Cindy had to be killed before then. Filter told him that he would not help kill Cindy, but he agreed to alibi for him if necessary."

Pulling the courtroom back to the image of Cindy as a person, Larry continued, "October 17 at Leguna Seca, just outside of San Francisco, was the last IRL race of the year. Michael confronted Cindy there in the presence of Sandi Fink and Becky Miller. They heard him beg Cindy to come back with him. She refused.

"Cindy stayed out west with Pete Twiddy. The two liked and respected one another. Then, all of a sudden, in the fall of 1992, they fell deeply in love. Cindy intended to move to Florida after the divorce from Michael to be with Pete.

"This relationship made Michael even more jealous and embittered. Michael came back to Indianapolis after the race. Cindy and Pete attended the IRL banquet and the Marlboro party in San Francisco, then did some sightseeing."

After they attended Al Unser's Halloween party in Albuquerque, "Cindy flew back to San Francisco and from San Francisco flew to Indianapolis."

Cindy. Home. The story should have ended there. Larry's voice picked up the wistfulness of Sandi and Becky's voices. He pictured the hurt in their eyes when they said *if only you could have known her.*

"She arrived home about 8:30 Sunday evening. She called a friend, Heidi Dras, who took care of the cats, Billy and Willy, when Cindy was out of town.

"Cindy's mother, Patricia Woodward, called about nine from her home in Ft. Lauderdale. They discussed Cindy's impending move to Florida. Cindy was tired, but happy. Cindy told her mother she loved her, then said goodbye, for the last time.

"Sandi Fink called about nine-thirty p.m. They agreed to meet the next day to go over the receipts from the Leguna Seca race." They would "submit an accounting to the Penske organization, along with the remaining money. She kept that cash in a black carryall bag. Outside of a few people in the Penske organization, only Michael Albrecht was aware of that money. Cindy told Sandi she was very tired, but intended to wait up for Pete to call after his flight arrived at ten.

"After Pete Twiddy's flight arrived in Fort Meyers, Florida, he rented a car to drive to his home in Naples, and then tried to call Cindy from his cell phone. No answer. He left a message for her to call him but she did not call. He continued to call her Sunday night and Monday, each time leaving messages on her answering machine. Cindy did not respond. With each call, Pete became more desperate, wondering where Cindy was."

Where was she? Of course, the jury knew this was a murder trial, so they knew she was dead. But Larry wanted to take them step by step, feeding them the anxiety one cruel bite at a time.

"On Monday, October 26, he called Sandi Fink. Sandi said she had talked to Cindy Sunday night. They had agreed to meet Monday to go over the receipts from the race, but she had not heard from Cindy yet.

"Pete continued trying to reach Cindy, leaving messages on her answering machine. On Tuesday morning, he could wait no longer. He asked Sandi to get over to Cindy's apartment. He said, 'This isn't like Cindy!'

"Sandi and Becky drove to Cindy's apartment and saw her pickup truck parked in front. They knocked on the front door. No answer. They went around back, up the steps to Cindy's balcony. The screen on the sliding glass door to the apartment was off the track, and set aside. Sandi used two fingers and tried the sliding glass door; it opened. They ran back to Sandi's vehicle and grabbed an umbrella and mace for protection against a possible assailant."

Larry studied the jurors' faces. He wished he could measure their heart rates. Were they following his chronicle of events as carefully as they appeared to be? Could they feel the dread? He hoped so.

He described the two women checking out the haunting, unlit apartment and their disappointment in learning that they were too late. "The money was gone and Cindy was gone," Larry said.

"Pete arrived Tuesday afternoon. He, Sandi, Becky and everyone in the racing community searched for Cindy. Police agencies were searching for her. While everyone was working feverishly around the clock trying to find Cindy, Michael Albrecht was vacationing in Florida.

"Just a week before, at Leguna Seca, he begged her to return to him. When police told him about her disappearance, he was so concerned about it that he went to vacation in Florida. Cindy had disappeared and everybody was trying to find her; everybody except Michael Albrecht, that is."

Larry knew he was delivering a lot of information in a short time, but no one looked distracted. They each appeared to be following the sequence of events. He wished he could apologize for what they were to hear next.

"On November 15, Cindy was found by three rabbit hunters about one hundred and ten miles north of Indianapolis. In a wooded area frequented by hunters and used as a dumping ground for trash, lay the body of Cindy Albrecht. She was on her back, naked, legs spread apart and partially covered in leaves. Her head had been sliced and sawed off and taken away.

"Indiana State Police were summoned to the scene. An exhaustive search of the area was conducted for any physical evidence. No evidence was found nor was her head.

"Cindy's headless body had lain there in the woods for three weeks. She had been dumped like a piece of garbage for the animals to ravage and the elements to rot. Substantial rains during that time washed away any trace evidence that might have existed. To this date, Cindy's head has not been recovered.

"Michael Albrecht told law enforcement officers that he was in Milwaukee, Wisconsin, from Saturday, October 24, through Monday morning, October 26. During the critical time period between ten p.m., October 25, and the early morning hours of October 26, 1992, Michael Albrecht claimed he was drinking beer with his buddy Bill Filter.

"For nearly five years, Bill Filter lied to the FBI, lied to the Indiana State Police, lied to the Speedway Police Department. He supported Michael Albrecht's alibi that they were together Sunday evening and Monday morning.

"Then something happened to change Filter's mind. Michael Albrecht was charged with murder and brought back from Georgia to be tried. And because Bill Filter lied about being with Albrecht October 25 and 26, he was charged with assisting a criminal, a class C felony, punishable with from two to eight years in prison. The Court set Filter's bond at one hundred thousand dollars.

"Bill Filter did not want to go to jail for Michael Albrecht. He decided they were not that good of friends after all.

"Filter gave a sworn statement under a grant of immunity, meaning that the statements could not later be used against him in any legal proceeding so long as he told the truth. After five years of lying, he finally told the truth.

"Michael Albrecht drove from Milwaukee to Indianapolis that Sunday evening. He strangled Cindy in her apartment, wrapped her in a comforter from her bed, carried her out the back sliding glass doors, down the balcony steps, through the woods, to the back of the Marsh store, dumped her lifeless body in the trunk of the car, then rushed back up Interstate 65 to Milwaukee and his ex-wife's, Kathleen's, house where he stayed until morning.

"On Monday morning, he went to see Bill Filter, who asked him if he did it. Albrecht said, 'Yes, she's in the trunk. Do you want to see her?'

"Filter took a step toward the car, and then said, 'Nah, I don't think so.'

"Albrecht left and met his father to retrieve five thousand dollars that he had stashed in his father's bank account to hide from Cindy while the divorce was pending. There was no need to hide the money now. Cindy was dead.

"After getting the five thousand dollars, he drove south on Interstate 65 toward Indianapolis. Exited at DeMotte/Roselawn. Went to a wooded area close by that he undoubtedly knew about. Hauled Cindy's body into the woods. Sliced and sawed her head off. Then returned to his Speedway home.

"Three days later, he drove his BMW to Florida and probably took Cindy's head with him.

"He wrote a letter, dated November 8, 1992, blaming his former employer, Antonio Ferrari, for the crime, and gave it to his sister-in-law, Mary Jo Albrecht."

Let them think about that. It was an obvious lie. The letter *was* dated November 8, 1992, a week before Cindy's body was found. But it said that Cindy was dead. Michael's letter blamed Ferrari, but Michael never mentioned Ferrari in any interview.

"In a December 4, 1992, telephone conversation with Antonio Ferrari, Michael Albrecht told Ferrari that Sandi Fink and her husband Mike killed Cindy. Albrecht did not know that Ferrari taped that conversation. You, ladies and gentlemen of the jury, will hear that taped conversation," Larry promised.

"The defense will also contend that Matthew Kernel, a crack cocaine addicted tree trimmer with whom Cindy had a passing acquaintance, killed her.

"Someone else did it. Not Michael Albrecht. They will claim that the police investigation was sloppy, that the police did not properly and thoroughly investigate the case.

"Sloppy police work, alibi, knife used to commit the murder. Sound familiar? Well, the defendant is not O.J. Simpson. This is not the O.J. Simpson case. Some facts are similar. The defendant and his wife were estranged, a knife was used in the homicide, the defendant has an alibi, and allegations of sloppy police work. But there is one major difference. There can be no claims in this case of a 'rush to judgment,' of immediately arresting Michael Albrecht for the murder of his wife Cindy.

"It took five years to properly investigate this case before murder charges were filed against him. It took five years to make certain that he was the one who killed her. And after you hear the evidence, you, the jury, will be certain too that Michael Albrecht murdered Cindy."

CHAPTER 27

The courthouse was a new and intimidating experience for Becky and Sandi. Sandi recalls glass doors leading into the prosecutor's office, a place she says was generic and needed updating. She remembers "really small, freezing cold bathrooms." The only thing in the entire building that felt welcoming to her was Larry.

Becky and Sandi had not expected the separation of witnesses. They could not think about anything but Cindy, but they were not allowed to talk about her. Their friends, other witnesses, were also conversationally off limits. They could not even support and encourage each other. Almost six years of effort had led to this, another brutal waiting game.

Michael had to come up a separate elevator and be brought in with care. No juror should see him in chains and be biased by his appearance. *Heaven forbid that they think he looked like a criminal!* the women thought. "But he came down the hall glaring, still playing the intimidation game," Sandi says.

Becky and Sandi were given the use of a small waiting room with some chairs and a soda machine. This small kindness offered some privacy and kept strangers from viewing their anxiety. They could hear the staccato clicking of each pair of shoes when people walked down the hallway. The steps never paused in their doorway. No one said, *It's time. You'll get your chance to speak now.* The friends had volumes they wanted to say. The wait for this trial had been years, a trial that also gouged open the wound of losing Cindy.

While Sandi felt squeezed in by their private waiting room, Becky focused on the details. There was white leather furniture and a little TV in the corner—not that they would be allowed to watch the trial—and there were two chairs and a settee. There was no room for pacing. They could go out into the hallway, but others could not come in. When victim's advocate Robbin Fitzpatrick came to get them, she had to knock to enter.

Having never been inside the city/county building before, Becky was impressed by the beauty of marble imbedded in the walls. She was equally aware of the people around her: other prisoners, other families, and a throng of toothless, poor, and decrepit people. She wondered if she would feel like one of those people, hurting and used up, at the end of Michael's trial.

The women could only speculate about what went on in the courtroom. Not knowing when they would be called, they bought new outfits for each day of the trial. Regardless of the outcome, they would look their best for Cindy.

Larry Sells was also dressed to the nines for Cindy, with his perfectly aligned tie and immaculately trimmed hair. He was a general and this was war. He could not go reassure the women, but he knew they had faith in him and he was determined not to fail. He began calling his preliminary witnesses.

Cynthia's mother, Patricia Woodward, approached the witness stand in a haze of misery. When asked about her last phone call with Cindy, she scorched out her words through trembling lips. She identified a photograph of her vivacious daughter; she pointed out the defendant, Michael Albrecht. At the end of her ordeal, she returned to her seat, shuffling like a burn victim.

Larry's next witness, Heidi Dras, was the last person known to be in Cindy's apartment before her abduction.

On November 10, 1992, Sgt. Joel Rush showed Heidi photographs of Cindy's apartment on October 27. What was different or missing?

The cat litter by the back door was there on Friday, Heidi recalled. No magazines on the coffee table but beneath it. No cigarettes or ash trays on the tables. Heidi had also seen no watches or bracelets in the apartment and no bathrobe on the bedroom door.

The patio screen door had been on its track and there had been no hanger on the sidewalk behind the apartment's downstairs back patio. The TV tray had not been on the back patio.

The bedspread missing from Cindy's bed was a pastel comforter with an abstract design in gray, mauve, and white. The pillows had been tucked in.

During their final conversation, Cindy, the animal lover, expressed concern about a stray cat in the woods behind her apartment.

CHAPTER 28

Sandi Fink remembers her arrival in court as "stepping into an episode of *Perry Mason*." Her initial view of the courtroom was a disheartening one. The windowless chamber, devoid of natural lighting, looked dingy and dreary. Intimidating. "There was no perception of time or weather in there," she recalls. The witness chair was a step up from the floor but it made her feel small.

Worse, she hated having to see Michael Albrecht again. But Michael did not look so intimidating seated at the defense table. "He was pretty pale. He'd been in jail a year." When Sandi moved toward the stand, he merely shook his head as if dismissing her.

Judge Jane Mangus-Stinson, though, had a calming voice that directed her to the witness chair. The judge was tall and slender with a pretty face, "and she was immensely pregnant," Sandi recalls.

"We were praying that she wouldn't go into labor before the end of the trial," Becky adds.

Larry stood to question Sandi and she wanted to tell Cindy's story, all of it. That was not allowed. The court system was constraining, limiting her speech to direct answers to direct questions. In this situation, she felt as handicapped as Cindy, who went into eternity with no voice.

The jury heard more than a dozen calls from Pete Twiddy to Cindy's empty apartment. There was one last desperate message from Patricia Woodward, Cindy's mother. "For

God's sake, call me. Please, please, Cindy. Okay? I love you, honey. Bye bye."

State's Exhibit Number 11 was an expense sheet from Penske Racing Association, the Leguna Seca race, dated October 13-17, and documenting $3,737.83 in expenses. Sandi confirmed that the record was in Cindy's handwriting. They had started the weekend with six thousand in cash.

Sandi was annoyed by defense attorney Rick Kammen. "He kept looking around," as if her words had no value. But when he stood to cross-examine her, Sandi found that the attorney had missed nothing.

Kammen was decidedly shorter than Larry and looked at Sandi eye to eye.

She focused on Kammen's questions, being careful to answer only what was asked. It was hard. He wasn't asking about Cindy at all. He merely asked her to confirm statements taken out of context and twisted to make Cindy appear to be a druggie and a whore.

Larry had told them to speak directly to the jury, but she wasn't being allowed to say the things she wanted the jury to hear. The attorney "was just painting this picture that just wasn't true," she relates. "He was just trashing Cindy."

Her anger was a fiercely shaken bottle of soda but she had to rein it in and trust the process. Summer weather was pounding its drums but Sandi had to wear turtlenecks to court to hide her rage. She answered Kammen's questions in an even, professional voice, but her neck flamed with indignity.

The process offered "no rights for Cindy; it was all about Michael."

Sandi bit back her fury and maintained unwavering faith in Larry's ability to win the conviction. "I never thought he was going to lose. I was in a bubble," she says.

In her interviews with Lt. Jones, Kammen asked, why did Sandi never mention the conversation between Michael and Cindy at Leguna Seca where he begged Cindy to stay with him? "He asked you to be sure and tell him everything you possibly could about what you knew about this situation?"

"Yes."

"You attempted to answer those questions, did you not?"

"Yes."

"You attempted to answer them thoroughly?"

"Yes."

"Completely?"

"Yes."

"And accurately?"

"Yes."

"And you trusted Detective Jones to write things down thoroughly; did you not?" Kammen continued. "And you did not tell Detective Jones about the alleged situation at Leguna Seca...where Michael was supposedly saying to Cindy, please don't leave... you didn't tell him that did you?"

Sandi did not recall specifically and Kammen had her look over her statement.

"I may not have that day, no," Sandi replied.

Kammen asked about Cindy, and David Dras, who also worked in racing. "Now, drugs and racing really don't go together, do they?"

"One of the rules of CART, which is the governing body, is you sign a waiver that you can be tested at any time," Sandi explained. Kammen left the subject dangling, implying that Cindy was a druggie.

Marlboro-Penske was considered the best team, one that "prided themselves on qualifying on the first weekend of qualifications... And in 1992, that happened, two or three cars qualified in the first week of qualification?" Kammen asked.

"I assume that's true," Sandi replied.

Was she aware that a Japanese racecar driver for Dick Simon named Hiro Matsushita "had a rather serious accident?"

Sandi's husband worked on that car and Michael Albrecht was the chief mechanic.

"And, in fact, Mr. Matsushita was injured and the car was destroyed, and they had to build up a second car for a driver by the name of Raul Boysell?" asked Kammen.

That was possible, Sandi admitted. "Dick Simon had several cars entered."

"I understand they had several cars entered, but when you're working on one car, they have to get another car ready to race; isn't that correct?"

True.

"And those cars take a lot of work?"

"Unless they're already prepared," Sandi deadpanned.

Next, Kammen tried to demonstrate that any number of men could have killed Cindy. He asked Sandi, "She confided in you, for example, that she went out with a fellow by the name of Jimmy Valini? And Tom Abler?"

Casual, friendly dates, Sandi insisted.

Other men, Mr. Kammen? Other men didn't kill Cindy; Michael did. Sandi's testimony wasn't at all what she expected. The attorney had shoved her onto an escalator going the wrong way. Sandi stayed focused, tamped down her wounded emotions, and tried to state the facts simply and truthfully.

She braced for the pain when Kammen turned to take his next bite out of her. Cindy had trusted Sandi with the truth that she occasionally smoked marijuana. "And trusted you not to betray that confidence to your employer, Penske Racing?"

Yes.

"To CART, correct?"

True.

"To her boss, Mr. Twiddy... You didn't betray her to those people?"

"No, I didn't."

"Now, in all the time that Cindy and you talked, over all the time that she shared information with you about her relationship and how it deteriorated, Cindy never indicated that Mike had physically threatened her in any way; isn't that true? Cindy never suggested to you that Mike had physically abused her at any time; isn't that correct?"

It was, Sandi testified, but Cindy had admitted that Mike would lose his temper, that he could be loud and forceful.

What did Sandi know about the Albrechts' sexual relationship? "She never suggested that there were things about Mike and his behavior towards her that she couldn't tell you; did she?"

"No."

The defense attorney turned his attention to the financial side of the racing world. He asked about the "unimaginable amounts of money" involved. "In 1992, I'm guessing that any individual race car was worth half a million dollars or more."

That was correct, Sandi agreed. The money came from sponsors, "who would underwrite the expenses of the team."

Better funded teams "can have more stuff," said Kammen. "Speed costs money, how fast do you want to go."

Kammen measured the glamour of the Penske team against the struggles of the Simon team, and then turned his attention to the Penske team's response to Cindy's disappearance. They thought police could do nothing but list Cindy as a missing person. They hired Don Campbell and launched their own searches.

"You and the other racing people scoured that area as best you could?"

Yes.

"Now I want you to understand that I'm not in any manner belittling your efforts. I know that you were very concerned and doing everything you guys could do. But you're trained in this?"

"No, we're not."

"You had no equipment other than perhaps flashlights... You had no search dogs?"

One area the friends searched was a secluded area at Salt Lake Road, five minutes from Cindy's apartment. Kammen had Sandi place a Post-it® on the map to show the jury the location. He asked her, "You perhaps didn't know that it was Mr. Kernel's property you were searching off Salt Lake Road?"

Sandi replied, "I'm not sure if we knew it at the time or not."

When Kammen took his seat, Sandi felt bruised.

Larry rose for redirect. Did Sandi remember seeing the chain lock on Cindy's front door? She did.

Larry said, "Mr. Kammen asked about the defendant's conversation with Cynthia, in which you indicated that he asked her to come back, try it again. And you also acknowledge that you didn't tell law enforcement about it. That wasn't the only time when you were aware that he asked her to come back; is that correct?"

"That's correct."

"How many times might that have occurred?"

"Two or three times to my knowledge over the summer," Sandi said. "Once for sure in Cleveland."

"Did that have any significance to you at all when you were talking to the police?"

Kammen rose. "I'm going to object. That's self-serving, Your Honor."

"Well, Judge," Sells argued, "he's the one that's cast her credibility into question. I think she has a right to respond."

Sandi's injured soul brightened a bit. "I didn't think anything of those statements because I'd heard them several times before and I knew what Cindy's intent was."

Had Cindy ever confided to her that she had a sexual relationship with either Jimmy Valini, who worked with Newman/Haas Racing Team in Chicago, or Tom Abler?

"No, she didn't," Sandi affirmed.

Larry asked about Simon's wrecked race car. "Do you know where Michael Albrecht was while you were at the Marlboro party?"

"Yes, sir. He was at home."

"He wasn't in the Simon garage?"

"No, he was not."

Michael had been at home when Mike and Sandi picked Cindy up to drive to the party. Sandi had been present when Cindy called Michael at eleven p.m. to tell him she would be late. Kammen had asked if Sandi knew whether or not Michael had physically abused Cindy.

Larry's question was, "Do you know whether or not Cynthia Albrecht was mentally abused by Michael Albrecht?"

"Absolutely."

CHAPTER 29

John Commons called Speedway Police Detective Lloyd "Dane" Morgan, who had been the first respondent when Cindy was reported missing. "And in shorthand, that's simply referred to as a run; is that correct?" Commons asked.

"Yes, sir. Basically, as responding officer, we generate the initial report and talk with the complainant to see if we can get more information about where the person might be."

Morgan's first step was "to knock on the door just to make sure that somebody wasn't possibly asleep in the apartment."

Step two was to examine pathways in and out of the area. Only one drive doglegged from the entrance to the exit of the apartment complex. "A creek, an old path, and a fence that runs along the back isolated the property. There's a gateway that leads to a little crossing for the residents to walk over to the grocery store."

Morgan instructed Sandi and Becky to remain outdoors at the bottom of the back stairs until he had checked the apartment. This was both for their safety and to secure the crime scene. Then he allowed them upstairs but instructed them to remain on the balcony. Minutes later, Detective Turner arrived. Five minutes after that, Morgan said, they left, securing the back door and locking the front one with the key lying on the coffee table.

Findling questioned Morgan about the missing Penske money, which totaled $2,268.17. "And what they had told you was, before you even got there, they had already looked in the black bag to see if the money was there; am I right?"

Morgan replied, "That I really don't remember."

"Did they indicate to you they had looked in the bag before you arrived?" Findling asked. "I mean, there's obviously natural curiosity on your part when it's revealed to you a large sum of money is missing and a person is missing; am I right?"

Yes.

"And Mrs. Fink was very concerned... she wanted to make sure that that money was deposited; am I right? They didn't tell you, my gosh, she has this husband who mentally abuses her, he's a suspect, go out and look for him. They didn't say that to you, did they?"

"No, sir, they didn't."

Police searched about a mile and a half of the wooded area behind Cindy's apartment. They also examined an old railroad track adjacent to the wooded area.

Findling asked, "Certainly if you were requested along with other officers to do that and search for any evidence, sign of a body, sign of her head, or anything forensic you can assist in, you obviously would not refuse such a request, but do your best to assist your department in solving this case; am I right?"

"Correct, sir," Morgan attested, "that's my job."

On redirect, Commons had only one question: "Did you have any information or knowledge whatsoever on October the 27, 1992, that would cause you to think it would be appropriate to go out looking for a decapitated head?"

Morgan replied, "No, sir, not for a decapitated head."

Larry called Kevin Jones, who did excavation work and had been a reserve police officer for the DeMotte Police Department for the past eighteen years. He described finding Cindy's body and said he had protected the crime scene.

Indiana State Trooper Rick Grisel was a crime scene technician assigned to the Lowell Regional Laboratory. His task was to recover and process evidence from the crime scene. Grisel took the crime scene photos of Cindy's body.

Grisel told the Court that Cindy's body was transported to the Tippecanoe County Morgue at Purdue University in West Lafayette. After the body had been removed, and as darkness fell, the scene was marked with crime scene tape. Kammen questioned whether Grisel had paid enough attention to details. "And I'm not suggesting you should have," Kammen said, "and I don't recall; did you post a guard there?"

"I don't recall," Grisel replied.

The next morning, Grisel related, ten to fifteen police officers converged on the scene to make a more thorough, daylight search. They found a silver and black jacket that had the inscription PPG on it about two hundred and fifty feet south of the dirt lane.

Grisel explained that during autopsy, he unclasped the fragile ankle bracelets and took fingernail scrapings from the hands. He found no evidence of defensive wounds beneath the nails. Grisel had Cindy's hands surgically removed so he could take them to another location to get fingerprints which were more accurate.

Kammen asked, "And then the hands, which were separate from the body at this point, were preserved, as is necessary, in case it became important later on in the investigation?"

That was a common procedure, Grisel explained, "for a body that's decomposing."

CHAPTER 30

Pete Twiddy took the witness stand next.

For Pete, going to court for Cindy was as complex as running the 1992 Indy 500. He said that the house of justice is "never the same as when you're in there and have something going on."

Pete thought he knew how to avoid the debris on the oval. He'd run the legal gauntlet three of four years earlier following a crash with a drunk driver. He'd gone through the deposition process, trying to get back his lost wages due to injuries. The process didn't work for him.

"Lawyers controlled the whole thing," he says. The woman testified that Pete caused the accident and she was believed. He ended up taking a total loss plus twenty percent. "When you go in that courtroom, you have no idea what's going on."

Pete was present on the first day of Michael's trial for twenty minutes, and then he had to leave. He was only allowed in during the time he was testifying, but he had the satisfaction of watching the final arguments and the verdict.

Newspaper writers had shadowed Pete but he could say nothing. He was under a gag order from his employers. Not for the first time. He said, "No one let me talk when I was trying to find her."

Now, in a court of law, it was his turn to speak. He had been designated as the voice of Cindy's family. "Her mother, she was an alcoholic, and her dad was milquetoast. Dad was not interested in finding out who did it," Pete says. Cindy's dad told him, "'You speak on behalf of the family,' and I had his blessing."

After his first courtroom testimony, Pete was disappointed. "I'm kind of an outspoken person," he admits, and the questions limited what he could say. There was "not a lot of latitude to answer the questions." His constant worry was, "Will I say the right thing?"

Pete made every effort to convey to the jury that Michael Albrecht was a lowlife killer. First of all, Pete said, "He was out looking for a killer" to rid him of his wife. "I think he knew from his law enforcement friends where to dump the body."

Pete wanted to tell the full story. He wanted to say that Michael Albrecht "acted weird, like a guilty person. He would come up behind people and put them in a chokehold. He did that to a lot of people."

Pete also wanted to talk about Cindy's courage. Everyone close to her sensed there was abuse going on, but Cindy denied it at least a hundred times. She acted scared around Mike but told Pete the relationship was amicable. She braved the pain of her broken teeth at Skeleton Lake, but when she called Mike to tell him, he ripped into her, yelling about the fortune he'd spent to replace her jaw.

Then there was that final moment at the Albuquerque airport when she insisted he drop her off and leave, as if she sensed something and felt the need to protect him from it.

Michael also "didn't have any mean things to say to me. Michael said sorry to *me* that it happened and that I got involved in it. I wanted to express what I'd seen in this guy," Pete said.

Pete grew to detest Kammen. Even during the deposition, Pete was "defying him in there and knowing I could." As hard as the trial was, it made him thankful for the damage done to him in his wreck hearing. He had learned to spot pitfalls.

He noted that in the courtroom, Michael had a dark and sullen look. "And Kammen looked greasy," Pete said. *And you want to defend this guy? Everybody needs a job but...*

Kammen claimed that he got Marlboro and Penske blurred and asked if Cindy worked for Pete in 1989. "I know one of the reasons Marlboro likes to sponsor Penske is that it does get blurred in the public mind. But there was a Marlboro hospitality tent and a Penske hospitality tent in '89?"

"Correct," Pete replied.

Kammen asked Pete about his responsibilities. "And part of your responsibilities, as you've told us, is being with the race cars, not turning wrenches, but sort of knowing what's going on?" he asked. "Because Marlboro spends an awful lot of money to sponsor Penske Racing?"

"Yes, they do," Pete replied. "They want to know what's going on with their investment." He stated that racing is a "very expensive sport."

Pursuing the topic as if he planned to teach Racing 101, Kammen asked about the camaraderie among the teams. "The people involved tend to know one another?" He said, "And perhaps the jury understands the working conditions for the people at the track are not always real glamorous."

"No, not at all."

"You know, you're working out of a trailer, but it might be a hundred degrees and high humidity, and you're outside all the time? Or it might be raining and you're standing around in muddy fields?"

"Very much so."

Kammen honed in on the idea that in such a small, closed community, stories circulated. "And sometimes they can be hard to stomp out, like all rumors?" Referring Pete to Sandi's explanation that Cindy was possibly asleep or running errands, Kammen said, "And you believed Sandi, of course."

"Sure."

When Pete arrived in Indianapolis, he went straight to the police department. "You asked the question, 'Have you brought in Mr. Albrecht for questioning?'" Had Pete been told that the police were doing what was necessary?

Pete said, "No, he told me that he knew Mike and Cindy, don't worry, she's just out on a binge." Pete was insulted by Turner's comments. Because the police were not keeping him updated, Pete said, that, at that time, he trusted only his private investigator and his friends.

Over the years, Pete contacted the Speedway Police Department at least a hundred times. Kammen asked if the police got frustrated with his continual contacts and Pete said, "I didn't feel that Detective Jones was treating me that way. I felt I became persona non grata with Police Chief Dine. I think he was the most tired of talking to me."

Roger Penske sent in his head of security, John McGinley. "John said, 'I'll talk to these guys, you better not be talking to them anymore.'" McGinley called the police department twenty or more times on Roger Penske's behalf.

The defense tore apart Pete's deposition. "They railroaded me and grasped on to statements taken out of context so that what was said was not what I meant." The process made him "leery of everyone.

"No one was on my side. Everyone was on their side." They were "trying to make it look like I had actually done it." Pete also remembers that the defense lawyer "cut me off a bunch of times but I could tell the jurors were listening to me.

"As soon as it happened, I looked over at Larry. He pulled me out of the courtroom, pulled out my deposition, and we went back in." With the context of his own words, Pete could better answer, but he felt that the damage had been done. There were people in that courtroom who might actually believe he could harm Cindy.

When it was time for him to leave, Pete ran into trouble. A gauntlet of media stood outside the front door of the courthouse. Pete would lose his job if he spoke to them, so he was escorted out the back way. That path took him past the judge's chambers. Courtroom employees objected, but he had no choice.

Pete really wanted to watch the whole process and "every single day in the newspapers, it didn't look good for us. Larry kept saying we're going to win this thing. Larry had prepared me mentally to stay in the game."

Pete's neighbor told him it looked like the prosecution was losing. "No, we are *not!*" Larry insisted; although up until the final moment, he was not certain himself. He knew he had to win, yet he was not certain that he could. The dissonance wore on him, causing him more aches than his continual sleepless nights.

More intense than the trial and more vital than the need to see Michael pay for his crime were the personal effects on Pete. He found himself doing some painful soul searching, and this enabled him to stick with the task.

Cindy's gift to Pete was "she let me learn and know what it is to be in love. Times with Cindy were some of the funniest times I ever had." He remembers her as fearless, that she "could drive the wheels off a car." One time, they raced two rental cars back to the hotel and Cindy performed stunt moves that took his breath away. Her daring upped his own game but he barely beat her back. "This girl is the coolest girl that ever lived," Pete says.

The memories were bittersweet and hurt so badly that Pete didn't want to go through the trial. But Cindy's dad kept saying that he didn't think Michael would do that. He wasn't prepared to defend his daughter at all. Then Pete thought of Cindy. "I couldn't see how anybody so brave and so strong—I wondered where she got those traits."

Still isolated outside the courtroom and famished for encouraging news, Sandi and Becky brightened a bit each morning with the appearance of their favorite television newscaster, ABC's Derrik Thomas.

Michael Albrecht's long-awaited trial garnered great public interest. In that era, the Indianapolis ABC affiliate emphasized coverage of major courtroom trials and it was not unusual for Thomas to cover murder trials "gavel to gavel."

In the '90s, a morning news meeting was a gathering of ten reporters. Now, with budget cuts, there are three or four. With the demand to produce three stories a day and take his own pictures, the veteran reporter has found the creative process has dwindled.

He remembers Michael's trial because it was long-awaited and there had been such a push to bring him back to Indiana. What brought the story to life for Derrik was "the passion of Larry that this was a murder and Michael Albrecht committed that murder and he was going to prove it."

As long as Derrik was there, Becky and Sandi believed that Cindy's voice would be heard. Derrik denies bringing anything special to the table. "I have no skin in the game," he says, "but I try to have empathy for the victims, always."

Derrik did not think it odd that Michael sat silent and sullen through his trial. He expected that. "Attorneys tell them [defendants] not to show emotion." Having been a reporter for thirty-six years, he found murder trials hold the most public interest—but not all murder trials. He covered the highest profile cases. "Usually stories choose me," he says.

Though he is a diehard Colts fan, Derrik says he was not a race fan until the Albrecht trial. He now makes it a point to attend the Indianapolis 500.

Seventeen years after the trial, Derrik still believes that Michael is guilty. "All these people loved her. Everybody loved her except him. Who else had a motive? His alibi was blown up by his friend." Michael had planned "to not only murder her but cut off her head. Who else talked about that?"

Derrik describes defense attorney Richard Kammen as an excellent and a very smart attorney. *48 Hours* on CBS covered Kammen's fight to win a "not guilty" verdict for former State Trooper David Cam. The officer was found guilty twice but Kammen got his trial moved to Boone County. Derrik was there for the opening statements of that third trial.

Another high-profile case he covered was that of the Ice Man, Kevin Aaron Conner, who killed three people and was executed in July 2005.

Derrik was chosen to do a one-on-one interview with President Gerald Ford, which he still considers an honor. Asked to name the best story of his career, Derrik says, "It means nothing to anybody but me." He found some Vietnam vets hanging around behind a liquor store. They were young men who had gone off as teenagers to fight for their country and came home to find that they were unemployable. "There are no jobs for killers," they were told. "No jobs for killers."

When he goes to court, Derrik says he hopes that good wins over evil. "For victims' families, those days in court are the worst days of their life. I want to be kind and sensitive; I want to be cognizant of that. They want to tell what was special about their loved one. They want their story told."

CHAPTER 31

Forensics testimony, oppressively detailed, is often the most vital evidence in a trial. In the Albrecht case, the missing head and murder weapon limited information, even by forensics. Possibly the biggest hurdle Larry would ever face in a murder trial was a big one: he could not prove how Cindy died.

John Commons called William Pender from the Marion County Crime Lab to the stand. On October 30, 1992, he met Sergeant Joel Rush in Cindy's apartment. He collected Cindy's bed sheet, pillowcase, and clothing. He added these to the items Rush had already collected. Upon examination back at the crime lab, he recovered fifteen possible hairs from the pillowcase and one possible hair from the t-shirt.

Pender also collected fingerprints from the patio door and dishes in the cabinet. "I printed the computer in the living room, the TV set, the stereo, the table. We were looking for what they call elimination prints."

Michael Smilko, who had worked with the crime lab since 1974, had prior experience with the Marion County Sheriff's Department in Indianapolis. He collected latent fingerprints from Cindy's residence and belongings.

Smilko described the process for the Court. "The processing at the police department and also at the residence basically was done strictly with the powder mechanism and also with a brush. The powder that we use has graphite mixed into it. You place the powder onto the item that you're printing. You work in a circular type direction. At that time if anything is there at all, you take and lift it with the tape and place it onto a card." He said that he prepared approximately nine latent print cards during this particular investigation.

Tape holds the print in place on the card.

Smilko identified a latent print card "from a Marlboro ashtray that came out of the bedroom at that location of 6140 Nalon Court."

Also witnessing for the prosecution was Dr. John E. Pless, Professor of Pathology at the IU School of Medicine and Director of the Division of Forensic Pathology. Dr. Pless was also board certified in anatomic, clinical, and forensic pathology.

"Within your fields of specialization, Doctor, do you perform autopsies?" Commons asked.

Dr. Pless did perform autopsies and he explained the purpose to the jury. "Well, an autopsy is a surgical procedure performed after death. It's an examination of the outside of the body and the interior, as well as the recovery of certain specimens from the body for microscopic examination. From that examination, determinations are made about the factors relating to death, and opinions can be developed concerning the significance of wounds or injuries as to what instruments may have been used to make those injuries."

Commons questioned, "Dr. Pless, did you have an occasion to conduct an autopsy in conjunction with a Dr. Albert Kaltenthaler back in 1992?"

Yes, he performed just one autopsy with Dr. Kaltenthaler that year and he co-signed the autopsy report. "Dr. Kaltenthaler did the initial examination on the 16th of November of 1992," Pless said, and he examined the body on November 27.

Commons handed Dr. Pless a photograph, asking, "Do you recognize that?"

"This picture shows the upper body of Cynthia Albrecht, in which there is an absence of the head and neck."

"Does that particular photograph depict an area which would help to explain the testimony that you might give in regard to the cause of death?"

When Dr. Pless said yes, Kammen asked to approach the bench. "Your Honor," he said, "this witness has previously testified under oath that he was unable to state to a reasonable medical certainty what the cause of death is. Given that statement under oath, it's hard to explain how the State's Exhibit Number 31 will help him testify as to the cause of death because I don't believe he can state today what to a reasonable—"

Larry Sells cut Kammen off. "No, that's not right. He said it was due to traumatic, rapid injury, in his deposition, head or neck injury, and it was much probably as a result of a gunshot wound, strangulation, or blunt force trauma. That's what he said."

"One of those three. I don't see how this is going to help him," Kammen argued.

The judge responded, "He said it did and that's the test. So overruled."

Dr. Pless' opinion was "the cause of death was traumatic injury to the neck."

"And how do you determine that?" Commons asked.

Dr. Pless based his opinion on the body's location in a remote area in a state of decomposition and "there was evidence of saw cuts in the bone."

The pathologist further testified that there were no signs of alcohol or "common drugs of abuse" in the body. "Most drugs are metabolized by the body and after four to six hours, are not found in the blood stream but may be present in the urine. Some drugs, such as marijuana, may be present for weeks to as long as a month after consumption."

"And at what point in time when a person dies, what is the metabolism process?" Commons asked him.

"The metabolism process or breakdown of drugs essentially ceases after death. And not until advanced decomposition, such as putrefaction, occurs do those drugs disappear." He added that the level of decomposition "may not occur at all during the winter months." As for drug levels, "I would say on the basis of this examination, that those substances were not present in the body at the time of death."

Dr. Pless cited the probable cause of death as "any kind of cutting or slashing injury with a sharp object such as a knife. Or manual strangulation or garroting or choking with the arm."

On cross-examination, Kammen posed a series of yes or no questions asking Dr. Pless to confirm there were no defensive wounds.

"And you examined her lungs to see if she had aspirated blood?"

That was correct.

"When a person's throat is cut and they are alive, it is likely that they will aspirate blood?" he probed. "And the most likely scenario, as based on your examination, is that she was decapitated after death?"

The doctor had found no evidence that Cindy had been bound or pinned down, and no injury to the trapezius, one of the neck and shoulder muscles.

Dr. Pless saved the vertebrae with the saw marks in order to compare it to a weapon. "And no saws were ever brought to you in the course of this investigation; isn't that correct?" Kammen asked.

Dr. Pless also confirmed that a headless body could be identified through fingerprints, footprints, scars and moles, or a chest x-ray.

"Now, it's obviously speculative, but there are many reasons why someone might want to remove a head; isn't that correct?" Kammen asked. He listed scenarios, such as "if a person is shot and the bullet remains in the head, they might know that that bullet can be identified or linked to a particular weapon."

Did Dr. Pless go to the site to look for the "lots and lots of blood most probably at the scene where the head was removed?"

He had not. Nor had he tested the area with Luminol to see if the ground had been drenched with diluted blood. "You found no attempts to remove any scars... she may have been strangled, you can't exclude that... she may have been shot... she may have been hit in the back of the head... In all likelihood, instantaneous because she aspirated no blood?"

That was correct, according to Dr. Pless, who also said that in all likelihood, Cindy's head was cut off after her death.

Commons, on redirect, asked Dr. Pless if it were possible that the head was removed on site but laid on some surface, such as a plastic sheet that could be carried away. Yes, it was possible, according to the pathologist.

Kammen approached for re-cross examination. "I hope it's obvious to the jury that—" he began.

Commons spoke out. "Your Honor, I object to the continued characterizations of questions when they are asked."

"I'm going to sustain that objection," the judge replied.

"I apologize," said Kammen. He asked Dr. Pless to reconfirm that there were no defensive wounds consistent with strangulation and that strangulation may not be instantaneous.

Kammen protested admitting the autopsy report into evidence. The judge responded, "He certainly was permitted to testify... No one objected at that time on the basis of speculation." Then Judge Mangus-Stinson had a question for the doctor. "Who hired you, let me ask you that."

"I was asked by the Marion County prosecutor, Jeff Modisett, to review the case with Dr. Kaltenthaler."

"Okay. Did you have any information about a particular defendant at the time of the autopsy?" the judge wanted to know.

"I don't know that I did. I don't remember."

Her Honor determined that Dr. Pless's testimony was cumulative "and I can see no additional prejudice."

The judge reminded Kammen that the contested issue was the cause of death. "That's in evidence without objection from the defense."

Then Kammen raised the alarm that Michael's one chance at a fair trial was being shot down by courtroom spectators wearing orange buttons that declared victory over violence. He said, "It seems to pertain to this case clearly trying to influence the jury. We would ask the Court to order those removed."

Larry said, "I didn't even notice it. Mr. Kammen is much more perceptive than I am."

The judge too had just noticed the buttons. "What does it say?"

Larry offered, "I'll bring it up to the Court. I don't see anything on here about the case." He said that the buttons had not come from the prosecution.

The buttons had come from Cindy's friend, Kim Graham, who had them made from the photograph on Cindy's Missing poster. She had been passing them out in the hallway to show support for Cindy and to signify their shared loss.

The judge said, "I don't want any witnesses wearing those."

Kammen said, "We would like to be heard further on this issue of these buttons. And we'd like to call some witnesses."

Drew Findling interjected, "Your Honor, I am deeply troubled that we... are actually considering a First Amendment right that would override the Sixth and Fourteenth Amendment rights of Michael Albrecht to a fair trial. It's clearly, Your Honor, intended to be recognized by the jury as these folks, and these nice folks who have considerable concern to be here—"

The judge cut him off, saying the jury had already seen the pins.

"We would like to know where the pins are coming from," Kammen persisted.

Someone among the spectators spoke out, saying that a woman had handed them out in the hallway.

The issue was resolved when the spectators offered to take the buttons off.

Inability to locate Matthew Kernel was a burning issue for Kammen. A subpoena had been issued but "it is our understanding that Matthew Kernel is a fugitive, that there is a warrant for his arrest...but we would like Mr. Kernel brought before the Court."

"How can I do that?" the judge asked.

Kammen said, "We're asking the Court to enforce our subpoena."

"I know, but he has to be served before I can issue a warrant for him, doesn't he?"

Commons said, "When he raised that the other day, we looked and have not found a warrant on the computer system."

The bailiff searched and found no warrant, but in the arrest records, he found "a Matthew Kernel, that's for a possession charge. However, that's a non-bond situation, but there's no warrant on that case."

"Looks like we know where he is," the judge informed Kammen.

"He's in the Marion County jail?" Kammen asked.

The bailiff explained, "He's in the jail under a no-bond situation."

"Looks like you could serve him," the judge prodded.

Police had interviewed Kernel's girlfriend, Cindy Bierman, but she was now residing in Denver, Colorado. Bierman had previously agreed to testify but was thirty weeks pregnant and Kammen questioned her ability to fly. He suggested that either the defense or prosecuting attorneys fly out to depose her.

The judge said, "My preference would be that you do that over the phone so that people don't have to spend the money to fly to Denver in the middle of a trial."

CHAPTER 32

Becky said it was a bad omen when she and Sandi were stuck in a crowded elevator in the courthouse. Things like that did not happen to her. Her nerves were a bee sting burn when Larry summoned her to testify.

Becky had dressed carefully for the occasion, trying to be respectful of the Court and demonstrate the professionalism of Team Penske.

She moved from the harsh, clacking hallway to the courtroom. The change was surreal. The room, with its stale air conditioning and dark wood, felt tense. Fear perched on her shoulder. She was deeply afraid of saying anything biased or anything that would give Michael's attorneys an edge in the trial. She wore a stretchy bracelet, borrowed from a friend, to help calm her nerves.

"It was like having the weight of the world on you," Becky remembers, "knowing that I can't screw this up." She felt like she could not breathe.

Then she scanned the courtroom. "Our side was so full. I bet we had ten women every day and people from racing. They took off work; their lives stopped." Michael's side, she said, was a smatter of a few people: Michael's parents and one day his daughters.

Judge Jane Mangus-Stinson, tall, thin, and pretty, wore her hair in a stylish pixie haircut. She was "very sweet," Becky says, and very pregnant. A well-spoken woman in her thirties, she wore a black robe and tended to lean back in her chair to ease the weight of her soon-to-be-born child. From the witness stand, Becky had to stretch to see the judge.

When Larry began to question her, Becky felt like she was taking her first real breath in years. He asked narrative questions, allowing her to tell the jury, in her own words, *what happened*. She talked about her friendship and working relationship with Cindy Albrecht.

Becky recalled the dwindling relationship between Michael and Cindy and said she became aware of a romantic relationship between Cindy and Pete Twiddy after the July 19 Toronto race.

"She started seeming like Cindy all the time. She didn't seem like she was depressed about her and Mike's marriage so much and it seemed like she was ready for a change in her life."

Becky saw Michael at the Laguna Seca race when the women delivered food. "We were coming back to our area and he stopped us, calling Cindy over and she asked Sandi and I to stay with her, to wait with her while he spoke with her." He wanted Cindy to sign insurance papers and they debated whether the divorce was final on the 24th or 26th.

Becky recalled another interaction at the August 9 Cleveland race. "He brought a letter over to Cindy at our kitchen trailer and I remember it because it made Sandi and I mad because it was right during the lunch rush and it upset Cindy. She started to cry when she read the letter and he asked her at that point if they could just talk about things and would she please not go through with the divorce, if they could just please talk about things."

There were other instances. "He would call our hotel room, sometimes to the point that I would go down to the office."

After the Laguna Seca race, Becky and her husband went to San Francisco. They returned to Indianapolis on Wednesday, October 21.

Becky described her trip to Cindy's apartment on Tuesday morning, October 27, finding Cindy's truck parked in the first slot in front of her apartment, covered in dew, stepping into the dark apartment armed with mace and an umbrella.

Shown photographs of the apartment, Becky confirmed they had found Cindy's abode just that way, a stack of clothing beside the dresser and luggage still packed. The bed neatly made. Larry Sells asked her, "Sometime after you were in the bedroom, did you have anything come to mind about the bed?"

"Yes. I believe it was on the twenty-eighth, possibly. We were trying to remember everything we could, what was there in her apartment, what could have been missing, and I remembered that her bedspread was missing off the bed."

Larry asked, "Other than using the telephone and looking in the closets, and Sandi Fink taking her fingers and opening the sliding glass door, did you or Sandra Fink disturb anything in that apartment before the police arrived?"

"I did look in her purse."

"Why did you do that?"

"I wanted to see if she had been robbed. I took her wallet out and I saw there were two twenty-dollar bills, there was forty dollars, and all her charge cards were still there." She had not gone through Cindy's purse but merely examined her wallet.

Officer Dane Morgan arrived followed by Detective Steve Turner. "How were your nerves at that point?" Larry asked her. "Your nerves. You. Yourself."

"I was—I had at one point started to cry. I knew something was wrong, I was very upset." She headed outdoors to smoke a cigarette and calm herself down but Detective Steve Turner "told me I could smoke in the apartment." She smoked one cigarette and placed the butt in the ashtray next to Cindy's couch.

Sandi mentioned the moneybag and Turner instructed her to look inside it.

Becky said, "It was unzipped and she looked in it and there were the receipts that we had from all the purchases we made in Laguna, but the cash and the change were all gone."

"Do you know how much money should have been in there?"

"Probably around twenty-five hundred to three thousand dollars."

"Before Dane Morgan and Steve Turner arrived at that apartment, had either you or Sandi looked into that briefcase or money bag?"

"No."

Shortly after this discovery, they all left the apartment. Turner left first. "Before you went back to Sandi's house, did you have a conversation with Officer Morgan?" Larry asked.

Yes, they did, "down on the sidewalk in front of Cindy's apartment," Becky said. "We said that we were afraid that Mike Albrecht had done something to her because their divorce was to be final the day before and that it had gotten very unfriendly. And we didn't want to speak in front of Steve Turner because he was friends with Mike."

Michael sagged in his chair and did not react to this comment. His graying hair was freshly trimmed. His new wife, Denise, carried a bible with her into the courtroom. He would turn to grin at his spouse, "showing off his jailhouse religion," Becky says. He always had a notepad with him.

Becky was also pleased to see Filter acting like a nervous wreck. She said, "You know what, you gotta get your little pieces. Every once in a while, a blind squirrel gets a nut."

Even though Michael was a prisoner, Sandi had found that seeing him face to face since the murder was intimidating. The man, she said, was "always mad."

Becky agrees, quoting a favorite saying of her dad's. "He was mad enough to hunt us with switches. He'd been walking free all this time and now…"

Becky was glad she had been able to tell her story. She describes Larry as "magical in the courtroom." But now the defense would have a turn at her.

The carpet hushed each footstep as defense attorney Elizabeth Rankin approached. Rankin, a short, dark-haired lawyer from Atlanta, Georgia, began her questioning. Becky's eyes flitted to the row of seats along the back wall. It looked like an escape route. Tempting. But Becky knew she did not want to escape. She was in court, under oath, and looking for an opportunity to speak, to make a permanent record about the brutal murder that ended Cindy's young life.

The prosecuting team and the jury were on the left. Larry had chosen the left side for that reason. Becky focused herself that direction.

Rankin asked Becky about events in Indianapolis after the Laguna Seca race. The attorney said, "I guess you were under the impression that Cindy probably had some errands to do, she had just gotten back in town, and it didn't concern you at all that the three of you were not going to get together on Monday?" Becky said no. "And you didn't make any effort to try to contact Cindy on Monday to find out?"

On Tuesday, "even though there was this conversation between Sandi and Pete Twiddy, you were not concerned and you had thought that when you would get to Cynthia's apartment that she would be home?"

"We would assume she—hoped she would be. We hoped she would be," Becky clarified.

Rankin countered, "Well, in fact, you expected her to be home? You believed that she would be home when you arrived there; is that correct?"

"No. We were hoping she would be there by the time we got there."

Rankin referred to Becky's December 4, 1992, deposition. "And do you remember during that deposition, Mr. Findling asked you questions about that morning and you stated that when you arrived at her apartment at 8:30, you expected Cynthia to be home at that time; do you remember that?"

Becky was not going to be thrown off track by semantics. "We knew from Pete's phone call she was not answering the phone, but we were hoping she would be there."

Rankin noted that the two women called Michael Albrecht and Pete Twiddy before contacting the police. "And the reason you didn't call the police was because Cynthia was an adult and at that point she was just missing and you really didn't know how serious the situation was; is that correct?" It was. "When you got there and saw she was missing, one of the things that jumped to your mind was maybe Cynthia had been robbed?"

"That was a thought," Becky responded.

When Officer Morgan arrived, Becky didn't mention that she thought Michael Albrecht may have been responsible for whatever had happened there. "Is that correct?"

"Like I said, I can't swear that his name was never brought up... I don't remember everything that was said when Dane Morgan arrived," Becky said.

Detective Turner arrived. "And again, there was no indication on your part that Michael Albrecht may have had some kind of involvement; is that correct?"

Becky answered, "I'm just trying to remember. Because at some point, I did have a discussion with Steve Turner that we were suspicious of Mike. But I believe it may have been at the police station later that day."

At some point, she did mention suspicions of Michael Albrecht to Lieutenant Jones or Sergeant Rush, Becky insisted, but she didn't "remember exactly, October 30 of 1992."

"Let me show you a summary of your statement taken by Lieutenant Jones—" Rankin began.

"Judge, I'll object to that characterization," Larry protested. "First of all, it's speculation on her part to respond to anything Detective Jones may have memorialized concerning the conversation she had with him unless she saw that memo when it was completed."

Rankin said, "Your Honor, I was going to use it to refresh her recollection."

"You can use anything to refresh recollection," the judge decided. "Overruled."

Becky saw that she had mentioned Michael's name twice in Lieutenant Jones' notes, and even though one reference was merely a mention of his buying car parts, "I don't know why I would be concerned about that if I didn't think he had done something with Cindy."

Looking at the memo again, she said, "I think right here also tells me we were suspicious of him, that we were watching his movements. I think our suspicions were very well known. I can't imagine ever having a meeting with them and not telling them of our suspicions about Michael Albrecht."

Then why had she mentioned hospitality worker Lori Wetzel as Cindy's enemy? Becky didn't know.

On redirect, Larry asked Becky, "Do you recall if you were asked by Detective Jones at that time whether or not you suspected Michael Albrecht on that specific date?"

"I don't recall," Becky replied and he directed her to read the second paragraph of page two of the memo. Did that refresh her memory? Becky remembered the interview now. "I believe it was, 'Other than Mike Albrecht, who are some suspects you can think of or who are some enemies in the racing organization?'"

In the entire racing community, he noted for the jury, Becky was able to name only one person who may have had differences with Cynthia Albrecht.

Directing Becky's attention back to the memo Rankin had given her, Larry said, "And you were specifically referred to an October 30 reference to Michael Albrecht buying parts for his BMW; do you recall that?"

"Correct."

"And I believe you were about to testify about another incident, perhaps one that occurred on the same day, on October 27, that caused you further suspicion?"

"Yes," Becky said, "I believe—"

Rankin cut her off. "Objection, Your Honor, this question is calling for hearsay."

"Judge, she brought it up," Larry pointed out. "She asked what in there shows that she said anything about suspicions that she had of Michael Albrecht. It's right in there. And it's not offered for the truth of any hearsay content, but to corroborate her statement that she gave and her testimony that she's given."

The judge agreed, saying, "I think he's allowed to rebut the inference attempted to be raised on redirect. You may answer."

"What did you tell—" he began.

Dissatisfied with the ruling, Rankin interrupted again. "Your Honor, may we approach?" She told the judge, "I specifically asked her just if she suspected that Michael Albrecht was involved in this. I mean, I didn't ask her about statements about what Michael Albrecht may have done on other dates."

Findling said Becky's statement was made to "somebody who's never been on their witness list, we've never been given an address of."

"An unknown person," Larry mocked. "You've been out there beating on everybody else's door. You could easily have found her."

"Have you given us one iota—" Findling began.

"You could have asked us. You're the one that put that piece of paper in front of her face, not me."

Rankin said the memo did not give Becky license to testify to hearsay and Findling added, "The question was, did she say the words 'I suspect him.'"

"No, that wasn't the question," the judge stated. "The question was 'did you not tell him anything about you being suspicious?' There's a completely different inference."

Findling objected again that Becky had referenced a conversation with someone "not in discovery, not on the witness list."

"Well, it's in discovery because it's right here," the judge told him. "Her address is right here... in the statement." Her Honor told Rankin, "She gave, in her mind, based upon what she said, quite specific information. He's not offering to prove it's true—"

"Of course, he is, Your Honor," Findling declared. "That is a fiction, Your Honor."

The judge overruled his objection.

Turning his attention back to Becky, Larry asked, "What else did you tell either Joel Rush and/or Lt. Bill Jones about your suspicions concerning Michael?"

"That Karen Welch had called me the day Sandi and I reported Cindy missing and told me that he was out in his driveway washing his BMW," Becky responded.

CHAPTER 33

The Albrecht family fastened glares of contempt upon Michael's brother, Randy Albrecht, when he was called as State's witness. Larry knew it had cost Randy dearly to break rank and testify against his brother. With the entire Albrecht family eyeing him like he was yesterday's sausage, Randy strode bravely to the witness stand and swore to tell the truth.

Michael wanted Cindy roughed up.

"Did he say why he wanted that done, why he wanted her roughed up?" Larry asked.

Randy answered, "Well, because the relationship was bad and he didn't want it to break up, and he had given her a lot of things." Michael "was angry because she had destroyed his life." These conversations came from phone booth to phone booth at Michael's insistence.

Did Michael have any money when he brought his personal effects from Indiana? "Did he tell you anything about five thousand dollars?" Larry probed.

"I don't remember."

"Or nearly twenty-three hundred dollars?"

"No," Randy answered.

"Don't recall that?" he asked. Other than living with Randy, did Michael appear to be paying his own way? Randy said he had. "And during this same time period, do you know whether or not he was using payphones?"

"I believe so," Randy recalled. "Occasionally."

Randy and Michael had a close relationship. He described Michael as "one of the more desirable family members." Their musical performance history reached back fifteen years. Then, in 1994, Indiana law enforcement contacted Randy and he was required to give a statement. This threw him and his nuclear family "into a state of turmoil." He had had no contact with his parents since then.

In a later conversation at a park in Hialeah with Michael and Willie Hernandez, Randy said his brother mentioned money being paid to Bill Filter in Milwaukee.

Randy also said Michael's neck muscle test "hurt" and could incapacitate a person. "It would cut off circulation on the, I believe it's the carotid," he said.

The witness passed to Findling, who curved the conversation back to the failed marriage. Hadn't Michael been gracious when Cindy first became successful?

"And when he told you things were going very well for Cindy, he told you that with great pride; isn't that true?"

Randy said it was.

A few months before the murder, Michael's conversations about Cindy morphed from happiness to concern. Findling said, "He indicated to you that Cindy was hanging around with Penske team members, and I'm using your words that you've given me before, and acting inconsistent with marital commitment in her behavior; is that a fair way you've summarized that before?"

Hearing an affirmative answer, Findling hammered the point. "His concerns were that she was wearing more revealing clothes?" "Looser type of clothes?" "Open top shirts?" "Tighter pants?" "She had dyed her hair?" "She was starting to stay up late at night?" "And go with people other than him? I'm not suggesting men, but going out with other team members late at night and just coming home late at night and not including him?"

"Correct," Randy answered.

Larry acted nonchalant, letting the jury see that he found this information uninteresting. Too bad the defense had not had time to interview some of Michael's sex workers. Those women could probably offer some sizzling testimony about his "concern."

Findling asked if Michael expressed concern about Cindy drinking excessively and using marijuana. Randy answered. "Cocaine. I don't remember about the marijuana."

Cocaine. That was a lie. Larry took note of it.

The defense attorney honed in on Cindy's alleged drug use. "He continued to be concerned about her use of cocaine? Now, you know, as a law enforcement officer, that when folks are involved with drugs, cocaine and things like that, sometimes that can be a very violent world; would you agree with that?"

"Objection, relevance," Larry challenged. "There's no indication there was such a conversation between the defendant and this witness. I don't know how it's relevant what this witness's experiences are." The objection was sustained.

Why, Findling pondered, did Michael want Willie Hernandez or a Cuban person to harm Cindy? Did many Cuban cocaine users inhabit Miami? "And Michael... never said to you at any point of that conversation, 'Randy, will you have somebody kill Cindy?' He never said, 'I want to have some part of her body removed,' did he?"

Satisfied that Randy kept agreeing, Findling offered, "He never said, 'I want it done and I want you to make sure that forensically that law enforcement can never figure out who did it,' he didn't say any of that, did he?"

No. Michael had said that he loved Cindy and wanted to get back together with her.

Findling pointed out that Randy did not take Michael's threat seriously or report it. "And when you talked about it with Willie, you basically laughed it off, didn't you? If you had thought at all that he was really serious about this,"

Findling said, "you… being a law enforcement officer, would have called, at the minimum, Cindy; am I correct?"

The defense attorney's next tack was to flatten the tires on Michael's alleged threat. He pointed out that Michael had not said to Randy, "If you don't do it, here are my plans… I'm an assassin and I'm going to do this so quickly and promptly and officially nobody will ever be able to tell; none of those kind of things ever came up when he talked to you, did it?

"And this is very, very important. He was going to move his things down from Indianapolis down to Florida; am I right? And you permitted him to do that knowing, okay, knowing that he had made the 'can you get her roughed up?' comment to you."

Michael had also told Randy that people would come to interview him. "And you understood that he had given out your phone number and your address so if law enforcement wanted to contact him, he could be contacted; am I right?"

Findling next swerved to cast suspicion on Antonio Ferrari. Larry objected, saying that Randy was testifying to what Michael said someone else told him.

The attorneys accused each other of making editorial comments and Judge Mangus-Stinson ordered them all to the bench. Her Honor said, "If I hear him say one more time that something is important, I'm going to object myself, okay? You ask questions, you make objections. Evidence comes from witnesses. So just ask your questions without any headlines of emphasis on how important this point is."

Returning his attention to Randy, Findling asked about Michael's suspicions of Antonio Ferrari. Michael "was concerned because… Cindy had done some work for Antonio Ferrari a while back. Antonio Ferrari had lost a good bit of money as a result of that… And he expressed to you that it was his understanding that Ferrari had some mob-like connections? And he was concerned that one of the possibilities is that Antonio Ferrari could have had somebody do something to Cindy; am I right?"

Was the guy reading a narrative or asking a question? Larry tried to gauge the jury's response to this tailspin on the facts.

Findling asked if one of Michael's scenarios was that Cindy's death was drug related. Randy said yes. "And at the time, it was not your belief that when he was expressing those things to you, he was just trying to throw you off track in any way; am I right?"

Larry shouted, "Judge, I object! That's speculation and irrelevant."

"It's his opinion," Findling countered. "He didn't do anything with the information and I think he should be entitled to explain why he didn't do anything with the information."

"It's still not relevant what his impressions were," Larry barked.

The Court said, "I'll sustain the objection. I don't think his opinion is relevant."

As an IndyCar mechanic, Michael traveled to Canada and Australia. The defense entered his passport into evidence as Exhibit J. "Randy, you had indicated you had had these extradition conversations with Michael back in 1992?" Randy said yes. "And he stayed in the United States; am I right?"

Regarding payment to Bill Filter, Findling said, "The amount of money, or whether it was a loan or a payment, you don't know the specifics, you just know there was some conversation about money with Bill Filter." Had Michael's comment about sending money to Bill Filter seemed important enough for Randy to mention it to the officers?

"I don't recall."

Randy's brother, Scott, suffered some years earlier from Guillain-Barré syndrome and had lain in a hospital for weeks on end, paralyzed. During that time, it came to the

Albrecht brothers' attention that Scott's wife was cheating on him. Did Randy recall making "a passing comment that you can find somebody to do something to her?"

Randy said it was possible that he had made that comment. He was upset.

What comments had Randy made, Findling wanted to know, when he discussed Michael's situation with his older brother, Mark? "Do you remember telling him that you had told Michael that you can get somebody to take care of Cindy?"

"No."

"Do you remember him saying that Mike is not that way, he's just a wimp?"

"No."

"You're telling us you did not make that statement to Mark?" Findling challenged.

Randy replied, "I'm telling you I don't remember."

Larry could have hoped for a better answer, but the defense had not buzzed past him with these allegations against Randy, and they were not going to.

He rose to question Randy. He maintained his poise, stepping out smoothly, demonstrating that Findling's clutter of questions had not thrown his case off track. He asked Randy about the life insurance money. Randy told the Court that Michael said he wanted the money to go to Cindy's father, Woody.

He asked about the request to have Cindy roughed up. "Michael… specifically asked you to attempt to find someone in the Cuban community, either Willie Hernandez, your friend, or someone he might know."

"Want me to elaborate?" Randy responded. "He referred to Willie because he felt since Willie lived in Hialeah and there were a lot of Latin people there and they work for low wages that we may be able to find somebody to do it for a relatively small amount of money."

"He didn't want to pay a lot to have it done?" Larry asked.

"Right."

Why did Michael want this violence done to Cindy? "Mr. Findling asked you if it had anything to do with her drug use," Larry pointed out. "I believe you testified on direct examination that Michael told you that he wanted to get her for destroying his life, she had been spending his money, she was dumping him and costing him his job, and that that's the reason why he wanted her roughed up."

"That's correct," Randy said.

What about Michael's insistence on using payphones? "Did he ever give you any sort of explanation for that peculiar behavior?"

"He believed that the phones were being tapped at my house. Or possibly his apartment later on, because of the murder investigation," Randy said.

Michael had told Randy that his chief suspects in Cynthia's death were Antonio Ferrari and Pete Twiddy. "Did he mention Sandra or Mike Fink as being suspects in her murder?" Randy had heard those names before but not in context.

CHAPTER 34

John Commons questioned Randy's wife, Mary Jo Albrecht, about Noel's 1992 visit. Was picking her up from the airport an issue? No problem, Mary Jo said, "we're very close to the airport."

However, when Mary Jo heard that Michael was also coming to Florida, she made some phone calls. "It caused us some concern if there was a warrant for Mike's arrest that he should not stay with us."

Deputy Prosecutor Commons showed Mary Jo an envelope that Michael had given to her. Findling objected. The attorneys took their arguments to the bench.

"Your Honor, its prejudice value outweighs any relevant value that it may have to the proceedings," Findling began. No one could prove who wrote the letter or when. "And because of that, we'd ask that it not be admitted."

"Our response is that by it having been delivered to her, it constitutes a communication. There is a date on the letter. It becomes a communication at the time it is communicated, which is at the time it was delivered." The letter should be admitted, Commons said, because it "contains allegations that were brought up by Mr. Findling... regarding the possible suspects in the case, particularly Mr. Ferrari."

The Court admitted the letter. Written to Lt. Bill Jones, Michael's letter claimed that Antonio Ferrari was behind Cindy's disappearance, that she was killed for "a number of mistakes" that cost Ferrari thirty thousand dollars. "He was very upset with her," the letter read. "I apologized and tried to explain that she was never very good with numbers." Michael claimed that Ferrari was keeping tabs on Cindy. "I thought it was just curiosity. But late in the season I found out that he was paying everybody else their money and holding back on mine."

The letter further claimed that Michael was safe only because he was in Milwaukee when Cindy was grabbed. He wrote, "The whole deal smells like a professional job" and "I can't make this statement to you in person because I think they'd kill me in a heartbeat—I know too much about his business dealings." The letter was signed November 8, 1992—one week before Cindy's body was found.

The bailiff passed copies to the jury.

Mary Jo Albrecht testified that Michael "asked me to hold onto it and if anything happened to him to mail it," she said.

In cross-examination, Findling mentioned that Mary Jo and Randy's son had been six years old at the time Michael came to stay with them. "During the next couple of months, things became somewhat uncomfortable?" Findling asked. "And during this period of time there were prank phone calls or hostile phone calls being made to your telephone?"

"I did not take any of those phone calls," Mary Jo replied. "There was concern that the phone could be tapped."

When Larry called Antonio Ferrari to the witness stand, the judge dismissed the jury from the courtroom.

In December of 1992, Antonio Ferrari was asked by the Speedway Police Department to place a call to Michael Albrecht, which he did. He taped that call and Kammen did not want that tape heard by the jury. Kammen complained that the call transpired while the State knew that his divorce lawyer Mr. Van Barteau represented Michael.

"And because he was represented by counsel, the State, we believe, was prohibited from undertaking such as surreptitious communication. And for that reason, this tape should be suppressed and excluded," Kammen argued.

Larry began to explain that Lt. Jones requested the tape but that the call came from Ferrari's personal phone at his residence.

The Court was more concerned about the issue of Michael having retained counsel. Kammen said, "There are other cases which hold that once an individual has exercised his right to counsel, the State is prohibited from maintaining surreptitious contact with the individual during the course of an investigation."

"Judge, I know that in the Massiah case the defendant was in custody and the government sent in an informant to obtain information from him," Larry countered. "I know of no case law that says that an individual not in custody, who has not expressly exercised his right to not talk based on Miranda, cannot have his telephone conversations taped."

Kammen argued that "your right to have counsel does not attach at custody, it does not attach at indictment, it attaches when you hire a lawyer… if you have a lawyer, the State cannot circumvent the lawyer simply by sending in some other party."

"What authority is there for that?" Larry challenged.

"Well, what authority is there that you can do it?" Kammen retorted.

Commons said, "We can do anything that the law doesn't proscribe us from doing." The defense started looking up cases.

Antonio Ferrari, an Italian citizen, lived in both Italy and Zionsville, Indiana. He had met Michael Albrecht in 1989 and Michael had worked for him sporadically as his chief mechanic.

Ferrari identified a photograph of Cindy, who had also worked for him. Ferrari said, "We were planning to have, in '91, a hospitality and I assigned her the job to prepare a program for hospitality." The plan did not work out. "We have a trouble with sponsorship that didn't pay for, so we interrupt this project. But when she worked for me, it was fine."

When Michael worked for Ferrari, they had friendly conversations several times a week. Around mid-June, Michael's marital problems erupted. "It was going deep and deep in the conversation... Kind of, I was the person, you know, kind of a counselor, a guide with which he can talk about his personal stuff."

"Did you try to draw information from him or did he volunteer it?" Larry asked.

"No. I was absolutely no interesting at all," Ferrari said. "I have an interest in my organization—"

Kammen cut in. "I'm going to object to the volunteered nature of the—"

The judge said, "Mr. Ferrari, you need to just answer the questions he asks you."

Larry continued. "How would you describe Michael Albrecht's emotional state at the time when he started telling you about the problems?"

"Well, I permit my English is no good; if I can say in Italian, I can explain better."

"I don't understand Italian," Larry apologized.

Ferrari answered, "I will say he was upset, he was mad. Progressively worst in the feeling." He mentioned being jealous. Since Ferrari served on the CART board and Roger Penske was the director of that board, Michael asked Antonio to approach Roger.

"He mentioned to me that Cindy maybe was having smoking drugs... and was not good for the Penske organization to have somebody in the hospitality that can be caught and do something like that. So he asked me to report to Mr. Penske this information."

"Did he tell you why he wanted you to do that?" Larry asked.

"He used the word to have her out of racing," Ferrari related.

Ferrari was not sure when he heard that the couple was divorcing, but "he really love a lot Cindy. I don't know after. Because the relationship definitely switched."

At the Lexington, Ohio, race on September 13, Ferrari said, "happening something a little different. Mike asked me an extra passes for a girls that he take to the track. And I thinks she stayed with him… on the team, we kind of joke about this because he was always mad and we was happy to see him with somebody else."

Several weeks later, "things got change again. And he was kind of upset."

A news story from Italy reported "the Mafia blew up the interstate and kill a judge with a lot of people in some car." This event ignited new conversations with Michael, who wanted to know if his boss knew anyone in the Mafia. "I thinks was for hiring something against Cindy.

"What he liked to do specifically, he used the word 'permanent' and put out of racing. He said 'if somebody's not able to do it, I will do personally.'"

John Carlos Incasa was the director of the clothing department for Fendi and Fendi, Antonio Ferrari's sponsor. He frequently called the shop from New York and he spoke Italian. Ferrari led Michael to believe that this man was a contact. Actually, he was just waiting for Michael to cool his motor. But as the Nazareth, Pennsylvania, race approached, Michael wanted action. They would be close to New York.

Michael told Ferrari that Cindy "carried cash for the hospitality, especially in Nazareth." He asked Ferrari if a robbery could be arranged "and so can hurt her during the robbery, and he mentioned the hotel where she stayed."

If Ferrari could make arrangements, Michael could pay. "And I asked how and he said, 'well, I have an insurance policy for fifty thousand dollars.' And I remember the fifty thousand dollars."

"On whose life?" Larry wanted to know.

"Well, it must be her."

Kammen did not like that answer. "I'm going to object to the conclusion that 'it must be her.' If he didn't say, don't guess. And I move to strike that."

"I'll strike that answer," the Court responded.

"During the time that Cynthia Albrecht worked for you, did she ever do anything that cost you thirty thousand dollars?" Sells wanted to know.

"No. No way."

"Did she ever do anything that cost you anything?"

"No," Antonio insisted, "zero. I am the only one sign check in the company. She actually didn't purchase nothing. I get some tools for the kitchen she get through another hospitality. Cost me zero dollar."

Larry asked permission to approach the bench and told the judge that he was close to wanting to play the tape. Kammen said he was "still looking" for cases that would block him.

The Court stated, "I found a court of appeals case directly in point. It says if proceedings have not begun, there's no right to counsel. The court of appeals explicitly held that the right to counsel attaches at the time criminal proceedings are initiated; that is either by arrest, arraignment, or indictment for a charge. None of that had happened at the time of the phone call in this case."

The tape was admitted, but due to time constraints, it would be played the next day. Kammen again objected and was overruled.

CHAPTER 35

Guillermo "Willie" Hernandez had been friends with the Albrecht brothers since 1987. When Michael decided to move to Florida in 1992, Hernandez flew to Indianapolis to help him pack up his house. Commons called him as a witness for the State.

"My understanding was that Mike wanted to get out of racing and come down to Florida since him and Cindy were going to divorce," Hernandez said. When they arrived, Michael's roommate, John Weland, informed them that Cindy's body had been found. Michael was taken in for questioning.

"From what I remember, Mike was very distraught. We went out for a walk and he talked about it."

The media talked about it too. Michael's house became a hub for reporters.

"I guess they were following him around." They even knocked on his back door." Hernandez said, "Whenever it would come up on the news, he would turn the TV off."

They left Indianapolis and drove the rental car to Milwaukee, "just to see his family, if I recall correctly."

"While you were on the trip to Milwaukee," Commons asked, "did Mr. Albrecht indicate anything to you about the discovery of the body?"

"About an hour outside of Chicago, we were driving north and he pointed to the right of me, east, and he said they found her body in that field, about a mile in," Hernandez related.

Commons wanted to know "from the time that John Weland had first told the two of you about the discovery of the body until you were on that trip to Milwaukee, had you received any information through the news media or any other sources while in the presence of the defendant regarding the discovery of her body?"

"From what I had seen," Hernandez answered, "when the news media would come on, they hadn't said anything about where they found the body."

During the visit, Willie Hernandez met Bill Filter at his dad's bar. The three of them socialized for a while and then Filter and Michael stepped outside for a discussion that lasted half an hour to an hour.

Hernandez and Michael returned to Indianapolis, packed up a U-Haul, and headed for Florida. It was not a pleasant trip for Hernandez; Michael was in a bad mood. "He had been doing most of the driving, so I asked him if he wanted me to drive... I had never driven a truck of that size and I would, you know, veer a little bit off the road... and he would kind of scream, 'keep the truck on the road!'"

Michael's driving didn't instill confidence in Hernandez either. "He drove pretty crazy. I remember a couple of instances on the rental car, coming back from Milwaukee to Indianapolis, it was raining fairly hard and he was speeding, going eighty or ninety or so."

Once he settled in Florida, Michael made several boat-shopping trips with Hernandez and Randy. "Initially, he wanted to live on the boat in case anything would happen, he could sail on out in the boat and he could be a free man, I guess," Hernandez said. "I can't recall the exact words, but it was along the lines of him escaping and not being caught."

He'd also asked Hernandez if he knew countries in Latin America or South America which he could not be extradited from.

Hernandez and Michael's friendship snapped in 1993. He said Michael's "attitude was he was always in a bad mood; he was pretty much an asshole most of the time."

Kammen rose to cross-examine Hernandez. Michael wanted Randy to find a Cuban to rough up his wife? Yes, Hernandez and Randy had joked about it. "But," Kammen said, "there's a certain stereotype in that; wouldn't you agree?"

"Sure," Hernandez replied.

"I mean, you know, you work, I think you're in the computer industry now?" But in 1991 and 1992, Hernandez was unemployed. He and Randy had worked together in the purchasing department for a company called Brent Metals, and later gone to Locklear. "So you work in an office environment?" Kammen asked.

"Right."

"And certainly, and I mean this very seriously, certainly had nothing to do with drugs? Nothing to do with violence? And the notion that just because you were Latin, somebody would suggest you knew anything about that was kind of offensive?"

"Yeah. It kind of ticked me off," Hernandez admitted.

Kammen circled. Hernandez and Michael had not heard where the body was found? Odd. He presented an *Indianapolis Star* newspaper from Wednesday, November 18, 1992. In it was an article stating that the headless body found might belong to Cynthia Albrecht. On page two of the newspaper was a map showing the location of the body.

Oh, he wasn't saying Hernandez was wrong, but there was confusion at Michael's house? "The phone is ringing off the hook, correct? Sometimes… the calls were short and had the appearance of crank calls?" Kammen asked.

True, Hernandez agreed.

Then Michael was taken in to be questioned. "As you recall it, it might have been as much as six or seven hours?" Kammen asked. Hernandez was in a strange city with no car and the only person he knew was gone. "He's gone off to be questioned about a murder?"

"Right," Hernandez said.

"And you said, 'if they arrest Michael, how am I getting home?'" Then the media staked out the house, cameras and trucks with different station numbers. "It was so bad you didn't even want to look out the window; fair to say?"

He had expected to fly to Indianapolis and drive home. Then Michael invited him to Milwaukee and Michael's parents welcomed him. Michael had not deserted him except to talk to Filter outside the bar.

"And I don't mean this anything other than factually; you were probably the one Hispanic guy in the place?" Kammen asked.

Yes. One more awkwardness that he endured. "And I suspect that sitting alone under those circumstances, no one to talk to, time was going pretty slow?" Maybe Michael and Bill tried to explain what they had discussed and "you just don't recall?" Hernandez said that was possible.

The pair returned to Indianapolis. Kammen said, "When you're packing up, he's not keeping you from touching anything? He's not saying, no, don't touch that box, no, don't touch this?"

Hernandez replied, "No. Just asked me to be careful with his tools in particular."

During the drive south, discussion turned to what may have happened to Cindy. "And he told you why he thought Ferrari had something to do with it?" Kammen asked.

"Yeah," Hernandez replied. "He said that Ferrari had Mafia connections and Cindy had lost a great deal of money to Ferrari... He's Italian, he's connected. I'm Cuban, I know people."

"And that's an unfortunate stereotype," Kammen agreed.

What about boat shopping in Florida? "Was that so rare?" Kammen asked. "You and Randy talked about buying boats?" They had. "But Michael never bought a boat, did he?" He did not.

Pressing his point, Kammen said, "And... you don't know whether Michael had the ability to leave the country or not? I mean, you don't know whether he had a passport? To your knowledge, he never made any efforts to leave the country?"

Not that he knew of, Hernandez responded.

CHAPTER 36

The defense did not intend to let Bill Filter testify. Larry Sells knew that during the lunch break, Michael's attorneys were whipping up their arguments. He decided to send them to the pits.

When the trial resumed, Larry stood to address the Court. "Based upon the discovery, it appears that the defense may attempt to impeach William Filter based upon two arrests, neither one of which resulted in criminal convictions... I think one was a drug arrest and the other an arrest for lewd and lascivious conduct."

The defense could say nothing to this. They had expected to catch Larry napping and get Filter's testimony thrown out, but had been surprised by Larry's gut punch. They might try to impeach Filter's testimony after the fact, but the jury would have already heard the words they wanted them to disregard. For now, they could only hope to undo some of the prosecution's damage on cross-examination.

Larry Sells abhorred Bill Filter. The guy was scum. He knew an innocent woman was going to be murdered and he didn't even call to warn her. Then he lied about it for five years, even tried to forget about it. What's a human life compared to showing loyalty to an old drinking buddy? Well, today Larry was going to scrape off some of the filth and reveal the raw truth beneath it.

He summoned Filter to the witness stand and made him state that he was charged with a felony that should have launched him into a cell for two to eight years.

"Are you testifying under a grant of immunity in these proceedings?" Larry asked.

He was. His Use Immunity Agreement, executed on June 12, 1998, said that his statements could not be used against him. Unless he lied.

Filter had met Michael Albrecht twenty years earlier at a hobby shop in Milwaukee where they did slot car racing. Michael built frames for the model cars and "kind of took me under his wing," Filter said.

Over a period of years, Filter became acquainted with Mike's wife, Kathleen, and later Cindy. By 1991, Mike had settled in Indianapolis and Filter saw him at an occasional race. "He was working in a pit crew and I used to walk in the pits. I kind of felt like a big shot because I knew somebody personally that was actually doing that."

"Did you have much conversation with Michael outside of the times that you visited with him at the track during that period?" Larry asked him.

"Not at that time," said Filter, "we didn't talk much."

The lines of communication opened when the two old friends attended the Milwaukee race in 1992. Michael was going through marital problems. Filter told him, "You can rely on me; I'll try helping you out." Filter had been through two divorces, so his friends considered him an expert. Later, Michael told Filter that he was getting divorced and "he wanted to see me."

When Filter came to the 500 race in 1992, the pair talked a lot. "Mike wanted to get some things off his chest," Filter recalled. "Michael said that he had some ideas; he wanted to do something to Cindy. And I was trying to say, you know, things will get better."

They drove around and ended up at Cindy's apartment complex. Michael pointed out Cindy's apartment and her red Nissan pickup truck. "What happened next?" Larry asked.

They left and circled to a "supermarket shopping center and he pointed. Through those trees is where the building is and you can get up to her balcony from that area, and there's not much lighting or anything so you can get there at night."

Sells asked him, "Did he indicate what the reason for going through that wooded area, through the path, and up to the balcony at night would be?"

"Well, we had talked, and he mentioned something about would I be willing to dispose of her, kill her?" Filter said Michael told him, "If you walk through those bushes and you're close enough to the back of the house, you'll be able to take the body out of there."

"What was your response to that?"

"I was pretty shocked," Filter admitted. "Just to appease him, I said, 'well, let me think about it,' hoping that by the end of that weekend he would be calmed down."

Throughout the weekend, Filter said he continually tried to talk Mike out of his plan. "I said I've been divorced twice and I've gotten over it. I was hurt, you know. Especially after my first one, she ran off with my best friend. I mean, I got over it."

Michael insisted that his case was more extreme. He had invested in Cindy. He told Filter that "he had a chance to get a real good job with the Penske organization and that he didn't take it because she would lose her job."

Another thing was her very extensive surgery in Milwaukee. "She had gotten this major dental work done and it did make her prettier... it cost him a lot," Filter testified.

Larry asked, "Did Michael Albrecht say anything to you with respect to... all that dental work? About anything in connection with her being killed and all the dental work?"

He had, Filter said. "That if she was going to be killed that her head had to be severed, that way they wouldn't be able to figure out who she was right away because of the dental work that was there. That it was some kind of alloy metal titanium or something in her mouth and that they'd be able to figure it out right away.

"But I was still at this point trying to talk him out of doing it."

The men shared a number of phone calls between the time of Filter's trip and the night of the murder. "He kept talking about how she had to be killed and this and that," Filter related. "I said I couldn't kill her. And then eventually he said, he asked something about being an alibi—"

Defense attorney Findling spoke up. "Your Honor, I'm going to object only because we just don't know which conversation it is."

Filter explained that he did not remember exactly. He did remember that when Michael came to Milwaukee on the weekend of the murder, they watched some football and drank a few beers at Rodeo's Bar in West Allis. "But at that point, he asked if I could be his alibi; it looked like he was going to have to possibly do this thing on his own."

"Do what thing?" Larry asked.

"Kill Cindy."

Michael helped frame the alibi. "He hadn't been to Milwaukee for a long time. Nobody would say anything if he went out drinking and sightseeing and went down by the lakefront. We got drunk and then I could use the drunkenness for forgetting things."

"Like times?"

"Exactly."

On the evening of October twenty-fifth, Michael made a short phone call to Filter. "I told him I didn't know if I could do it, be his alibi. He says, 'go through the motions.' As far as I knew, I was still being the alibi."

On Monday morning, the twenty-sixth, Filter was painting a house, "and all of a sudden, Mike came up behind me." They moved away from Filter's co-worker. "He says, well, I did it. And I kind of looked at him and I says, you kill her? And he says, yeah. And I says oh. And I says what did you do with the body? He says it's in the trunk of the car. And he says you want to see it? And I kind of made a gesture to go that way and I just, no. I don't even want to know."

Larry asked if the timing of the killing been important?

"Yes," Filter answered. With the divorce looming and life insurance on the line, "He said it had to happen before the twenty-sixth."

Filter had stood firm when questioned about Michael's whereabouts on the night of Cindy's abduction. After the body was found, Michael and Filter had a conversation outside Filter's Place bar.

"About what?" Larry wanted to know.

Filter replied, "What was going on, they found the body, you know, am I still on line with the alibi." Then Michael returned to Florida.

Phone conversations between the two men were sporadic for a number of years. Mike met Denise, his current wife. "But they were just kind of going out and he was even having a couple of problems with her. As I understand it, he had told her the whole story about the Cynthia thing and the murder and she was having a hard time with that."

After Mike's arrest in 1997, the two had more phone communications. Filter said, "I was having a hard time remembering the time frames that we were supposed to have been together."

Then Michael was extradited back to Indiana. Filter said, "I was really shook up. I had heard from his sister that rumors were going around that I was arrested. I said, well, that can't really be because here I am in Milwaukee and I'm free."

Lt. Jones contacted Filter and advised him to seek legal counsel. If the Marion County prosecutor's office had not been contacted by nine-thirty a.m. on Monday, "there would be a warrant for my arrest." Filter was accused of assisting a crime. The bond would be hefty, "like a hundred thousand dollars."

Filter contacted Milwaukee attorney Pat Knight, "to keep me out of jail, basically."

For the purpose of the Albrecht hearing, Filter was giving Knight permission to testify in open court about the matter. "Everything I've said to him in confidentiality can be used here in this court to defend me."

When Larry passed Filter to the defense, Findling postured, like he was armed for battle. Did Filter recall being questioned by Special Agent Daniel Craft of the Milwaukee branch of the FBI during the investigation into the disappearance of Cynthia Albrecht? Yes, on November 4 and November 9 of 1992.

During those interviews, Filter had complained to Special Agent Craft about private investigator Don Campbell. He told the FBI agent that Campbell tried to get him to change his explanation of the events that took place the weekend of October 24-26.

Filter again recited his story to Special Agent Craft. He and Michael had been out drinking together during the time of Cindy's abduction. But this time, Special "Agent Craft was a little bit more intense with the interview; he was coming at you a little harder?" Findling asked. Yes, but Filter had told Craft that he would do nothing to jeopardize the life he'd made for himself. "And that you would not lie to protect anyone; isn't that what you told him?" Findling demanded.

Craft had explained to Filter "the consequences of misleading a federal agent in an investigation" and Filter had insisted that he spoke the truth, adding that Michael would have confided in him if he had done anything wrong.

After Cindy's body was found, Craft questioned Filter again. He repeated his story: Michael had been in Milwaukee with him when Cindy went missing.

Filter lied for years, Findling pointed out. "So up until the time you get the phone call from Lieutenant Jones, not one person on the earth had heard anything different than what you were saying up until that point to Lieutenant Jones, to Krueger, and repeatedly to a member of the Federal Bureau of Investigation; am I correct?"

"Correct," Filter acknowledged.

He had been trying to help Michael by maintaining his alibi. "You were trying to be helpful to him in December," Findling challenged, "when you told them that he said Cindy was a bitch, you were really trying to help him out, right?"

"Right," Filter insisted.

Findling dug harder. "When you told them that Michael sometimes said, 'I just wish she was dead,' that's when you were helping him with this made-up and fabricated alibi defense; am I correct?"

"Yes."

But the story changed, didn't it? The moment Filter was threatened with arrest and a hundred thousand dollar bond? "And at one time you thought, heck, I could even be looking at the death penalty or a life sentence, didn't you?"

"Well," Filter explained, "that was before all this happened, that if I was an accessory, that the accessory gets the same as the principal. I don't know who stated that to me."

"And when you came down to meet with the prosecutors, you weren't met at the state lines by law enforcement officers, were you?" Findling asked. "You weren't put in handcuffs, were you?"

"Not at that point. I was that day though," Filter replied. When he arrived, Larry guided them to a parking spot and joined them for coffee.

"So you weren't in shackles when you were suspected of assisting a criminal in a murder case?"

That was correct. Filter had been treated very nicely. He had been granted immunity and then he gave his statement to the prosecutors and Lieutenant Jones. "And your understanding of immunity," Findling said, "was that what you said at that time was going to be the truth?"

"I was going to tell them the truth, right," Filter echoed.

"And if they liked what you said, you may not be looking at a hundred thousand dollar bond; am I right?"

Findling mused that Filter must have made the prosecution very happy since he paid no bond at all.

Findling asked, what about the money, and Filter said, "I do remember the numbers hitting. The twenty-five hundred dollars and also the twenty-five thousand dollars."

Findling also wanted to know if Filter could "remember the affidavit specifically saying in there that Michael Albrecht had stated that if it was going to happen to her, her head would have to be cut off because of the extensive dental work?"

Definitely.

Remarkable, Findling scoffed, that after all those years Filter could remember so many details.

Did Filter remember that Michael said his conversations with Ferrari took place before anything happened to Cindy? What did he remember about the bedspread after he "got the immunity break?"

"He said there was a big bedspread, right," Filter acknowledged. Michael was going to wrap the body in it.

Findling bantered about Filter conveniently remembering this detail after "it was later learned that a bedspread was missing from Cindy's bed." Then he asked Filter, "By the way, let me ask you this, do you understand that you are still being charged with assisting a criminal?"

"Yes."

"And you understand that as you sit here today," Findling continued, "testifying before the members of this jury that you are looking at up to eight years in a state penitentiary for that charge? And that the prosecutors who are going to make a recommendation for a court to consider with regard to your testimony are the same prosecutors who sit at this table here; am I correct?"

"Right," Filter agreed. "It was also stated to me that I had to tell the truth."

"I understand that," Findling replied. "And only you know whether what you're saying is the truth?"

"Judge, I object to that. I have a pretty good idea myself," Larry asserted.

"Well, they weren't with you that night—" Findling began. Then he turned. "You just did not have any explanation or understanding in that statement or in what fashion, what method she was killed?"

"I didn't know exactly how she was killed," Filter replied. "The only thing I know is that her body was found headless."

The defense attorney honed in on Filter's drinking. "Is it hard for you to remember a lot of the details of what you did that weekend?"

Filter stated clearly that two weeks prior to Cindy's disappearance, he spent time in Indianapolis with Michael. They went to Hooters and the Slippery Noodle. Filter also took a bus tour of the Speedway.

"And it's during this weekend that Michael Albrecht is telling you, okay, that he wants to kill his wife?"

Findling asked Filter about his back problem. "In May of 1992, you were having radiating pain in your back and in your shoulder?" He had "throbbing and sharp pains" in those areas at that time?

Yet, despite all the pain and treatments, Michael was asking Filter to "go up the stairs, kill her, come back down the stairs; carrying her, I assume?" Findling asked. "And then go through the woods with her to get to your car in the parking lot somewhere… it was proposed to you to do this during this period in which you were in all this tremendous pain; am I right?"

Then it was proposed that Filter become an alibi instead. "And you became uncomfortable with that, you're telling us?"

Was Filter frequently "trashed"? Hadn't his girlfriend, Eunice Beckendorf, been trying to get him into treatment?

Larry objected, saying that the description of Filter's condition that night was merely Eunice's opinion.

"She has been concerned about him. She testified about it in front of Your Honor," Findling argued.

"Why is Eunice's concern relevant?" Her Honor asked.

Filter had claimed he was not drunk that night and Eunice's concern said he probably was, Findling said. The judge said she had enough evidence already about Filter's drinking problem.

"The evidence—" Findling protested.

Larry cut him off. "Are we continuing to argue about the Court's rulings?" He added, "Judge, proof that somebody is a drunk is no proof that the person is drinking on any particular night."

"Now why can't I show that the behavior that he testified to previously is consistent with his general behavior?" Findling complained.

"Because the law doesn't allow it," the Court declared.

Filter's claim that he was sober the night Cynthia Albrecht was murdered stood.

Still trying to discredit the witness, Findling listed the interviews in which Filter had insisted he was telling the truth; so why did the truth change when he was threatened with jail? "You never went to anybody else in confidence, your loved ones or your family, and said, 'I'm not telling the truth'; am I right?" No. The story changed because "Michael Albrecht… does not have the ability to offer you immunity, does he?"

On redirect, Larry asked Filter, "Just so we all know, do you have a photographic memory? Do you remember everything that you said back in 1992? Do you remember everything you said September 3, 1997?"

Filter confessed that he was sketchy on the details of the stories he'd told over the years but agreed with Larry that his actions had made him guilty of the crime of assisting a criminal, a class C felony. "And that assistance," Larry clarified, "is that you aided your dear friend Michael Albrecht in concealing evidence of a murder, the murder of his wife, Cynthia Albrecht?"

"Your Honor, that is leading," Findling complained.

Larry changed the question and asked Filter if he wished he had told the truth from the beginning. "After I told everybody, I felt rather relieved that I was able to get it out and I just felt like it was a real heavy burden off my shoulders," Filter responded.

CHAPTER 37

State's witness Angela Gray was Manager of Corporate Security for Ameritech. She researched calls from July 1992 through November 1992 for both William Filter and Michael Albrecht's telephone numbers.

There were no calls between the two numbers from April 7 through August 7, 1992. The billing period up through September 7 showed one call on August 9 from Albrecht to Filter. The billing period that ended October 7 listed seven calls from Albrecht's number to Filter's. The following month's bill, ending November 7, listed sixteen calls.

The Court passed a summary to the jury.

Judge Mangus-Stinson arrived early on Monday morning and immediately called for a bench hearing. Larry Sells, eager to move on with the trial, found these hearings time consuming and often nitpicking, but in some ways, these private discussions were as essential as the trial. The judge and attorneys examined details of the hearing, making sure that the defendant received a lawful and fair trial.

Larry was determined that Michael Albrecht would be convicted. But he wanted that conviction to be right. And legally right. He would allow no missed detail to equip Michael with a key to freedom once he was behind bars.

When Judge Mangus-Stinson had arrived at 8:09 that morning, she had seen two jurors, numbers One and Seven, in the hallway when six prisoners were escorted in. The deputy sheriff reported to the judge that Albrecht was in the line in the middle of one group of three.

"Mr. Albrecht tells us that it's his belief that he saw the jurors before they saw him," Kammen reported. "He notified the deputies and sort of turned and pulled people back. And it would be his belief that they probably didn't see him, that it happened so quickly. Given that, it seems questioning by anybody is going to create more problems than it's going to solve."

Kammen didn't need more problems. His was a cross-examination case. His efforts went into discrediting the State's witnesses. The defense had no witnesses who could declare that Michael did not kill Cynthia.

Time was a factor too. The racing people would be leaving for Portland as early as the next day.

Antonio Ferrari took the stand for his delayed cross-examination. Kammen asked him to verify that Michael had said he wanted something "permanent" to keep Cindy out of racing and had never used the word "kill."

Ferrari said that the two terms had not been used together. "Permanent is one thing. Put out of racing is another. Do something permanent, period. And using another conversation, say put out of racing."

Antonio had kept his conversations with Michael to himself but when Cindy disappeared, he went to the authorities immediately. Kammen asked him, "And after knowing she disappeared, you were worried that maybe the conversations were more significant that they seemed to you at the time; fair to say?"

"Yes."

Those conversations, Kammen insisted to Ferrari, were about getting Cindy out of racing because Michael said she was having affairs with other men and he didn't want to work in the same environment with her.

The two solutions Ferrari said he offered were one, for Michael to find another woman, and two, that he could speak to Roger Penske for Michael, saying that Cindy "has gotten using possible drug." In other words, get her fired.

As a CART director, couldn't Antonio have insisted that Cindy take a drug test? Ferrari said he did not have that authority.

1992 had been a tough year for Ferrari. His father died. Also, his money was tight. "But not for my father, for other reasons," he said. He was in danger of losing his CART franchise. Since he had two franchises, he was required to attend every race and run two cars at each.

"And you were in danger of losing the franchise throughout the season because it was difficult for you to have the money to have cars at all the races?" Kammen asked.

"Because Johnny (Jovy) Marcelo died," Ferrari answered. But his money had been tight for years. "I would say has been the constant of my life in nine years in the States." His franchises were worth over a hundred thousand dollars each back in 1992, more in the present.

"When those race cars come into the pits, they're going fast, there can be fires. Lots of things go wrong that can injure people who are close to the race cars; true?" Kammen asked. Because of those dangers and the fact that repair costs came out of Ferrari's pocket, he needed mechanics "who are paying attention to detail so you don't have to use your limited funds to rebuild wrecked race cars, true?"

With two cars, Ferrari needed six or eight full-time mechanics to maintain the cars between races. Michael worked on a day-to-day basis when work was available.

Ferrari frequently traveled to Italy? Did he actually know what went on in his shop? Especially when his father's health failed? Perhaps, Kammen suggested, since the team joked about the Mafia, Michael's request to get a Mafia guy to stage a robbery was also a joke?

"Okay. You're not in the Mafia, are you sir?" Kammen asked.

Ferrari was not amused. "You ask a very strange question."

Kammen apologized, saying he realized that Ferrari would take offense at the stereotype.

"I've had family kidnapped from Mafia, that's why I'm so upset," he told him. He had never intended to call John Carlos Incasa for Michael; he knew John Carlos would be offended if he did, even as a joke.

"It's a strange way to present racing," Antonio replied, "but it's your point of view, not mine. In the twenty-two years of racing, I never considered racing in this way. So I can't understand it in your mind."

Kammen next asked about his potential hospitality team in 1991. He had an Italian driver who expected to bring in $1.9 million in sponsorships. "It was a fraud," Ferrari said.

Plans for hospitality lasted about two months, and then he realized the money would not be coming in. "But in that two months, an order for forty thousand cups and napkins had been placed; isn't that correct?" Kammen asked.

Ferrari said the amount was thirty thousand. Remnants of the order were stored in Ferrari's basement. He still used them. A lawsuit was filed in 1991 into 1992. "And it was alleged in this lawsuit that Cindy Albrecht had been the one that who had placed the order for this material; is that correct?"

"Subject of the lawsuit was an invoice that was not supposed to be issued," Ferrari argued. "Not even the making of the goods, but the issue of the invoice."

Kammen honed in on Ferrari's taped conversation with Michael on December 4, 1992. The police did not supervise the call. "I thinks he asked me to speak with Mike and let Mike talk," Ferrari said.

From the transcript of the tape, Kammen pounced on the word "scared." Ferrari said repeatedly that he was scared and wondered if Michael was scared that someone had overheard their private conversations.

Larry almost chuckled. Would the jury really believe that a businessperson like Ferrari would take someone's life over paper cups? He strolled over to shred that ridiculous theory in redirect.

Larry asked Ferrari to read the part of his statement Kammen had not referred to "that is pretty much sandwiched in between the other matters that Mr. Kammen asked you about." He read the section and responded that he had been afraid of "what he asked me before Nazareth." He said it referred to the conversation about having the fictional Mafia person do a favor for Michael.

The conversation ended, Larry noted, with the men on good terms and Ferrari offering to hire Michael as a mechanic when things calmed down.

Larry asked Ferrari about the paper goods lawsuit.

Kammen objected, saying that lawsuit was irrelevant. "It happened in 1993."

"Judge, it's our position that he knew all along the lawsuit had no basis and that's exactly what was proven true later," Larry said. The Court told him to ask how the lawsuit affected Ferrari's state of mind in 1992.

"Less than nothing," he replied.

Michael had worked for him for a hundred dollars a day and was present at every race from early June through October 1992, Ferrari said.

"Could you tell the jury anything about how persistent Michael Albrecht was with respect to you with helping him find somebody that could do something permanent to Cynthia Albrecht? Was it something that was only discussed once or was it discussed more than once?"

"More than once," Ferrari responded, and "more frequently discussed" by the time of the October fourth race at Nazareth.

How was the Italian Mafia person to be paid?

Ferrari gave a chilling response. "He mentioned that there was available fifty thousand dollar life insurance if we need it."

CHAPTER 38

Steve Womser was a special criminal investigator for the Prudential Insurance Company. Prudential carried life insurance policies on Michael and Cindy Albrecht. On March 22, 1993, Michael sent a request for insurance benefits. The form listed Cynthia's date of death as October 25, 1992. Mary Jo Albrecht witnessed Michael's signature.

Womser testified that Michael Albrecht had requested a lump sum payment. If he died before the claim settled, the money went to his three daughters, Noel, Melissa, and Dawn Marie.

When Michael filed the claim, the case was turned over to the federal district court. "And the reason for that," Rankin said, "is because if he was in fact responsible for Cynthia Albrecht's death that he would not be entitled to the fifty thousand dollar life insurance policy; is that correct? And the Court then allowed anybody who had information pointing to his guilt or evidence of his guilt to come forward regarding that lawsuit and share with the Court that information that they had; is that correct?"

Womser denied knowing the process. "We made the payment to the court and the court decided." On April 29, 1994, the federal district court ordered that Michael Albrecht receive the proceeds of the life insurance policy.

Cindy's divorce attorney, Jack L. Bailey, told Commons that in July 1992, he had her fill out a financial declaration, which is standard practice throughout the state of Indiana.

Declarations from both parties are used to fashion a property settlement agreement.

Bailey testified that in the case of the Albrecht's divorce, a final hearing had been waived because they agreed to the property settlement. Neither was required to appear in court.

The Petition for Dissolution was filed August 26, 1992. Bailey said, "The Court doesn't have jurisdiction to entertain a decree of dissolution until sixty days after the filing of the Petition for the Dissolution of Marriage." His normal practice was to file for the date; in this case, October 26, 1992, "and then advise the client to contact our office on October twenty-sixth and let us know if the dissolution was still to go through."

Kammen asked if had Cindy signed all the paperwork for the divorce? Did she have an appointment to see Bailey on the twenty-sixth? Any reason to come into his office? Could she have acknowledged her agreement from New Mexico or Florida? Yes, Bailey said.

Having faithfully investigated the crime and kept careful records over the years, Lieutenant Bill Jones finally had his day in court. Larry Sells let him describe his investigation. Jones had noticed many details. A phone and answering machine were in Cindy's bedroom. There were three photographs of Pete Twiddy in the apartment.

On October 28, Michael was called to police headquarters for questioning. He arrived about 11:20 a.m.

Findling reminded the judge that the defense had blocked the use of Michael's statements to law enforcement. The judge responded, "For purposes of the record then, we'll show that all previous arguments raised and made by the defense in pretrial proceedings with respect to the admissibility of any of the defendant's statements are preserved for the record."

Jones continued to testify. When he asked Michael about his and Cindy's marital differences, Michael told him that they split up at the Milwaukee race in early June. He went to stay with his parents and she stayed in the hotel by herself. Two letters from someone named Pat triggered a confrontation. After that, she moved to her own place.

Michael had been in the apartment eight to twelve times after she changed the locks on July 29 and was aware that Cindy was seeing Pete Twiddy.

Jones testified that Michael had said the divorce would be final October 19 or 23. At the conclusion of the Leguna Seca race, Michael knew she planned to attend Al Unser's Halloween party in Albuquerque, New Mexico. He expected her home on October 31 or November 1.

Questioned again on November 20, Michael told Jones that he had not known when Cindy might return. Jones interviewed Michael on October 28, November 4, and November 20, 1992.

"Now on any of those dates or on any later date, on any other date, did the defendant, Michael Albrecht, ever mention to you that he suspected Antonio Ferrari as being involved in the disappearance or death of his wife?" Larry asked.

"Michael Albrecht never told me that," Jones responded.

"Did he ever mention that he suspected a drug dealer to be involved in the disappearance or death of his wife? Did he ever mention Sandi or Michael Fink as being involved in the disappearance or death of his wife Cynthia?"

"No," Jones answered. Michael had never mentioned Pete Twiddy or any other suspect to Jones. "He said she didn't have any enemies. Zero."

Regarding the weekend of Cindy's disappearance, Jones said that Michael "actually told us two different versions… two different locations where he was at on Sunday night." First, he said he was at Rodeo's, which happened Saturday night, and then he said he was driving around with Bill Filter beginning around nine-thirty or ten p.m.

On November 20, Jones told the jury, Michael "said that he had to remind Kathleen that he left the house at around nine-thirty… I believe it was on November the fourth he told us that he had left the house around six-thirty or seven o'clock."

During the October 28 interview, Michael said nothing about the five thousand dollars his father was holding for him. Nor did he mention visiting Bill Filter on Monday morning, October 26. He did tell Jones that Cindy sometimes opened the sliding patio door for the cats, that the sliding door came off its track easily, and that Cindy showered before bed.

Shown a photograph of Cindy's apartment building, Jones indicated the path from the apartment complex to the Marsh Supermarket behind it. He said he had been to the site during both day and nighttime hours and had never found the gate to the path closed.

Jones said, "The path is, I believe, an old abandoned railroad line that I've been familiar with since I came on the police department in 1977. It's back here somewhere. But you could actually drive a car up here and along this old abandoned railroad line."

On October 28, 1992, on his way home from work, Jones drove the path and observed that he could see Cindy's back patio and door, and that if the curtains had been opened, he could see into the apartment.

The lieutenant's records showed that the last phone contact with Cynthia Albrecht was at approximately 9:39 p.m. on October 25, 1992. Pete Twiddy failed to reach her when he called at 10:45 p.m.

Larry asked, "Did Michael Albrecht ever contact you or attempt to contact you on or before November the fifteenth, 1992, regarding the disappearance of his wife Cynthia Albrecht, other than at your request?"

"No."

"Following the discovery of her body on November 15, 1992, did Michael Albrecht ever contact you with respect to how the investigation was going other than at your request?"

"No."

"Just one other matter. Did you hear William Filter testify as to what he understood about the surgery that Cynthia Albrecht had to have done in Milwaukee and the titanium and some other metal that she had placed in her jaw during the surgery?"

"Yes, I heard that," Jones responded.

"In the probable cause affidavit, did you mention titanium or the other metal at all?"

He had not.

CHAPTER 39

On Monday, June 16, Kammen argued about DNA evidence brought in by the State. He said, "There was material submitted to the FBI laboratory, I think, in 1995. I suspect that we could bring in witnesses who will then testify that the FBI laboratory has been substantially discredited."

Larry said he wanted to use the evidence "just to show the thoroughness of the investigation and how he (Jones) relied upon different information that he received and what he did as a result."

The judge said, "He didn't do anything as a result of the FBI analysis."

"Well, if we had received any results anywhere along the line that exonerated the defendant," Larry responded, "we would have dismissed the charges." The hair in John Weland's car, in the front side driver's side floorboard, microscopically matched Cynthia Albrecht's hair and definitely had blood on it. "There was no forensic evidence linking Matthew Kernel to the offense. They argued to the jury that the police investigation was totally lacking up to and including the time of the trial."

"No," Kammen argued. "I think up to the time of the arrest."

Findling complained that adequate attention had not been paid to Virgil Vandagriff, a private investigator, who took statements from Matt Kernel. Findling said that Vandagriff's questions focused on "whether or not he was responsible."

Larry argued, "Any opinion that Virgil Vandagriff arrived at as a result of his interrogation of Matthew Kernel relied in part, if not entirely, upon his interpretation of polygraph results."

The judge said the defense could raise the issue of why investigators did not explore Vandagriff's findings and "Detective Jones will have to explain why that didn't happen."

"That opens a can of worms," Commons countered. "Part of Detective Jones' answer to that explanation will be a voice stress analysis that was done on the tape that we heard yesterday. He gave that to Virgil to listen to and Virgil said based on that, it sounded like Albrecht was lying. That's part of the rationale. How dependable were those tests?"

"I think the distinction is," said the judge, "if he didn't follow up on the further questioning of Kernel, he is entitled to say it's because I believed Michael Albrecht was the suspect."

Pat Knight, a former public defender who practiced law in Milwaukee, Wisconsin, represented Bill Filter. When he learned that Filter had lied about Michael's alibi, he urged his client to confess to Marion County prosecutors.

Larry told Knight, "Just so you'll know, William Filter has agreed that you can testify as to any matters that you and he discussed."

Knight contacted Lieutenant Jones on Filter's behalf and met with his client again on Sunday, August 24, 1997. The climate-controlled office building was stifling. No windows opened and the air conditioning shut down over the weekend. At that meeting, Knight shared the eight page probable cause affidavit from Indiana with Filter. His client began to sweat from more than the heat.

Filter flipped through the document and was surprised to see that other witnesses had claimed that Michael said he intended to harm Cindy.

"I advised Mr. Filter that it's important that your attorney not be surprised by information that may come up and be damaging to you. It would be best to discuss that with me now so that I could be prepared to represent your interest." Knight said, "Bill, at that point, became somewhat emotional and he advised me that his statement the he had made to law enforcement authorities on a number of occasions in the past was false, and that he had been asked to provide that statement by Michael Albrecht."

"As his attorney," Larry asked, "did you expressly ask him whether or not he had been directly involved in the death of Cynthia Albrecht?"

"Oh yes."

"And what was his response?"

His response was that he had not been involved in Cindy's death. Even though he knew of Michael's expressed intentions and had had conversations with the defendant after Cindy's death. Knight said that Filter "largely convinced or tried to convince himself that somehow it happened by some other means."

After their discussion, knowing that his confession was protected by attorney/client privilege, Filter formally retained Knight as his attorney.

Knight told Filter that appearing voluntarily would be to his advantage. Knight contacted the Marion County prosecutor's office. Prosecutors agreed to modify their bail request to five thousand dollars, under the conditions "that Mr. Filter appeared, that he submitted to an interview, that he truthfully answer questions, and that he cooperated."

After Filter gave a revised statement, Filter and Knight signed a Use Immunity Agreement at the prosecutor's office on September third. Then Filter was released on his own recognizance.

Taking his turn with the witness, Findling asked Knight if he had told Filter that fighting extradition could land him in jail for a lengthy period. Had Knight told his client that "to go to a jury trial would be a lot more expensive venture for him than entering a plea?"

What would have happened, Findling wondered, if Filter had come to Indianapolis and repeated his story that he had been with Michael until one or two a.m.? Would the bond have remained at one hundred thousand dollars?

"And when Mr. Filter came down, you didn't have him come down here with the things that he may need if incarcerated; is that correct?" Findling asked.

Knight replied, "My understanding is you don't get to take much in when you're incarcerated." He had not been able to guarantee his client a reduced bond, but there was a possibility.

During the five-hour drive from Milwaukee to Indiana, Knight testified, he and Filter had talked about a number of things. Findling wanted to know, was it possible that Filter had read the affidavit on that drive? Possible, Knight agreed, but he had not suggested information to Filter going into the meeting.

John Commons re-called Angela Gray, a record keeper for Ameritech. He wanted to know if Filter's number had called Michael's number on October 25, 1992. "Yes," she responded.

"What time of day was that call placed?" Commons asked.

"11:54 a.m." The call, she said, lasted one minute.

Findling asked her, weren't phone records normally destroyed after eighteen months?

She said they were.

"Now, you have one particular page there and you're obviously familiar with the information regarding that bill?"

She was.

"Now that bill, so you can explain to us, there are some calls I believe on October twentieth of 1992, to 1-900 numbers?" He pointed out that there were also thirty calls to a Houston number.

Findling argued that the full bill was pertinent because it showed that Filter's calls to Houston normally occurred when his girlfriend was not around and, "on the twenty-fifth, he's not making his usual phone calls to Houston, Texas."

Lieutenant Jones returned to the stand for cross-examination. Findling asked him about his initial interview with Michael Albrecht on October 28, 1992. Though the breakup seemed amicable, Michael claimed Cindy had issues. Hadn't Michael "become a little alarmed about the money she was going through… and at one point I think had to borrow some money from him because an expense check or something like that from Penske was a little late?"

Then she developed a relationship with Pete Twiddy and went to Al Unser's party with him. The officer's interview indicated that Michael said Cindy would be home around October 31 or November 1, 1992. "That's what he said," Jones acknowledged.

The litany continued with Findling asking no questions beyond whether or not Jones agreed with his written report of the interview.

Reading Jones' and Krueger's interview of Michael Albrecht on November 20, 1992, Findling laid out Michael's agenda of where he and Filter had gone the night of October twenty-fifth. They had been to bars, the airport, the lake, driving John Weland's car because Michael's BMW had clutch problems. Findling noted from the interview that Filter's truck had clutch problems too.

Findling also noted that while the November twentieth interview was part of a homicide investigation, the interview on November fourth was a missing person's investigation, and on the twentieth, Michael had cleared up his statement pertaining to Rodeo's Bar, stating that he was there on Saturday night rather than Sunday.

A homicide investigation was labor intensive, was it not? Multiple law enforcement agencies working together, taking interviews, investigating. "It is extremely important to everybody involved to conduct a complete investigation? And most of all a fair investigation for everybody involved?" Findling asked Jones.

If everybody was a suspect, then why the tunnel vision, why the focus on Michael?

Focusing now on the persons Cindy may have dated, Findling asked Jones, "And it was your obligation to look into the possibility that perhaps one of these people may have been involved in her disappearance and her murder?"

"If I had reason to believe they were involved, yes," Jones answered.

Well, there was Matthew Kernel, and there were stories that he had been involved, Findling reminded Jones. "The neighbors of Cynthia Albrecht never on the evening or any time of the day the twenty-fifth or twenty-sixth of October 1992 indicated that they identified Michael Albrecht as being around Cynthia Albrecht's apartment."

Cindy's neighbor, Joseph Joyce, had stated during the investigation that a black vehicle had parked in front of Cindy's apartment building at various times, and didn't Matt Kernel own a 1977 black Jeep?

Jones had heard that but "didn't know" himself.

Findling then took Jones through the details of Kernel's date with Cindy. They met, went out, kissed. Days later, he returned to her apartment unannounced and she asked him to leave, explaining that she'd had a call from his girlfriend, Cindy Bierman.

The defense attorney asked Jones again to examine his reports and verify that all officers involved had made their reports in an accurate and timely manner, realizing that each investigating entity depended upon the others to gather accurate information. The Speedway Police Department, the Indiana State Police Department, and the FBI netted eighteen to twenty reports regarding Michael Albrecht's whereabouts the weekend that Cindy was abducted and killed.

And yet, Findling pointed out, there was no written report nor any tape of the telephone call with Mary Ann Kernel, Matt Kernel's mother, who was Kernel's only alibi witness for that weekend. On October 24, 1997, Jones had testified in front of Her Honor that he believed Matt and his mom had been together at the hotel where she resided in Clermont on the weekend of the murder. But his interview with Matt Kernel on December 15, 1992, placed them together at Matt's cabin.

Findling said, "There was never an attempt to get any of the hotel records to maybe indicate whether or not she was staying at that motel."

While investigators had gone to great lengths to verify Michael's alibi for the weekend, even using the services of Special Agent Craft of the FBI, the search into Kernel's alibi had been nominal.

Investigators had looked for evidence, hadn't they? Jones had gone to Phoenix, Arizona, to examine John Weland's car. Jones had never obtained a search warrant for Kernel's black Jeep, had he?

Continuing to ram Jones's extensive investigation of Michael Albrecht, Findling asked if the investigator had given adequate credence to the fact the Kernel owned a tree trimming business complete with vehicles, bucket truck, dump truck, and saws. Someone transported the body, right? "And possibly, the head that was never found could have been transported as well; am I right?"

"That's possible," Jones answered noncommittally.

What about the fact that Kernel hunted and owned a cabin in northern Wisconsin? Cindy's body was found in an area frequented by hunters.

Investigators also had not searched Kernel's property. Nor had they dredged the two ponds on the property in search of Cindy's missing head. No one attempted to search Kernel's cabin in Wisconsin. "You never sought the consent of Matt Kernel to take any of his saws and have them tested by the medical examiner so they can be compared to the bone that had evidence of saw marks. You never did that, did you?" Findling demanded.

Larry objected that Kernel's tools were not in evidence.

Still honing in on the investigation of Kernel, Findling asked Jones if he had searched the hotel room where Kernel's mother resided. He had not. He had collected phone records from the Albrecht family and Findling. Had he collected Kernel's phone records? No.

Had Jones and his department adequately interviewed potential witnesses at Cindy's apartment building?

Findling also questioned the time of death. He asked Jones to read over Defendant's Exhibit R, a forensic entomology investigations report of diagnostic laboratory examination. Entomologist Neal H. Haskell, the forensic entomologist at Purdue University, generated the study of the maggots found on Cindy's back.

According to Haskell's report, the twenty-six larvae were blowflies in the second larval stage. The maggots' stage of development, combined with National Weather Service's data of days on which the local temperature would have supported blowfly activity, pinned the time of death as before sunrise on October 26 or 27. At temperatures below six degrees Celsius, the report explained, "the required energy units these species of blowflies need to complete specific stages of their respective life cycles... are expressed as degree days (DD) on a per day basis with a base temperature of 6° C (DDB-6) below which development ceases."

Furthermore, according to Haskell's report, "Blowflies do not fly at night, and there were only three days in the last week in October (26th, 27th, and 28th) with temperatures exceeding the minimum threshold temperature for blowfly activity. The age of the larvae indicate that oviposition most likely occurred around the 26th. It is very unlikely that female blowfly activity could have occurred after these dates because the daily temperatures were too low." Therefore, "the body would have been in the location where it was found for approximately the entire period the individual was missing."

The defense attorney also questioned Jones about daylight savings time. On October 25, 1992, Wisconsin's time fell back one hour at midnight on Saturday but the time in Indianapolis did not change.

Findling had tried to make Lieutenant Bill Jones appear inept, but Larry knew the detective's investigation had been thorough. The attorneys approached the bench. "Nearly everything I ask from him from now on will be considered hearsay. It will be related to the investigation and its thoroughness," Larry said.

The judge told the jury, "I think, ladies and gentlemen, that we're about to hear a series of questions. The party who is asking the question isn't offering it to prove the truth of the information, but to show what information was discovered or available to the detective during the course of the investigation"

Larry asked Jones if he had determined where Cindy's Nissan was from October 12-25, 1992. Jones replied, "I determined that that vehicle, 36022A, was at the long-term parking at Indianapolis International Airport."

"Can you tell the jury whether in Cynthia Albrecht's personal effects, anything you found in the apartment, there was the name of Matt Kernel appeared? You looked at her address books? Telephone, personal telephone numbers, and books?"

Jones said he had found no reference to Kernel.

Was Jones present when investigators inspected John Weland's car? Did he see the evidence collected? How did the results of hair analysis affect the investigation?

"It continued me to believe that Michael Albrecht was involved in the death of Cindy Albrecht," Jones stated.

Michael drove Weland's car on the weekend of the murder because his BMW had clutch problems. Yet Jones observed the BMW in Florida when he went to question Michael on November 4, 1992, and Michael told him that he drove the car to Fort Lauderdale three days after Cindy's disappearance.

An examination of Kathleen Albrecht's phone records indicated that she had called Michael's number in Indianapolis on October 25 at 12:13 a.m., 11 a.m., and 3:29 p.m. There was one call made on the morning of October 26 at 7:13 a.m. "So there were no phone calls that you observed that were made after 3:29 p.m. on October twenty-fifth and before 7:13 a.m. on October twenty-sixth?" Larry asked.

Jones said that was correct. During that period in October and November of 1992, Kathleen worked at Quarles and Brady, an accounting law office. Jones stated that from November 12-19, two calls came into the office from Fort Lauderdale.

Jones made a couple of trips from Indianapolis to Fort Lauderdale. "Did you ever search Michael Albrecht's white BMW, the one that you indicated he drove to Florida?" Larry asked.

He had not.

"Anywhere near that area, are there ponds or swamps?"

"All over the place," Jones replied.

"Did you make any effort to dredge any of those?"

No.

"Now, at some time during the course of your investigation, did you personally eliminate Matthew Kernel as a suspect?"

Yes, Jones said, around June of 1993.

"By then, had you received any hospital records concerning Matthew Kernel?" Larry asked. Findling objected four times based on hearsay and leading, but Judge Mangus-Stinson allowed Jones to answer.

Jones eliminated Matthew Kernel as a suspect because his alibi was confirmed by a witness named Bret McCarty, and by Kernel's medical records. "I chose to preclude him from further investigation and continue my efforts on Michael Albrecht," Jones said.

Larry asked, "Other than alibi information… concerning the whereabouts of Michael Albrecht October 25 and 26, 1992, have you received any other information that would cause you to look at someone else as a suspect, other than Michael Albrecht?"

Jones said he had not.

"If other information had come to you after that period with regard to any other leads on any other suspects, would you have pursued those leads?"

"Objection, Your Honor," Findling said. "It calls for a self-serving response. It also calls for conjecture on his part."

"On that basis, I'll sustain it," the judge said.

Changing his question, Larry asked, "Did any other information come to you after June 1, 1993, either about Matthew Kernel or any other suspect other than Michael Albrecht, in the investigation of the disappearance and death of Cynthia Albrecht?"

"No," said the lieutenant, and stated that he still considered Bill Filter as a suspect in Cindy's disappearance because he had never been able to explain how his head hair ended up in the trunk of John Weland's car.

What about Bill Filter? Could anyone verify his alibi? Where was he was on the night of Cindy's abduction? In the course of Larry's questioning, Findling objected seven more times.

"Have you considered the fact that more than one person may have been involved in the disappearance and death of Cynthia Albrecht?"

Before Jones could answer, Kammen called out, "Your Honor, may we approach?" The attorneys moved to the bench and Kammen said, "I know that this is not my witness—"

"Why don't you wait until your co-counsel gets here?" the judge suggested.

Kammen continued. "The State has committed to a theory of prosecution. The theory of prosecution is that Michael Albrecht alone committed this crime. The State is not privileged to change its theory of prosecution in the middle of the trial. Now it was Michael and Filter, Michael and somebody else. And that's something they are not allowed to do."

"According to who?" demanded Her Honor.

"The various cases," Kammen responded. "There's case after case after case in Indiana that says that the State may not change its theory of prosecution."

"Judge, we didn't have a theory of prosecution," Larry answered mildly. "We charged the defendant with having committed the crime and that's what our proof is going to be. I can't vouch for William Filter's involvement." One more move that would keep the defense up late. Larry loved it.

Kammen argued, "The point is that if the theory is he acted alone, and they've committed to that theory—"

"I don't know that they're committed to any theory," the Court responded.

Kammen tried again to hammer home his point. "In their opening statement, they committed to the theory—"

"They charged him with killing," said the judge.

Jones' statement that he had considered more than one killer remained in the trial record.

Larry submitted Matt Kernel's medical records from Methodist Hospital. Kernel was in the emergency room at 1:20 a.m. on October 25, 1992. Listed as a crime victim, Kernel was unable to open his right eye. A CT scan showed trauma to the orbital socket. The fracture required serious pain medication, and the ER doctor referred Kernel to a specialist.

Findling's re-cross of Jones looked like a rookie trying to monopolize multiple lanes. He asked Jones to examine a Midwestern Climate Center official report for October 25 though November 15, 1992, then asked him to confirm the data in the report and asked no other questions about it.

Then Findling asked Jones about the cards from Pat Hawley. "In one of the cards, it indicates when the time is right, we will both know it and the magic will happen. Thanks for the great weekend in Portland, it was great. That's contained in one of the cards; am I correct?"

Jones said he was.

Again shifting gears, Findling asked about Matt Kernel's medical records. Jones had continued to interview people about Kernel's potential involvement for a couple of months after he received those documents. "So, you testified to the jury that in June of 1993, the reason why you chose to no longer pursue Mr. Kernel was because of receiving a medical report that you actually received six months before reaching that decision; am I correct?"

Larry objected. "That's a mischaracterization of the evidence. It was one of the reasons that he considered. That was his testimony."

"You do not reference anywhere Mr. Kernel said that the injury was so debilitating that he was unable to continue in his employment for any period of time; am I correct?" Findling asked.

"No, I did not put that in my report," Jones responded. He had also not interviewed any medical care professionals who had told him the injury was debilitating.

"And you understand," Findling continued, "that the kind of work that he does, the tree removal business, requires some physical strength?" Did trauma to Kernel's orbital bone affect his ability to use his hands, his arms, and his strength?

"Now, Sergeant Rush interviewed a guy named Bret McCarty," Findling continued. "Bret McCarty indicated that Matt came to his place afterwards and stayed there and got there about two-thirty in the morning... and stayed on his couch until about two in the afternoon on Sunday, October 25, 1992?" Findling asked.

"Correct," said Jones, who also acknowledged that McCarty and Kernel had joked that Kernel killed Cindy. Other information McCarty had proffered about Kernel was that he had a cabin somewhere and McCarty was never impressed with Kernel's hunting skills.

Jones investigated Filter's finances and credit report. He found no sudden influx of cash. "And, in fact, during that time period, he actually filed bankruptcy; am I correct?" Findling asked.

When prosecutors offered Filter immunity, Findling asked, was Jones in on the questioning? Had Jones read the immunity agreement? "If there was any deviation from that statement, he could subject himself to a charge of perjury; am I correct?" Findling asked. "And during that statement, at no time does he say that he physically had anything to do with the abduction and killing of Cynthia Albrecht; am I correct?"

"You're correct," Jones responded.

Findling honed in. "His statement, from your vantage point, was inconsistent with your belief of his involvement; am I correct?"

Jones said no. "It confirmed that he knew a lot of details about the apartment and those areas surrounding it."

Jones and the prosecution team had never asked Filter if he was "physically involved in the abduction and killing of Cindy Albrecht?" Findling challenged. "The information that was gathered was just going to be used with the threat of prosecution in deviating for perjury so that Michael Albrecht could be prosecuted for murder; am I correct?"

"Judge, that's been asked and answered," Larry objected.

"Sustained."

Before calling his next witness, Larry submitted documentation of Cynthia Albrecht's life insurance policy with the John Alden Company. Attached to the billing was a note from Cynthia dated August 4, 1992.

It read: "At this time, please remove Michael G. Albrecht from my policy due to a changing marital status between us."

CHAPTER 40

Gerold Albrecht did not remember going to the bank with his son to withdraw five grand. Larry Sells asked, "So your testimony here today is that you don't remember any of that; either telling them that or that it ever happened?"

"I don't remember anything about it," Gerold said. "I remember talking to the guys. I don't even remember the date."

Kammen also questioned the elder Albrecht and confirmed that the man's memory was fading.

Matthew Kernel, called as a witness for the defense, said that his attorney Steven Allen had advised him to take the Fifth Amendment and refuse to testify

The Court responded, "Well, he can't take the Fifth in the presence of the jury, so I'll have to bring him in."

"And I want to be real clear," said Kammen, "the questions that we intend to ask him deal with events in 1992 for which to the extent they may invoke other crimes, the statute of limitations had run. So he has no Fifth Amendment privilege to these issues."

The judge replied, "I don't think he's going to testify today, because if he wants to invoke his right to counsel, I'm not going to deny him that."

Kammen fumed that the door on Kernel's willingness to testify slammed shut "all of a sudden, now the prosecutors run down there... I'm not suggesting anything improper."

John Commons whacked the table with a folder, creating a thunderclap. "You just made an improper suggestion! I am going to call evidence to show that you should be cited to the disciplinary commission for creating an inference that there is no evidence to support. And in fact, we have direct evidence to the contrary, Mr. Kammen!"

Commons turned to the judge. "Your Honor, for the record, I will call a deputy if necessary, but we sat down at the table with Mr. Kernel, and he started to ask what is going on when the deputy said to him, 'Are you going to tell the prosecutors what you just told me?' And that's how the issue of the Fifth Amendment came up."

The defense probably intended to elicit Kernel's confession of the crime to free their client. Larry said, "I wouldn't be sitting here for the last week and a half if I felt that Matt Kernel is the one who committed this murder."

With Kernel's refusal to testify, Kammen tried a common but ineffective strategy. He moved for a directed verdict and judgment of acquittal on the grounds there wasn't evidence on every material element of the offense.

"There is," Larry challenged.

The judge ruled, "Denied."

The only way a judge would acquit a defendant before the defense presented its case was if the prosecution had no case. Larry had never seen this happen. Kammen and Findling needed a way to prove Michael's innocence. It looked like their strategy would be to fling out theories like strings of cooked spaghetti and see if any of them stuck to the wall.

With his star witness racing for the bleachers, Kammen struggled to negotiate the unexpected turn. "Judge, we had four or five witnesses, but obviously this changes."

"Let's do what you have on line for today," the judge told him. "Don't scramble to get any more." But Kammen was scrambling and Larry struggled to keep a straight face. *Gotcha!*

Beginning his defense, Findling called Mark Good to the stand but Commons stalled him. "We at least need a couple of seconds to get organized, because yesterday afternoon, Mr. Kammen crossed Mr. Good's name off."

Forced once again to change strategy, Kammen called Mary Ann Kernel.

Matthew Kernel's mother staggered to the stand like an overloaded donkey. Findling asked about her background. She turned and stared at the wall behind her. The judge explained to her that she needed to face forward and speak up. "Okay, he's going to ask you a question," the judge nudged.

Mrs. Kernel said she was sixty-nine years old. "Do you have a son, any children?" Findling asked her.

"Do I have what?" She appeared too drunk to know who was asking.

She eventually confirmed that she had three sons. Kammen moved to the time of the crime. She said that she was living in Clermont, Indiana, in a motel refurbished into apartments. Her son had never visited her there. She had spent time in his cabin in July of 1993, while workers remodeled her apartment.

On cross-examination, Mrs. Kernel told Commons that she had heard about Matt's eye injury but never seen it. She did not know when it happened. She had not been to the cabin at the end of West 34 Street since the summer of 1967 or 1968. Maybe she had been there to visit.

"Could you have been to Matt's cabin during '92 sometime?" Commons asked.

Ms. Kernel said she did not recall visiting Matt's cabin that year because she "took care of a person that had cancer for five years and he died in '93."

Defense witness Mark Good, Cindy's former downstairs, Apartment B neighbor, had worked at Methodist Hospital for nineteen years. Good did not know Cindy but believed she was a smoker. He could smell the smoke and the apartment directly above his was vacant.

On October 25, 1992, Good said that he watched football on television all day and went to sleep about ten-thirty p.m. He claimed to be a light sleeper.

On the night of the abduction, Findling asked, "Did any loud noises or vibrations awaken you after you went to sleep?"

No. Between five-fifteen and five-thirty, he said, "I was watching the news and I heard a man and a woman's voice open up the door from the outside and walk up the stairs."

The couple used a key to open Apartment C. Their visit was short. "I did hear a little walking. And a few minutes later, I did hear them walking back down the stairs." He could not identify the couple, having seen only their backs. They left in some type of four-wheel drive vehicle. Good also claimed that Cindy Albrecht's pickup was parked in front of the apartment building for "close to two weeks."

Good's deposition read that the couple went up the stairs on Monday. In court, Good said, "I might have been confused."

"So... you were confusing Sunday and Monday?" Findling asked.

"Possibly." Good did not sound certain.

Findling passed the witness to Larry Sells.

Good told Larry that he had never seen Cindy with any man, and that the woman who climbed the stairs on Monday the twenty-sixth was not her. What about the truck? Larry asked, "Did anybody else in that apartment complex have a similar type truck?"

Good didn't think so.

Larry kept firing questions. Good was vague about the people climbing the stairs. He had never seen Cindy's cats, and he did not recognize the defendant, Michael Albrecht. "And you heard nobody around eight-thirty or nine...

coming in the front door to the apartments carrying a whole bunch of luggage, toting it upstairs?"

No, he had not.

Good's bedroom faced the outside wall to the hallway. "From that location, it is then difficult to hear things in the back of the apartments if you'd been asleep?" Larry asked. Possibly, Good agreed.

Findling asked for more clarification. When the man and woman entered the apartment building, wasn't it their conversation that alerted him? Had he seen the woman's face? "Can you say whether or not it was Mrs. Albrecht?"

"No." The couple must have entered Cindy's apartment because Good heard no footsteps in Apartment D above him.

Larry approached the witness. "Mr. Good, I don't want to quarrel with you, but I thought for sure on cross-examination you told me that the woman that you saw coming out of that apartment building was not Cindy Albrecht? I thought for sure that's what you said, isn't it?"

Good's reply was vanilla pudding. "Yes. Possibly it was. I can't say."

"So, you've changed your mind somehow between cross-examination and redirect examination. Now that you think about it some more, you're not sure?"

"No."

"I have no further questions," Larry announced. *And you no longer have credibility with the jury.*

CHAPTER 41

Defense witness Dick Simon had been in IndyCars since 1969. "Ninety percent as an owner/driver and the other ten percent as consultant engineer," he told the jury. He retired as a driver in 1988.

In 1992, Michael Albrecht was his chief mechanic for Hiro Matsushita's car. Simon's team had prepped two cars. Matsushita crashed the first one, injuring himself and breaking his leg.

On Sunday, the week of qualifications, Raul Bozell took Matsushita's place, driving the second car, sponsored by Panasonic. Simon told Kammen that, as an owner, he had to have absolute faith in his chief mechanic, who was "totally responsible for the driver's safety."

Sponsorships were hard to obtain and maintain, Simon explained. While sponsors with deep pockets like Marlboro's could host gala parties and events, most sponsors considered IndyCar as business. They would attend during the race weekend to see how their promotional dollars fared. If they hosted a business dinner, the crew, if included at all, was dismissed early.

"And did you have any policy with respect to people who worked for you attending other teams' functions?" Kammen asked.

Race cars have a basic design, Simon explained, "but we have many secrets in Indy racing that helps us to stay ahead of the next team. If an employee makes his best friend one of the people on another team, that's not good."

Michael Albrecht had worked for Simon for years, Kammen said, so why did he leave the team at the end of May in 1992?

"All I recall is I didn't want to see Mike go," Simon said. "He was probably one of the most meticulous people that I've ever seen working on a car. I don't believe I would have fired him at all."

What about the mechanics' toolboxes? Would there be any reason for an IndyCar mechanic to have a hacksaw in his toolbox?

None, Simon responded.

He became aware of Cindy's plight when "I received calls from a couple of sponsors asking me what in the world to do about the fact that Mike showed up in a Panasonic uniform in the media. They were very concerned about it. If racing was that type of coverage, they might not want to stay in it."

Michael had already left Simon to work for Antonio Ferrari, claiming that he would make more money. Did Simon know Ferrari? "And does Mr. Ferrari have a reputation?" Kammen asked.

The man was known for deceit, according to Simon. "He always takes advantage of an opportunity that may benefit him."

Larry rose to question Simon's hard assessment of Ferrari. "That's not necessarily a reputation that might not apply to others involved in auto racing, is it?" he asked.

"I would say that he's one of the worst that I've ever seen," Simon declared, "if not the worst."

"Mr. Simon," Larry began, "I believe it's your testimony that you believe that Michael Albrecht voluntarily left your racing team after the 500 in 1992?"

"That's exactly what I remember," Simon replied.

"Did you advise the Speedway Police Department that you finally had to take Albrecht off the team because of his negativity?"

Simon stonewalled. "I don't believe I said that. Maybe one of our other employees did. I don't believe I had anything much negative to say about Mike. Michael was an excellent mechanic."

When he had finished questioning Simon, Larry approached the bench. "We'd like Mr. Simon to search his records to see if his employment records show how Mr. Albrecht's relationship was terminated."

The Court ordered Simon to mail a certified copy of the records.

As expected, the records showed that Michael Albrecht had been terminated from his job. The jury received copies of the paperwork.

Kammen summoned Dana Smith, who had been an electrical engineer for Indianapolis Power & Light for ten years. He was a member of the BMW Car Club of America. In October of 1992, Smith took a course at Road America at Elkhart Lake, Wisconsin. The four mile track was in a secluded area with hills. "It's a real tough track to learn," he said.

Smith's BMW blew a head gasket that weekend and he had to have it towed to the Little Car Shop for repairs. He caught a ride home with other students. Once the car was repaired, the mechanic phoned and suggested that Smith contact Michael Albrecht to try to get a ride to Milwaukee. Smith had never met Albrecht, but they were two car buffs and had plenty in common. Smith said Michael did mention that he was recently divorced. His testimony helped confirm Michael was in fact in Milwaukee on October 24.

The defense was still struggling to get Matt Kernel on the stand. Judge Mangus-Stinson said she wanted to talk to Kernel and would have him in court during the jury's lunch break.

Michael's defense team moved forward and prepared to take the lead, bringing the entire Albrecht family—minus Randy, of course—to the witness stand. How could a killer possibly come from such a nice family?

Michael's eldest daughter, twenty-seven-year-old Noel Albrecht, testified first. Kammen asked Noel about her trip to Florida the week after Cindy's disappearance. The trip had been planned for some time and her dad bought her airline ticket, she said.

The neck muscle test? Noel said it was just an old wrestling move. Kammen invited her to try it on him. "I do it with my son," she said, implying that the neck squeeze was harmless to four-year-old Devin.

When Michael came to Milwaukee the weekend of October 24-26, 1992, Noel knew he was coming. She told Kammen that "he always called ahead of time to let us know so we'd make sure we had time set aside to spend with him."

On Saturday, October 24, 1992, Noel traveled to Great America, a theme park midway between Milwaukee and Chicago. She rode with her friend Celia in a little blue Omni. As the girls pulled in sight of the roller coasters, they discovered that the car had a problem. It would not shift out of drive. They finally turned off the key and placed a brick under the tire.

That night, the car had not recuperated from its ailment. They could not shift it out of drive or into neutral or start it at all. Noel called her dad, who was having dinner with her aunt and uncle, April and Kevin Hafemann.

Noel charmed the jury with her tale of being rescued, coming home around one a.m., and waking up to her dad cooking a special breakfast with homemade hash browns.

Noel next saw her dad around four-thirty p.m. that Sunday. They made dinner together. Noel had been dating the future father of her child, Shawn Sundholm. Shawn arrived for the meal about six-thirty. The two of them played in dart leagues. That night, their games began between seven and seven-thirty.

"And when you left between seven and seven-thirty, was your father still at your mother's home in Milwaukee?" Kammen asked.

"Yes, he was."

"Did you know Cindy Albrecht?"

"I knew her pretty well," Noel replied. "She was a good friend to me."

Larry stepped forward to cross-examine Noel. "Are you okay, Ms. Albrecht?" Her voice was iffy. Perhaps she was choking on a few lies? Or she felt stressed from morphing between imaginary timelines?

"Yes, I'll be fine," the young woman said.

Larry asked her to take time to compose herself. His questions were simple ones. "But I want you to make sure that you're in a frame of mind where you can talk to me. Do you feel like you are?"

"I'll be fine," she parroted.

Did she remember her trip to Florida in 1992?

Halloween and she stayed a week.

Her dad's trip to Milwaukee the weekend of the abduction and murder? It was planned, "I believe you said, for weeks?" Larry asked.

"A couple of weeks, probably." Her responses sounded practiced.

"A couple of weeks," he echoed. "Had your father been in Milwaukee just the Monday before that weekend?"

"I don't remember."

Odd. She could remember hash browned potatoes from six years ago but an entire weekend seemed to have slipped her mind.

"You don't recall him coming up to Milwaukee on October the 19 to pick up a gear box, and then spending Monday night there at the house, and driving back to Indianapolis Tuesday morning?" he asked.

Her babbled response shuffled like a dog-ate-my-homework excuse. "He came, you know, every couple of weeks to see us. So I don't exactly remember every time that he was there."

"And you don't know that it was at that time," he questioned, "he said he was coming back the following weekend to test drive his BMW?"

"No." She recited again, "He would tell us a couple of weeks in advance so that we'd make sure that we had time to spend with him." Cindy was a close friend of hers, she repeated. She did not come to Indianapolis like her sisters did, but that was only because she was older and had a job.

She did recall that on the day of her good friend Cindy's abduction and death, her dad went to her grandparents' home to watch the Packers game. She believed the game started at noon and that he returned at four-thirty p.m.

Did she know her father's telephone number in Indianapolis? Larry recited the number for her. "On Sunday at 12:13 a.m., did you call that number from your mother's home?"

"I don't know."

What time did she get home from the Great America trip?

"After midnight, maybe one a.m.," she said.

"Would there be any reason why you would have called your father's house?" he asked.

"No," Noel told him. "He was with me."

Larry fired back, "So do you recall whether or not later on that morning, at eleven o'clock, you called your father's home in Indianapolis?"

"I would have no reason to," Noel insisted.

"How about 3:29 p.m., did you call your father's house from your mother's phone?"

"No." Her mouth formed the word but her face lacked confidence.

Before she could think it over, he continued. "At 3:29 p.m., your father—as you understood—was still at your grandparents?"

"I think so, yes."

"No further questions."

Daddy's little paragon of virtue left the stand looking slightly derailed.

Michael's brother-in-law, Kevin Hafemann, related that Michael had eaten dinner with his family at his apartment on Saturday, October 24, 1992, around six p.m. Then Noel had called, reporting that the vehicle she was in had a failed transmission. Kevin said they arrived at Great America around ten p.m. when the park was closing and everyone was leaving.

Michael "disengaged the transmission from the drive train so we could at least get it into neutral and tow the vehicle home. Mike rode in the towed vehicle because he did have experience being towed in a disabled car. And I drove the pickup truck to tow him."

Back in Milwaukee, the group first took Noel's friend and her car to her home on the southeast side of Milwaukee. Hafemann believed that they arrived back at his apartment around twelve-thirty a.m. He did not see Michael at all the following Sunday or Monday.

Michael's sister, April Hafemann, remembered specifically that on the night of October 24, 1992, Michael came to her house for dinner and they had mostaccioli with spaghetti sauce, garlic bread, and salad with Italian dressing. She told Kammen she was certain of that "because Mike thinks he makes better spaghetti sauce than I do. He doesn't." It was a competition between the siblings. Michael arrived around six o'clock and left around nine o'clock to rescue Noel. They returned around midnight or twelve-thirty. She saw Michael momentarily when they arrived and did not see him for the remainder of the weekend.

The jury asked Mrs. Hafemann what the driving time was from her apartment to her mother's house. Twenty minutes in light traffic, she responded. She did not see what vehicle Michael drove that night.

It looked like the defense was struggling to prove Michael's innocence, but Larry knew better than to get cocky. In the courtroom, you never knew when you'll run into a blind curve. He stayed focused.

Kammen's next witness was Gwendolyn Albrecht, Michael's mother. She listed her children in order: Michael, Mark, Scott, Randy, and April. Mrs. Albrecht told the Court that the first time she was questioned by Sergeant Krueger and Lieutenant Jones she had been returning from an art class.

The two officers interviewed her at her kitchen table. Krueger asked questions while Jones took notes. She complained that Krueger seemed antagonistic and kept changing the subject. He also misstated what she had said. She paused the interview to have her earlier response read back to her and discovered that she was correct. She never saw a report of that interview.

When Michael came to Milwaukee the weekend of October 19, 1992, Gwen and her husband were closing their summer cottage, located two hundred-forty-seven miles north of Milwaukee, near the Canadian border. Michael had called her that weekend, asking if she would be home the following weekend, October 24-26.

"He said he wanted to come and be with his family, that he didn't want to be alone because his divorce was going to be final that weekend," Gwen recalled. He arrived about twelve-thirty on Sunday afternoon, missing the beginning of the Packers game. He left after four-thirty.

That afternoon, Michael and his father began winterizing the pool and finished the job on Monday morning. She believed he left for Indianapolis around ten-fifty a.m. on Monday.

Larry asked Gwendolyn about Bill Filter's calls to her home. Did he call on Friday night, October 23, looking for Michael? She was not sure. Larry gave her a portion of her statement to read. She said, "And I do not recall having told Lieutenant Jones that there were numerous phone calls from Bill Filter" on Sunday morning, October 25.

Kathleen Albrecht married Michael in 1969 when she was twenty years old and he was nineteen; the marriage lasted sixteen years. She and Michael had remained good friends throughout his marriage to Cindy. Kathleen found it awkward to be around Cindy, but the daughters seemed to get along with her.

Kathleen testified that Noel planned her trip to Florida for months. Noel had vacation time coming from work, had some boyfriend problems, and wanted to get away to spend time with her dad. Upon her return, Noel told Kathleen that they "had a good time when they weren't being followed" by local law enforcement.

Kathleen worked at Quarles and Brady Law Firm in the accounting department, handling cash receipts and doing billing for the top managing partner. She was at work when FBI Special Agent Craft called, saying that he wanted to meet with her. "And he said pick a time and I said I don't know, and he said I'll be there in two minutes and there he was two minutes later."

"And did he ask, when he arrived, whether that was convenient or not?" Kammen asked.

No, he had not. For want of a personal space, the interview took place in an office kitchen that served as a break room. It was not private. "Our human resource director kept coming in and out. It was also right across the hallway from our executive director and his secretary and she could look right in the door… she could hear everything."

At the time, Kathleen said she thought Cindy had simply not come home. Special Agent Craft did not inform her that Michael was a suspect in her disappearance. "He just let me believe that it was just an interview. He didn't make it sound important at all."

In late November, Craft again called Kathleen at work, again giving her a two-minute warning. By that time, Kathleen knew that Cindy's body had been found. Had she discussed that with Michael? "I had conversations," Kathleen told Kammen, "but not about that... not about Cindy."

The weekend of Cindy's disappearance, Kathleen made several trips to Saint Helen's Catholic Church, eight blocks from home, to open or lock the doors. She was the security person.

After dinner on the evening of October 25, 1992, Kathleen cleaned the kitchen. Her daughter, Dawn, watched television in the living room with her father. She estimated that Michael went out with Filter around nine.

There seemed to be some confusion about the time, Kammen stated. Kathleen's explanation was that she at first said he left at six p.m., confusing Saturday and Sunday. He left at six p.m. on Saturday. Then she had said between seven and eight because that was when Noel left. Now, she said, she was certain that Michael left around nine p.m.

She was equally certain that he returned at two a.m. She had given him the wrong keys, forcing him to knock on the door. Awakened, she looked at the clock. It was definitely two a.m. She smelled beer on him. He was still there the next morning when Noel came home to change clothes before going to work.

On May 30, 1998, Sergeant Krueger filed an Indiana State Police Supplemental Case Report. He and Lieutenant Jones had traveled to Milwaukee on May 13, 1998, to speak with Kathleen Albrecht. The meeting took place at the law offices of Quarles and Brady in the presence of Matthew Flynn, Kathleen's attorney.

Krueger's report read: "Kathleen stated that she had been made aware that Bill Filter had changed his story around and was now saying that Michael had the body in the car over the weekend. She had become 'good friends' with Denise (Michael's new wife) and this is who she had heard it from."

Kathleen stated that she had been corrected. Noel and Shawn's dart game began at eight p.m. rather than seven, and Dawn and Michael had watched a Star Trek movie on TV later that night. She further asserted that Michael arrived home at two a.m. She could see the clock plainly and had already set it back for daylight savings time.

Krueger reported, "Kathleen said her memory now was better than when she was interviewed by Agent Craft because she had had time to think about it." Krueger's report concluded, "Kathleen said that she was positive that Mike came home at two a.m. She had no explanation as to why Bill Filter would be telling such a story about Michael."

CHAPTER 42

Matthew Kernel appeared in court with his attorney Steve Allen, who was present to ensure that he gave no testimony that would affect the outcome of his current charges. Questions referring to his current case were ordered "in limine" by the Court. Judge Mangus-Stinson explained to Kernel, "Nobody can talk about it until I say they can, and they have to come up here and get my permission." Also, "you cannot talk about having taken a polygraph."

Her Honor questioned Kernel about his willingness to testify. She told him he had the right to invoke the Fifth but "that can't ever be done in front of a jury."

Kernel assured the Court that he would testify willingly. He returned to jail until early afternoon.

Larry Sells cross-examined Kathleen Albrecht. "Do you recall having a thirty-five-minute telephone conversation on October 17 with Michael Albrecht?"

Kathleen said she didn't remember. He could have talked to his children.

What about a twenty-one-minute call at 6:22 p.m. on October 18?

It was possible, Kathleen said, "but that night I would have been at my mother's house." Michael had been in Milwaukee though on the nineteenth and had spent the night with Kathleen.

Larry said, "I believe your testimony was that on Saturday afternoon, October 24, Michael Albrecht was at your house until he left to go over to his sister April's house for dinner?"

Kathleen said that was correct.

"But you left—how many times did you leave the house that afternoon?" he asked.

"The last time I left the house that afternoon was at five-thirty to go close up the church," said Kathleen.

"But he was still home when you got back?"

Kathleen said, "Yes. He was just leaving when I—"

"And you had left the house one other time in the afternoon?"

"Before he came there, I had the church opened because we had a craft fair going on in the basement of the church," Kathleen explained, "and I had asked Father if I could keep the church doors open and he said no problem."

"And Michael Albrecht arrived at your home initially in the afternoon at what time?"

"Somewhere after two o'clock in the afternoon," she responded.

"And as far as you know, he was there from two until five-thirty?" Larry pressed.

"Yes."

She seemed quite sure until he asked her, "Did you know that he told law enforcement authorities that on that Saturday afternoon, he was in fact at Rodeo's Bar with Bill Filter?"

Kathleen responded, "I never asked which bar they went to."

"On Saturday afternoon," Larry clarified. "The time when you said he was at your house."

In Michael's defense, she said that he could have gone to the bar before he came over. He was a good man who made his child support payments "like clockwork."

"Do you recall Special Agent Craft advising you that you'd be interviewed concerning the whereabouts of Michael Albrecht during the weekend of October twenty-fourth through the twenty-sixth, 1992, and any knowledge that you might have concerning the disappearance of Cynthia Albrecht?" he asked.

"That's what he said when he called, yes. And in two minutes, he was there."

"You did not consider that important?" Larry asked.

Kammen interrupted. "Excuse me. That's not what she testified to. She was talking about his attitude."

"Judge," Larry complained, "this is cross-examination and I don't think he needs to be testifying for her."

On November 3, 1992, Kathleen told Special Agent Craft that Michael left her home on October 25 at six p.m. to go with Bill Filter. "But I had meant it for Saturday," Kathleen argued. If Craft "would have read that back, I could have corrected it at the time. But he never read back the statement to me."

Larry asked, "You did correct it then, later, on November the twentieth?"

"Yes, I did."

"The second interview?"

"Yes," she blurted.

"Did you know—"

"I knew it was after Noel had left," Kathleen asserted.

"—between November the third and November the twentieth, did you know that Michael Albrecht had given a statement in Fort Lauderdale, Florida, indicating that he left your house at seven-thirty or eight o'clock to go visit Bill Filter?"

Kammen scurried to the bench, seeking permission to warn Kathleen not to speak about the polygraph. Permission was granted.

Larry turned his attention back to Kathleen. On November 20, 1992, Michael Albrecht had told the Speedway Police Department that he left her house at nine-thirty p.m. On November 4, 1992, his stated time was seven or eight o'clock.

Was Kathleen also confused about the time?

Kathleen said that the interview had taken place at work and that while answering, she had been distracted by other employees.

"But in a period of thirty days what had been—at least in the impression of law enforcement—the six o'clock p.m. time became three hours later at nine o'clock?" Larry queried. "How sure are you of that two o'clock time?"

"I'm a hundred percent positive," Kathleen told him.

Referring back to her interview with Special Agent Craft, Larry asked her, "And you didn't tell him that you were not positive of the time because you were asleep and woke up momentarily when he came in?"

"No," said Kathleen, "I never said—"

"You never told Special Agent Craft that?" he asked.

Kathleen's somewhat convoluted explanation was, "Well, my clocks are set fifteen to ten minutes fast. Quarter till two is around two a.m."

He glided past her mistake in calculating the time. "How far again is Michael Albrecht's parents' home from your house, in terms of minutes to drive?"

Kathleen estimated ten to fifteen minutes on city streets.

"You did not make that call on October the twenty-fifth at 3:29 p.m. to Michael Albrecht's phone in Indianapolis?" Larry asked her.

"No, I did not." She said she was at the church.

He handed her copies of telephone records. "I'd like you to look through… the dates of November the tenth through November the thirtieth, 1992. Would you please look and tell the jury how many of the calls charged to your calling card were made to your home number and how many made to your work number?"

Kathleen examined the records and found three calls to her home and eight to her place of employment.

"I don't suppose you were allowing anybody else in Fort Lauderdale to use your credit card, were you?" Larry asked.

When Kathleen tried to suggest that some of the calls could have come from her daughter, he told her that Noel had already testified that she went to Florida on Halloween and returned a week later.

Kammen asked Kathleen when she had received a copy of her phone records. She replied she had received them from Kammen in the past week. When questioned repeatedly about Michael's whereabouts that fatal weekend, "Were you trying to be just as forthright and honest as possible and give them your best memory?" he asked. "Now, did they ever say to you, in November or December, well, gee, we have your phone records and, you know, you may be wrong; did they ever say that?"

"No."

"And did they ever allow you to compare the phone records with your memory to see if maybe you were wrong?" Taking the role of best friend and confidant, he followed with, "And where were you for, the most part, eight of these calls? At one of the biggest law firms in the state of Wisconsin. And so there's no secret about where you were?"

"Right," Kathleen agreed.

The defense called Joseph Joyce, who had lived in Cindy's building in Apartment A when she disappeared. At the time, Joyce had worked at Allison Transmission. Police interviewed him in October after Cindy's disappearance and death.

"Within a day or so prior to her disappearance, did you see anything unusual that attracted your attention?" Kammen asked.

"Yes, sir. The crime unit parked outside the apartment, sir," Joyce replied. "White vans and so forth."

Kammen asked, "Before you saw the crime unit, the day or two before, did you see anything unusual that you told the police about?"

He had. "There was a dark four-door sedan parked in front of Cindy's apartment. Just to the right of the door." The parked car faced away from the door with a person inside whom Joyce could not see.

What was unusual, Joyce explained, was "as cars would pass, he would seem like to follow them around the complex and then come back and do it again. He did this like two or three times."

Joyce also recalled that "they asked me if I saw any Orientals in the area and I had seen two come out of her (building) door previous to that."

Commons said, "Mr. Joyce, I don't mean to embarrass you by this, were you on medication at the time?"

Joyce believed his medications were called Prolookson and Theratal.

"And for what condition was that prescribed?" Commons asked.

"It's known as schizoaffective, sir."

Kammen asked Joyce, "Did your medication interfere with your ability to see?"

"I believe my medication helps my ability, sir."

CHAPTER 43

The defense planned to swoop ahead of the prosecution when Matthew Kernel took the stand. At the time of Cindy's murder, Kernel lived in a log cabin owned by himself and his father by Eagle Creek Dam. The cabin included 19.2 acres of wooded property and a lake. Another pond joined the property behind the cabin.

"And had you ever gone fishing in these lakes?" Findling asked. He had, but not always alone. Prior to 1992, he had shared the cabin for five years with a friend, Jeff Wright. The roommate worked for Kernel. They employed themselves in construction, tree trimming, and landscaping.

"Okay. Now what are the tools of the tree trimming business, what are the kinds of things that you had to keep in order to be in that business?"

Kernel had used chainsaws, pruners, bowsaws, a chipper, and a bunker truck. He had a number of employees and could earn four or five hundred dollars a day. He said he used the money for "equipment, insurance, gas, eating."

Back in 1992, had Kernel used any of his money "to buy any type of illegal drugs?" Findling asked.

"Illegal drugs?"

"Yes, like marijuana."

"No."

"Did you, back then, buy any cocaine?" Findling asked.

"I may have." He said he had used cocaine a couple of times but never sold it.

"Okay, and after using the cocaine, did you become violent with your girlfriend, Cindy Bierman?" Findling asked.

"No, sir," Kernel insisted.

"Mr. Kernel, what type of effect does cocaine have on you?" Findling asked.

"None that I know of."

Findling tried again. "Mr. Kernel, if the cocaine had no effect on you, why would you use it more than one time?"

"Uh, just to have a good time with my buddies, probably."

Kernel had difficulty remembering the details of the fight outside the Idle Bar at 10th and Tibbs the night of October 24, 1992. He thought he had been jumped and robbed by ten to fifteen people who took cash, a check, and his tennis shoe. He believed he'd been punched in the eye with a fist.

The ER doctor suspected he had been hit with a pipe. He received a dozen stitches above his eye and four more below it. The orbital bone was fractured and Kernel could not see out of the eye at all.

"Isn't it a fact," Findling continued, "that shortly after that incident, you ran into Jeff Wright and told Jeff Wright that the fight was over a cocaine purchase?"

Kernel vowed that he recalled no such conversation.

What about his hunting experience? He had a hunting cabin in northern Wisconsin. What kind of hunting equipment did he have in October of 1992?

Kernel doubted he even had his shotguns at that point because someone had stolen "all my guns at my log cabin." He filed no police report.

What vehicles did he own in October of 1992? Kernel told Findling that he had a bucket truck, a dump truck, and a green pickup truck. He also had three or four other pickup trucks and a '77 Jeep, all black. Sometimes he drove his dad's black Ford Ranger pickup truck.

Kernel and Cindy had dated casually until about a month before her disappearance. Their first date was dinner at Steak and Ale, followed by a movie. Then they returned to her apartment where they drank Crown Royal and she may have smoked marijuana. The intimacy was limited to kissing.

Any chance he had been in her bedroom? Findling asked the question repeatedly and Kernel continued to deny it, but Findling referred to Kernel's five-and-a-half-year-old statements that said he had.

"I may have sat down on the bed," Kernel allowed. "She was showing me some different shirts from the racing crew, different teams."

Findling badgered him for details. Why hadn't he sat on the couch to see the shirts? Why had he earlier described the intimacy as "heavy kissing" instead of "just kissing"? He wanted Kernel to relate the details of his relationship with Cindy but Kernel recalled little of it.

She gave him a couple of racing shirts, a sweatshirt, and a jacket. He did not know what happened to these items but said his shirts got torn up all the time.

He dropped in once while in the neighborhood. Cindy told him never to come unannounced again. His girlfriend had found her number and called.

"What were you doing that Sunday night, October 25, 1992?" Findling asked.

"I was laid up in bed all weekend," Kernel said. He had left the hospital around four a.m. and slept on Bret McCarty's couch for about twelve hours. Then McCarty drove him home because he was unable to drive. His mom was there at the cabin, cleaning, and doing laundry.

Kernel did not remember going out in the days after the fight. He saw a specialist for his fractured orbital bone. "My eye was in too bad of a shape… I had to go to the doctor to get some x-rays taken," he said.

According to Kernel's medical records, Findling pointed out, there were no injuries to his hands, his arms, his feet, his legs.

Back then, Findling reminded Kernel, the police had taken samples of his hair and blood. "But there was never any search of your house or anything like that; am I right? No search of your property? No search of your lakes?"

That had not happened, Kernel said.

Did he recall a conversation with his roommate Jeff Wright "where you offered him your opinion about if you killed somebody how you would dispose of them?"

"I don't remember," said Kernel.

"Do you remember saying something about putting their body in a wood chipper? Do you recall saying anything about then spewing the parts that were destroyed by the wood chipper into the lake so the fish can eat it?"

Kernel denied saying any of that. He said he'd heard such a conversation but did not recall who said those things.

On re-cross-examination, Commons asked Kernel, "How big is a wood chipper?"

"It's about half the size of a car."

"Half the size of a car," Commons contemplated. "You could put a whole body through a chipper, couldn't you?"

"Yeah."

"Did you kill Cynthia Albrecht?"

"No, sir."

CHAPTER 44

Next, Findling questioned JoAnne Delaney, Michael's former next-door neighbor. Mrs. Delaney had lived in her home for the past forty years and been married to her husband Jim for forty-five years.

Mrs. Delaney told the Court that the Albrechts had lived next door to her for close to two years and that the first spring they lived there, they gave her a key to their home so she could "look after their house, maybe get their mail in on short trips."

Was she still holding the key, still looking after the house when, in October of 1992, Michael Albrecht moved away to Florida? "The locks never changed?" Findling asked.

"Not that I'm aware of," she replied.

Mrs. Delaney said she kept a life calendar, recording the events of her days. Findling asked her to refer to her calendar for the weekend of October 24-26, 1992. "Were you in town that weekend?" he asked. She was. Michael was not.

"I would've known, like I said, any activity that went on over there, you're aware of because you can hear it and see it. We have a swing in our backyard, and if you sit there, you could look right over that way too, face their house." She did not see Michael that week until Wednesday morning.

She had come home on Tuesday evening, the twenty-seventh, from her bridge club and saw the story of Cindy's disappearance on television. "So the next morning I was in the bedroom and I happened to see Michael out in the driveway, and I yelled at him and asked what had happened."

Findling asked about Michael and Cindy's roommate. "Big John, that's how he was introduced to me, Big John," said Mrs. Delaney. "Every May, John Weland would come and then after Cindy moved out, he stayed on with Mike."

After Cindy's disappearance, Michael "was very down," asserted Mrs. Delaney, "and he would break into tears any time he would speak of Cindy." After Cindy's body was found, media cameras were trained on Michael's house.

"He would come over every so often and sit and talk to us," Mrs. Delaney reported. "He was devastated, and he said, 'I wonder what she went through before, you know, before they found her.' That seemed to upset him."

No law enforcement questioned the Delaneys, but Don Campbell came. "Sandi Fink called me and asked me if she could bring him over so that he could talk to me," she said. "That was the only interview."

Commons asked Mrs. Delaney about her records. Did she keep records of when the neighbors were out of town? Only for a planned outing like a race, she responded, "so that I would know where they were if anything happened to their house."

Had she written down when Michael left for Florida? She stammered. "You don't keep track. I'm not really Mrs. Kravitz." How many days was he home when he came home to pack? "That's six years ago, you know."

Findling asked, "From your bedroom, what can you hear coming from Michael Albrecht's house?"

"Now, if my windows was open," she replied, "and his door was open, you could hear conversations, and I'm sure they heard us at times."

"And you could hear cars pulling in? Basketball being played?" Findling inquired.

She could.

"And can you tell us whether or not you were home all day long on Sunday, October 25?"

"Yes." She sounded almost triumphant. "Because we had guests. That was on my calendar."

Mrs. Delaney's husband Jim was the next witness for the defense. His story matched his wife's. Cindy moved out and he went over to help with some heavy items. He learned about Cindy's disappearance when his wife saw the news on television.

Jim Delaney sometimes went over to shoot baskets with Michael after work. One night, Jim went over for an evening round of basketball. "Well, it's out of character for me to pry," he related, "but I remember I just picked up the ball and shot it and I said, 'You seem kind of depressed.' And his answer was this is the final, the divorce becomes final today. So I didn't ask anything more than that."

Kammen summoned John Weland, who now lived in Stuart, Florida. In 1992, Weland worked for a team originating from Long Beach. While in Indianapolis, he stayed with Michael and Cindy. He told Kammen, "Well, it wasn't efficient for the team to run out of California because all the races were here in the Midwest. So, during the summer, we would base here."

In 1992, he stayed with the Albrechts until June. "Once that trouble became apparent—I left." He moved in with some other friends. After Cindy left, Weland returned to Michael's house. "He was concerned that with the loss of her income, he might have trouble making ends meet, and I agreed to rent a room from him. I stayed there until just before Thanksgiving."

On the weekend of Cindy's murder, Weland was in Phoenix visiting family when Michael called, asking to use his car for a trip to Milwaukee. No problem. "I got a lot of mileage out of teasing him that his great BMW wouldn't run and that he was going to have to use my piece of Detroit iron."

All seemed normal when Weland returned home. The first indication they had of trouble was later that night or possibly the next when one of Cindy's girlfriends, possibly Sandi, called looking for her.

Kammen wondered, "During the time that you and Michael and Cindy lived together, would it be fair to say that Cindy Albrecht rode in your car?"

"Many times," said Weland. "They wouldn't really take any rent or anything, so I'd try to take them out to dinner and stuff. So we'd all pile into my car and go eat."

Kammen passed the witness to Larry, who asked Weland if he knew Bill Filter. Weland said he vaguely remembered meeting someone by that name. "Do you remember describing him as a smoker and being a nervous person?" Larry asked.

Memories of the man seemed vague to Weland "but I remember the nervous guy smoked. I didn't particularly like him."

How much had Weland and Michael discussed the divorce?

That was a topic he tried to avoid, Weland said. It was never a pleasant conversation. Michael seemed to be angry about it but not angry toward Cindy. "He would cry and be miserable."

Larry asked Weland, "Do you know whether or not on November the twenty-fourth, 1992, you had a discussion with Lt. Bill Jones of the Speedway Police Department in which you indicated that Steve Turner was paying Albrecht by the hour for working on cars Turner was repairing to sell?"

Weland wasn't sure.

"Did you describe Michael Albrecht as having very strong hands, or would you describe him at least back in 1992 as having very strong hands?" Larry wanted to know.

"Sure."

"And do you know whether or not Michael Albrecht was fired from Dick Simon racing after the Indianapolis 500 Race in May of 1992?" he queried. "Did you know that Michael Albrecht had hired an attorney by the name of Forrest Bowman to sue Dick Simon for being fired?"

"No, I didn't know that."

"And you were living with him in July of 1992?"

They were roommates, Weland explained. They did not share their personal business with each other.

Neither attorney had any more questions but the jury had a few.

What about the mileage on Weland's car? Was it consistent with a round trip from Indianapolis to Milwaukee? Weland responded that he did not keep track of mileage.

Was Weland on a racing team in 1992? Was his team a rival of Dick Simon's? Weland told the jury that, yes, he and Michael served on competing teams.

What had Weland been doing on the Tuesday and Wednesday after the murder? "Probably played golf," he said. Since Michael did not play golf, he didn't have any clear memories of what Michael was doing those two days.

Eunice Beckendorf, testifying for the defense, lived out of state. The Court explained to the jury that her written testimony would be read to them, Ms. Beckendorf role-played by Rankin, and questions being read by Findling. Eunice had been sworn in before Judge Mangus-Stinson. The jury was informed that the testimony was taken October 17 of 1997 in this courtroom.

Eunice's testimony was that she had been living with her boyfriend, Bill Filter, for nine years and had met Michael Albrecht through various race events. At the time, she worked for the VA hospital. It was common for Filter to go out with friends and drink beer.

Findling asked about Eunice and Filter's relationship. "It was okay," she said.

"If you were upset about something, would you share it with him?" Findling asked.

She would.

"If he was upset about something would he share it with you?"

"Eventually."

"Prior to Cynthia Albrecht's death, did he ever come to you and say that Michael Albrecht is talking all kinds of crazy things that he wants to do to his wife Cynthia?"

"No."

Had he ever talked about Michael hiring someone to kill his wife?

"No."

Was he violent?

Eunice hesitated and then said, "Verbally abusive, but not physically." He never got into bar fights but he did sometimes lose memory from drinking too heavily.

On work nights, Eunice normally went to bed around ten p.m. Filter sometimes went out for drinks but didn't always tell her. Eunice said that he confided nothing to her about Michael and Cindy except the fact they were getting divorced.

Had she ever believed he lied about his whereabouts on the night of Sunday, October 25, 1992?

No. Bill told his little white lies like everyone else, but nothing on that weekend waved a flag of doubt.

"Well, I'm just going by what Bill said," Eunice related. "I never heard Bill leave, I never heard anyone come to the house. So he's told me that he took off with Mike in the middle of the night, so that's what I'm going by because that's what he said."

Larry asked Eunice about telephone calls between Michael and Filter.

"Once Mike knew that he was going to get a divorce, he called Bill. There were a lot of phone calls. But prior to that, I don't recall any phone calls," said Eunice.

CHAPTER 45

The defense recalled Matthew Kernel, now with the jury present. Kammen asked Kernel how much cocaine he was using in 1992. "Not very much." Kernel said he'd used it a couple of times, possibly only twice during that year. On each occasion, he said, he used about half a gram.

"Now what was the effect of cocaine on you in those two times; did it make you happy, sad, angry, violent, what was the effect?"

"Happy," Kernel responded.

"Happy," Kammen echoed. Not the response he had expected. "And did you ever, in those two times in 1992, use cocaine and alcohol at the same time?"

"Not that I recall, sir." He drank, he admitted, but the effects of both alcohol and cocaine on him were that they made him happy.

"Now, specifically, you told us yesterday that you were dating a woman by the name of Cindy Bierman. And did you ever hit Ms. Bierman?"

No. He did not recall ever hitting his girlfriend. Nor did he recall slamming her face into the couch. He was not aware and did not recall any of five instances when he supposedly ingested cocaine in front of Jerry Dillehay. He did not remember taking cocaine to his cabin. He did not remember ever becoming violent due to drugs or alcohol.

Stonewalled, Kammen ran out of questions.

Michael's divorce lawyer, William Van Barteau, had a practice in Speedway where his firm represented, among other clients, eight or ten race teams. After Cindy disappeared, Michael approached Van Barteau about doing criminal defense work. Van Barteau's advice was "they should discuss it and try and fix in their minds the exact times that these things were taking place because it was kind of vague."

Van Barteau told Findling that Michael did not move to Florida because of "callous indifference" but because "the racing community is a very small community and Michael Albrecht, in the minds of that community, had been charged and convicted already. And I said, well, you don't have a job here; you're not going to be able to make a living. I said go to Milwaukee, go to Florida, go somewhere where you can make a living."

The attorney also advised Michael to file for Cindy's life insurance benefits. "If he didn't file it, it would look suspicious," Van Barteau said. The life insurance funds, over fifty-one thousand dollars went into Van Barteau's trust account. He took one third of the money, slightly over seventeen thousand, for legal fees.

After Michael's arrest in 1997, Van Barteau went to Atlanta to meet with his client and a local attorney. Bill Filter also contacted Van Barteau, complaining the press was bugging him and asking what he should do.

Van Barteau said, "Well, do you have any information that would be harmful to Mike, and he said no. And I said just tell them what you know to get them off your back."

Larry loved questioning another attorney in court, circling his rival, seeking the soft spot in his belly. He asked for specifics of the released life insurance money. "Was there any sort of an evidentiary hearing held in federal court with respect to a federal lawsuit of inter-pleader action?"

Van Barteau responded that in pretrial conferences, "Judge McKinney, who was the judge on the case, told the attorney for the estate that, gave him a certain amount of time to… show why Mr. Albrecht would not be entitled to the proceeds. That time passed and none was presented and the judge ordered the money released."

Larry narrowed his eyes. "Law enforcement officers were never involved in that proceeding, were they?"

"Well, another attorney might have talked to Jones," Van Barteau hedged.

Larry asked about the Florida vacation.

Findling asked to approach the bench and said to the judge, "You know, I talked to him awhile back, but I'm starting to get real nervous about him bringing up the polygraph."

"Oh," said the judge.

"Really nervous about it," Findling continued. "I mean, we've talked, but I just didn't want…"

No. He didn't want to jury to know that Michael conveniently left town just before he was to take a lie detector test. That might help prove his guilt. Who knew that Van Barteau had advised him to flee? But Larry was not out to prove Michael was a coward with a shady lawyer. He was out to prove the man was a murderer.

He went back to questioning Van Barteau, trying to learn when he had advised his client to go to Florida. Was it when his wife disappeared? Was it after Cindy's body was found? Was it after his November 20, 1992, interview with law enforcement when Van Barteau was present? Van Barteau claimed that he had talked with Michael so many times he couldn't pin it down.

Findling called Michael's brother Scott to testify for the defense. Findling asked Scott about his former wife, Susan Striker Albrecht. They were married from 1973 to 1990 and had seven children together.

In 1987, Scott became ill with Guillain-Barré, an illness similar to polio, which left him paralyzed for six months. His only form of communication was blinking: once for yes, twice for no. During his illness, his wife Susie "believed I was going to pass away so she decided to have an extra-marital affair." Scott's brothers were angered by her infidelity.

The divorce battle was prolonged and bitter. Scott took two of the children to Michigan and she stole them back.

Randy proposed "that he had a couple of friends that could take care of Susie and make it look like an accident," Scott said. "I told him he was nuts."

The defense also called Michael's brother Mark. Findling asked Mark about Scott's 1987 illness and about his brother Randy.

In February or March of 1989, Scott was living in Michigan. Scott's estranged wife, who lived in Milwaukee, called Mark's wife and asked where her children were going to school. Then she picked them up from school and took them back to Milwaukee. "And Scott was pretty upset. A little depressed about it. And I talked to Randy about it shortly after that."

Mark claimed that Randy said they should have Susie taken care of, at least scare her or have her legs broken. "And I said, 'Randy, that's a dumb thing to say.'"

How involved was Mark when Michael's marriage to Cindy became rocky? "I didn't talk to Mike that much," said Mark. "We weren't really tremendously close. We just lived kind of different lives."

Findling asked, "Mark, what is the neck muscle test?"

Mark said he did not remember a specific move called the neck muscle test. As boys, he and his brothers played together, imitating World Wrestling Federation moves like the neck massage and the sleeper.

Dawn Albrecht, age seventeen, was eleven years old at the time of Cindy's murder. On the weekend of October 24-26, Dawn, a late sleeper, said she first saw her dad sometime before noon on Sunday morning, October twenty-fifth. Her dad was making breakfast and Dawn heard the story of him rescuing Noel from Great America the previous night.

Her dad left for a period, Dawn recalled, and returned in time for dinner between six and seven. The diners included herself, both parents, her sister Noel, and possibly her other sister, Melissa. After dinner, she and her dad watched the movie *Star Trek V*. She thought it was on cable.

"Now how do you remember that you watched *Star Trek V* and how do you remember it was on this particular weekend?" Kammen asked her.

Dawn said, "Well, I remember it because it was the first time I saw it... And I also remember because my dad's a Star Trek fanatic...And it was just something I did with my father, which, you know, was seldom done."

She said after the movie they went to Leon's for ice cream. Then she went to bed. When she awakened for school the next morning, her dad was making instant coffee.

Larry asked Dawn, "Ms. Albrecht, do you recall back then, October twenty-fourth, twenty-fifth, twenty-sixth, 1992, whether you in that household had either Cinemax, HBO, or Showtime?"

She was not sure. "We could have rented it or we could have watched it on TV."

He offered Exhibit 75, a certified copy of a TV listing in the *Milwaukee Journal*, Sunday, October 25, 1992, three p.m. through one a.m. on October twenty-sixth. State's Exhibit 76 was a certification from New World Communications of Milwaukee, Inc. The television program *Women of Windsor* aired on WITI-TV-6 from seven to ten p.m., Sunday, October 25, 1992.

Larry asked, "Your testimony here today, Ms. Albrecht, is that you may have been watching a video?"

"Yes," she said, but she seemed to know that Larry had cast doubt on her story.

"Did you tell your mother on October 25, 1992, that you and your father were watching a TV program that started at seven o'clock?" he asked.

She did not remember.

The jury wanted to know how long the video was.

Maybe two hours but she could not be precise.

Asking another question for the jury, Kammen said, "Now, during the time you were at home, do you have any recollection of your dad placing any, or did you place any, phone calls to your father's house in Indianapolis on this weekend?"

"No."

CHAPTER 46

Melanie Sells, Larry's wife, arrived on Saturday, June 20, to hear final arguments. She found the courtroom, with its metal trim and dark wood, dated, like something resurrected from the 1970s. She said it was "industrial looking."

Larry's mother Mary Sells was also there. "She was his biggest fan," Melanie recalls. "She believed in him, believed he could not fail. Larry could do no wrong in Mary's eyes."

A friend sitting with them helpfully tried to point out that the case could go either way. Larry was trying to win a conviction on circumstantial evidence after all, and Michael did appear to have an alibi, and no one could prove how Cindy died. Mary did not bite the woman but...

Melanie was not as outspoken as her mother-in-law was, but she knew she had not driven downtown to see her husband lose. Larry had proven repeatedly he could rule the courtroom, especially when a particularly hideous crime made him angry. In the case of Cindy Albrecht's murder, he was charging-bull mad.

Finding himself finally at the finish line, Larry Sells raced toward the checkered flag. In the final arguments of a criminal trial, the State speaks first and last. Larry was exhausted, had forgotten what sleep was, but a beautiful, vivacious woman who had been brutally beheaded would go forever without justice if he did not win this final argument.

He stood erect and spoke to the jury. For two weeks, he had memorized their faces, their demeanor. Had they seen the truth of the matter? He prayed they had. Michael Albrecht was still at his station, looking bored, as if this hearing had nothing to do with him. If the Court released him, well... he had already proved his savagery. Maybe he would not make mistakes with the next victim.

Speaking clearly and with an energy fed by rage at this inhumane crime, Larry began.

"Thank you, Your Honor. Ladies and gentlemen of the jury, I want to express my appreciation on behalf of the State of Indiana and the Marion County prosecutor's office for your service in this case. The criminal justice system could not work without you. You are here to help us find justice.

"Back in 1990, '91, early 1992, Michael Albrecht was on top of the world. He had a beautiful wife. He was a chief mechanic working on race cars and was at the peak of his profession. Then in April and May of 1992, his life started to unravel. His marital relationship was rapidly deteriorating due to his controlling and obsessive behavior. His work for the Dick Simon Racing Team at the Indianapolis 500 was affected. That resulted in his separation from the team at the end of May following the race."

He did not look at the defendant. Michael didn't matter. Only the jury mattered now.

"Near the end of summer, matters became even worse for the defendant. He discovered that Cindy was involved with Pete Twiddy, a tall, good-looking guy, who had a great job working for Marlboro and the Penske Racing Team. Penske was the top team in IndyCar racing. Albrecht was working part-time for an 'also-ran' with no other prospects in sight while Pete had everything the defendant wanted.

"Michael Albrecht became enraged with jealousy. 'For jealousy is the rage of a man: therefore, he will not spare in the day of vengeance.' From the Book of Proverbs, chapter 6, verse 36. Never more true than in the evidence you have heard the last few days.

"After Cindy's disappearance, the defendant told his brother Randy that Pete Twiddy might have had something to do with it. *Now, come on, folks; you just know that ain't true.*" Larry pointed to the tape recorder, reminding the jury of Pete's messages on Cindy's answering machine.

"How could anyone, after listening to those woeful messages, think that Pete Twiddy did anything? By the way, hear any messages from Michael Albrecht on that answering machine tape?

"Cindy had no enemies. But Albrecht told his brother that maybe it was Pete Twiddy. Maybe it was a drug dealer. Maybe Matthew Kernel. You think Matthew Kernel committed this crime? Just use your common sense.

"The defense wants you to believe that this guy with one good eye, who was maybe drunk or messed up on cocaine, this guy stumbled into Cindy's apartment and somehow killed her. He managed to get her body out of there and drive over a hundred miles north of Indianapolis, dump her body, cut her head off, drive back to his cabin. And that he did it without leaving any evidence, or disturbing her apartment or disturbing her neighbors.

"This one-eyed, coke-crazed tree trimmer did not do it. He had neither the physical capability nor the motive.

"The defense also wants you to believe that Antonio Ferrari might have killed Cindy. If you do not fall for that, then they hope you will think that Ferrari is a liar and his testimony about what Albrecht told him is not worthy of belief.

"Albrecht wrote a letter dated November 8, 1992, addressed to Lieutenant Bill Jones, and left it in the safekeeping of Randy Albrecht's wife, Mary Jo Albrecht. The letter was to be given to Lieutenant Jones in the event something happened to him. Mary Jo later turned the letter over to Detective Jones. You read it.

"In the letter, Albrecht wrote that he suspected Antonio Ferrari had done something to Cindy. Done what? She could have been vacationing in Florida like he was! Her body was not found until a week after the date on the letter. Freudian slip? After all, he already knew she was dead. He wrote that Cindy cost Ferrari thirty thousand dollars. Ferrari testified that Cindy had nothing to do with the contract and he did not lose any money anyway.

"Albrecht even had the temerity to suggest that one of Cindy's best friends, Sandra Fink, and her husband, Mike Fink, might have done it. You saw and heard Sandra Fink testify. Based upon her demeanor and her obvious feelings for Cindy, do you think there is even a remote possibility that she had anything to do with Cindy's death? She and Rebecca Miller spent nearly every waking hour with Cindy. Those brave girls entered Cindy's apartment armed only with an umbrella and a can of mace, not knowing what they might encounter.

"They devoted hours, days, weeks, with the help of others in the racing community, searching for their dear friend. Then when Cindy's body was found, they mounted a crusade to see her killer brought to justice. No, Sandra Fink did not do it.

"HE DID IT!" Larry pointed a severe finger at Albrecht. "And now he is finally being brought to justice.

"All the credible evidence points to the defendant. The person who committed this barbaric crime had complete control of his thoughts and actions, unlike Matthew Kernel. It was done with planning and precision by someone on a mission. The defendant decided to do it himself after he could not enlist the help of Antonio Ferrari or Bill Filter.

"This murder was done by someone familiar with Cindy's schedule and habits. You saw the photographs of the apartment. No burglar did this. A burglar would not have bothered hauling the body away. And no mess was in there except what the cats left. There was evidence of a disturbance at the sliding glass door by the balcony. The door was unlocked and the screen had been removed from the track. Also, the comforter was missing from her bed. The Penske bag, which had contained over two thousand dollars, was lying on the living room floor minus the money. And yes, Cindy was gone.

"Think back to the testimony of Detective Bill Jones. He told you that Michael Albrecht admitted being aware of Cindy's habits, one of which was she kept the sliding glass door open with the screen door closed so the cats could look outside. How in the hell was he familiar with that detail? He did not live there. He told Jones that Cindy always slept in the nude or in some light nightshirt. Coincidentally, Cindy's large Garth Brooks t-shirt was missing. That she always took a shower at night before going to bed. Eerily, it sounds as if he was actually there on October twenty-fifth. *Because he was.*

"Before Michael Albrecht returned to Indianapolis from the Leguna Seca Race on October eighteenth, he made one final effort to reconcile with Cindy, to get her to call off the divorce. Sandra Fink and Rebecca Miller overheard the conversation." He stepped to the side. Twelve pairs of eyes shifted with him. Good. He had their full attention. "Cindy refused. She was going through with the divorce, which was to become official on October twenty-sixth. Perhaps that is when he knew for certain he was going to kill her. Maybe he had planned to kill her for weeks. He tried to get his brother Randy to find a Cuban to do something to Cindy. He asked Antonio Ferrari to contact a Mafia type to do something permanent to her. In early October, he encouraged Bill Filter to help him kill her.

"Bill Filter is neither a likeable nor honorable person. He lied for five years to protect a killer. Yet his testimony was convincing and worthy of belief. He testified that he came to Indianapolis in early October and went with Michael Albrecht to scope out the area behind Cindy's apartment. From his description, it is obvious that Filter was actually there. He said the defendant took him to a tree line up on a hill behind the Marsh Supermarket, from which he could see through the sliding glass door into the apartment.

"Detective Jones verified that one could actually see into the apartment from that location. Albrecht told Filter that he would have to cut off her head because of all the dental work he had paid for. Albrecht told him she had titanium and other metal in her jaw.

"How would he know those things unless Albrecht told him? Albrecht asked Filter if he would do it or help him do it. Filter testified that he told Albrecht that he was crazy. Then later agreed to support the phony alibi.

"The defendant killed Cindy in her apartment, then transported her body, first to Milwaukee, then to where he dumped her. Sandra and Rebecca testified that Cindy would not have voluntarily left there without her cigarettes and purse, yet they were left in the apartment."

Larry gestured with his hands and body, encouraging those in the courtroom to visualize the crime scene.

"It was obvious from her clothing on the bathroom floor and her bathrobe that she had taken a shower after she got home Sunday evening. None of her clothes were missing except the Garth Brooks t-shirt. Her clothes were still packed in her travel bags. Where was the comforter from her bed? Obviously, it left with her. Did she walk away into the October night wearing nothing but an oversized t-shirt and wrapped in a comforter? Of course not.

"The defendant drove John Weland's Chrysler Lebaron to the back of the Marsh store. Went to the tree line up on the hill. Saw Cindy just out of the shower wearing the t-shirt, maybe on the couch smoking a cigarette. Sensing the time was right, he went through the wooded area, up the steps to her balcony. The sliding glass door was open for the cats to look outside, just as he told Detective Jones it often was. He may have caused the screen door to derail when he opened it, just as he told Detective Jones it often did.

"If she saw him, I am certain she would have been startled, but probably not afraid. Remember, she told Pete Twiddy at Leguna Seca that she was not concerned for her safety around Michael Albrecht? She should have been. He may have come up the stairs to the back door on other occasions. That is likely how he knew the door would be open and that the screen might go off the track.

"Maybe he punched her on that expensive jaw he paid for, knocking her out, then got her in the strangle hold that you witnessed his brother Randy demonstrate. This big guy choked the life out of her. Saw the black Penske bag on the floor. Knew she had not had time to deposit the cash leftover from Leguna Seca. Greedily grabbed up the over two thousand dollars. That greed caused him to make a major mistake. Because he was one of just a few people who knew about it. He left the bag and everything else a burglar would have latched onto. Then snatched the comforter from the bed. Wrapped his dead wife Cindy in it. Headed out the back door. Pulled the door to so cats would not get out. Thoughtful guy! Then hurried back to the car. Stuffed Cindy in the trunk. Back up the interstate to his ex-wife Kathleen's bed.

"I am not saying that the murder had to have happened this way, but it certainly fits with the evidence presented to you. What the evidence does prove beyond a reasonable doubt is that Michael Albrecht killed Cindy. His motives were jealousy and revenge. Jealous because she had escaped from his controlling clutches into the arms of another. Revenge because he blamed her for destroying his life, for ruining his dreams.

"Randy Albrecht, Broward County, Florida, Deputy Sheriff, was a reluctant witness. He did not want to testify against his brother. But he told you that during the summer of 1992, Albrecht was depressed and angry. Then he asked Randy to find a Cuban in the area to rough Cindy up when she came to Florida to visit her mother. Randy put him off.

"Then Michael Albrecht went to his boss, Antonio Ferrari. Albrecht asked him to find someone in the Mafia to do something *permanent* to Cindy. That it could happen at the upcoming race at Nazareth in eastern Pennsylvania. Perhaps one of Ferrari's contacts in New York could arrange it. That Cindy would be staying at the Sheraton with her two friends. It could be made to look like a robbery.

"Albrecht told Ferrari that Cindy had a fifty thousand dollar insurance policy that could be used in the future to pay for the hit. Ferrari said nothing to police at that time because he just thought Albrecht was blowing off steam.

"The defense, recognizing how damning Ferrari's testimony was, tried to convince you that Antonio Ferrari was not a credible witness. So they brought in the defendant's former boss, Dick Simon.

"Simon testified that Albrecht was a great mechanic. He knew that Albrecht was having difficulties with his wife Cindy, but it did not affect his work as chief mechanic. He said that he did not fire Albrecht. That he voluntarily left the Simon Team after the Indy 500 in order to spend more time with his family and earn a better income with Ferrari. *Yeah right!* Going from making nearly seventy-five thousand dollars a year with Simon to a hundred dollars a day part-time with Ferrari is not exactly a better income. And what family was he going to spend more time with?

"Simon testified that Ferrari was deceitful and dishonest. You, the jury, know who was deceitful and dishonest. It was Dick Simon. You saw Albrecht's personnel file from Dick Simon Racing. It clearly shows that Albrecht was fired. And Simon told at least two Speedway police officers that he had to let Albrecht go because he was a disruptive force with the team. Hell, nearly everyone in IndyCar racing knew Simon fired Michael Albrecht. You can flush Simon's testimony right down the crapper where it belongs.

"Give me one good reason why Antonio Ferrari would come in here and testify falsely against Michael Albrecht.

He considered Albrecht an excellent mechanic. Couldn't afford to pay him on a full-time basis, but he was glad to have Albrecht working on his race car. But on October thirtieth, as soon as Antonio Ferrari heard about Cindy's disappearance, he reflected on his earlier conversations with Albrecht, then immediately came forward and told Detective Jones what he knew. And his account about what Albrecht wanted done to Cindy is remarkably similar to that of Randy Albrecht and Bill Filter.

"Albrecht told Randy that Cindy was spending his money, she was dumping him, and she cost him his job with Simon. He wanted to get her for destroying his life. Randy also told you about Albrecht's paranoia, especially his using all of those payphones. He asked Randy and Willie Hernandez where he could go to avoid extradition. He talked about getting a boat to flee the country if he got wind of the fact he was going to be arrested. He was going to flee the country. The defense wants you to think that it does not show consciousness of guilt. What exactly does it show then? Book of Proverbs, chapter 28, verse 1: 'The wicked flee when no man pursueth: but the righteous stand bold as a lion.'

"The defense has presented evidence of an alibi: Albrecht could not have murdered Cindy Albrecht on the Sunday evening of October twenty-fifth because he was in Milwaukee and West Allis, Wisconsin, during that time. The primary evidence to support that alibi defense came from two sources, Kathleen Albrecht and Bill Filter.

"Bill Filter has admitted that he lied about Albrecht being with him on Sunday. He testified that he went out drinking with Albrecht on Saturday night, and then did not see him again until Monday morning when Albrecht showed up at a site where Filter was working. Filter's memory of that event is pretty clear, as one would expect."

Larry pantomimed and described Michael driving up in Weland's car, Filter painting a house. Filter looking uncomfortable and asking if Michael "did it." Then Michael boasting, "Yeah, she's in the trunk; you want to see her?"

Going through the motions, Larry helped the jury see Filter stepping toward the car, then back, and saying, "Nah. I don't think so."

He said that Filter's "description of events is so striking, so compelling it resonates truthfulness. Besides, if Filter wanted to lie to help himself, he could have said he looked in the trunk and saw Cindy's body, thereby removing any possible question whether Albrecht had killed her.

"Kathleen Albrecht has provided multiple, conflicting accounts as to the alibi. Although she is Michael's ex-wife, it is apparent that she would like to have him back. Not saying that Kathleen wanted Cindy dead, but it was no secret that Kathleen wanted Michael back. Michael and Kathleen were still intimate.

"On November third, Kathleen told Special Agent Craft from the FBI office in Milwaukee that Michael had been at her house Sunday, October twenty-fifth. That he left about six p.m. to visit his friend, Bill Filter, who lived nearby. That he returned to her house at two a.m. or later, October twenty-sixth.

"Detective Jones testified that, driving the speed limit, one could travel from Kathleen's home to Speedway, Indiana, in a little over four hours under normal conditions. The speed limit did not mean much to Michael Albrecht. When Willie Hernandez accompanied his friend, Michael, from Florida to pick up his belongings in Speedway in November after Cindy's body was found, Albrecht drove eighty to ninety miles an hour in the rain in a U-Haul truck. When Willie complained, Albrecht said, 'Don't worry about it, Willie. I'm in the racing business.' Well, he was 'in the racing business' the evening of October twenty-fifth.

"Cindy's body was found on November fifteenth, just off Interstate 65, the most direct route from Speedway to the Milwaukee area. Agent Craft again interviewed and re-interviewed witnesses in and around Milwaukee. On November twentieth, he again met with Kathleen Albrecht.

"Agent Craft was not aware that Kathleen had talked to Michael by telephone several times since the November third statement was taken from her. She had provided Michael a credit card to charge the calls. Telephone records show that Michael called Kathleen from nine different telephones. He was bouncing around, using payphones, just like his brother Randy said. Paranoid? I guess. For good reason. He was afraid he would be caught.

"Michael made eleven calls to Kathleen in November using the credit card. Kathleen tried to tell you that he was calling to talk to his daughters, but her phone records clearly revealed that eight of the calls were to the law office where she worked." *Bingo! Caught her in a lie.*

"Mysteriously, after all the calls from Michael, she changed her story about what time Michael left her house to go to Filter's on October twenty-fifth. Told Agent Craft she had been mistaken. That Michael left about seven or eight p.m. Later, the time that Michael left was said to be nine p.m. Kathleen even tried to make it appear that Michael returned home before two a.m.

"Mr. Kammen tried to convince you that Michael, this guy 'in the racing business,' could not have driven to Speedway and back in the limited time frame. But you know he did. He drove to Cindy's apartment, killed her, threw her in the trunk of his friend's car, drove back to Kathleen's, and had sex with his ex-wife."

The next morning, he had finished up his business. He touched base with Filter and withdrew the five thousand he'd stashed in his dad's account. "No need to hide that money any longer," Larry told the jury. "Cindy was dead in the trunk.

"Now to get rid of that damn body. Know the perfect place. She would not be found right away. But eventually hunters who frequented the area or people who discarded their worn-out appliances, furniture, or other trash there would find her remains. He wanted her found, just not right away. Certainly not on the day the divorce was to be final. That would focus attention on him."

He drove to a place just off the interstate that was isolated, where he would not be readily observed. "He carried Cindy's body. Sliced and sawed her head off. Oddly, he cut the head off down by the collarbone. Took a lot more effort to remove it there than up by the throat. Perhaps that was to hide how she was killed. Punched in the jaw, then strangled with that hold he and Randy knew so well." Larry clenched his hands slowly, as if enraged.

"Left Cindy on her back with her legs spread open to make it look like some crazed, sex fiend, serial killer had raped and murdered her. Slight problem with that. Cindy was on her period. Had a tampon in her vagina. Guess he didn't notice that. Wrapped the head in the comforter that Cindy had been in, and took it from the scene.

"How could he do that to a fellow human being, especially someone he supposedly loved? How could anybody do something so grotesque?

"Cindy's head has never been found. Maybe he took it with him when he left for Florida in his cute little BMW on October twenty-ninth.

"He also took along the five thousand dollars from the Milwaukee bank, as well as the money from his bank account in Indianapolis, and the $1,425 he collected from Antonio Ferrari on October twenty-seventh. Let us not forget the nearly twenty-two hundred dollars that was taken from Cindy's Penske carryall bag in her apartment. Pretty tidy sum. Makes one wonder if he ever intended to return from this so-called vacation.

"The divorce was to become final Monday, October twenty-sixth, after the required sixty-day waiting period. Michael and Cindy had already signed the necessary paperwork, including a waiver of appearance. That meant they need not attend court to finalize the divorce. Once her attorney filed the papers and the judge signed them on October twenty-sixth, the divorce would be official. That never happened because Cindy disappeared.

"Remember, Filter testified Albrecht told him he needed to kill Cindy before the divorce became final because of the life insurance. What life insurance? Cindy had purchased her own policy through John Alden Insurance. Her father was the beneficiary. Well, her father was not the beneficiary on the life insurance policy she thought she dropped when she decided to divorce Michael. She no longer paid for that policy.

"Guess who did? And guess who was the beneficiary on that policy? Yep, it was Michael Albrecht."

Larry then held up a white poster board. On the right-hand side were five substantially enlarged copies of checks, arranged by date in chronological order from top to bottom, made payable to Prudential Life Insurance for the premium on Cindy's life insurance policy. All checks were signed by Michael Albrecht. On the left-hand side of the diagram were written descriptions of activities occurring while Michael was sending the checks to Prudential.

Larry said, "Let's examine those checks submitted to Prudential by Michael Albrecht, and what was happening at the time.

"Check number one on the diagram. Michael knew Cindy had hired an attorney to represent her in the divorce. She wrote a one hundred-fifty dollar check to retain that attorney on July thirteenth. The defendant is such a great guy that he paid her life insurance premium on August third. The policy was term life. It was not the type allowing the holder to cash it in at any time. The person named in the policy had to die, and then the policy amount, which in this case was fifty thousand dollars, was paid to the beneficiary. Hell, the only thing Cindy could realize from this was her death.

"Check number two. On August fifth, Cindy changed the beneficiary on her new policy from Michael to her father, Louis Woodward. She was not aware that Michael had continued to pay her Prudential policy premiums. Probably would have caused her some concern. The nice guy, who stands to benefit should something happen to Cindy, made another premium payment on August thirteenth.

"Check number three. On August twenty-sixth, Cindy actually filed for divorce. Those divorce papers were served upon Michael Albrecht on August thirty-first. That very same day he deposited five thousand dollars in his father's Milwaukee bank account to keep Cindy from getting any of it. In September, Albrecht asked his brother Randy to find a Cuban to rough her up while she was in Florida. Albrecht made another premium payment on September fourteenth. Getting the picture yet? Bad things are happening between them, yet he kept paying those premiums.

"Check number four. Late September, early October. Albrecht asked Antonio Ferrari to find somebody, an Italian Mafia type, to do something permanent to Cindy in Nazareth. That person could be paid in the future with fifty thousand dollars in life insurance. As you know, the only way that policy benefit would be paid is if Cindy died. Ferrari put him off. Albrecht said he would do it himself. In early October, Bill Filter visited Indianapolis. Albrecht tried to talk him into killing Cindy. Filter told him he was crazy. Albrecht told him the same thing he told Ferrari: 'I will do it myself.' Filter and Ferrari did not even know one another. Did they just coincidentally come up with that same line: 'I will do it myself'? Hell of an amazing coincidence! While this stuff was going on, old, reliable Michael made another premium payment on October twelfth.

"Check number five. At Leguna Seca on October seventeenth, eighteenth, Albrecht made a final attempt to get Cindy back. She rebuffed him. On October twenty-seventh, Sandra Fink and Rebecca Miller called him from Cindy's apartment and told him she had disappeared. On October twenty-eighth, he was interviewed by Detective Bill Jones. Jones told him Cindy was missing and foul play was suspected. That very same day, he made another payment on the policy. Could not stop now. Her body had not yet been discovered.

"On November fifteenth, Cindy's body was discovered. Albrecht made no further payments. But he did make a claim for the life insurance benefits on March 22, 1993, just five months after killing her. Unfortunately, he eventually received the fifty thousand dollars. Who says crime doesn't pay?

"Well, you folks can tell him it doesn't. I have asked you for justice, justice according to the law, justice for Cindy's family and friends, and justice for Cindy. The evidence in this case proves beyond a reasonable doubt that Michael Albrecht brutally murdered Cindy Albrecht.

"Your duty is to find him guilty. These good people, who have lost so much, have waited six long years for a jury to convict him for killing their beloved Cindy. I implore you to give them and Cindy" Larry looked toward the heavens, "at least that measure of justice. The decision will soon be in your hands. May God be with you."

Larry sat. Had he convinced the jury? Usually he could read a jury. But not today. Not one face flickered a readable expression. He could only hold onto an agonizing hope as Findling rose to speak.

CHAPTER 47

Note: Michael Albrecht did not testify nor could he be compelled to. The Fifth Amendment to the US Constitution guarantees that privilege. However, the defendant has every right to tell his story to the Court and jury. And in a case like this, in which Michael Albrecht was charged with such heinous atrocities, you would think he and his lawyers would want the opportunity for him to proclaim his innocence, not simply sit silently in the courtroom while evidence of his guilt was presented. There is one overriding reason why he did not testify: he would have been ripped to shreds on cross-examination.

Drew Findling began his final argument with questions targeted to elicit doubt. "Can I tell you who killed Cynthia Albrecht? Can I say it was Matt Kernel? Can any of us say it was Matt Kernel? There is no way that we can give you that answer.

"For no explained reason, this case languished for years. You heard no investigation after January of '94, when Randy and Mary Jo Albrecht and Willie Hernandez met with police down in Fort Lauderdale. Then it languished, nothing. Until Michael Albrecht was arrested in the summer of 1997, and we'll talk about why.

"We'll talk about the evidence that gave nobody the confidence to really prosecute this case until one last ditch effort was just made.

"But can we tell you who did it? The answer is no, but can we give you effort? Can we show to you, and have we showed to you, there were things that could have been done? There was a way to avoid the tunnel vision that plagues this case.

"Michael Albrecht looks like the guy that should have done it. The total effort as you heard yesterday from Mr. Van Barteau was to focus on Michael Albrecht, the easy guy to look at. Don't go the extra yard. We'll talk later about how we learned that sometimes you can make an effort.

"You know, like yesterday. Perhaps one of the greatest accomplishments in the investigation of this case was June eighteenth of 1998, when people got around to interviewing Mrs. Kernel. Got a little ambitious and talked to her family and we got an opportunity to actually talk to Matt Kernel. The guy that they were told to keep on questioning, and we figured, well, what the heck, here's our client charged with murder, let's finally do some questioning. Let's do some work.

"To consider Michael Albrecht a suspect was obvious. To consider his statements to Antonio Ferrari and Randy Albrecht should have been done, but he worked for Antonio Ferrari. He was obviously going through a vulnerable time. He expressed to Antonio Ferrari how upset he was.

"And then it transformed into this I want her permanently out of racing.

"Antonio Ferrari's doing business at Speedway. His competitors are completely involved in this investigation. So Antonio Ferrari comes and tells us what Michael Albrecht said, but he knows he's in a jam. So he is going to pull the pressure off himself.

"I'll tell you why, because when Michael talked to him about these concerns, does he say, hey, man, you are whacked out, dude? You need to go to therapy! You need to just settle down and just relax," Findling said.

The defense attorney looked anything but relaxed himself. He was intense, his feet constantly in motion, his voice commanding.

"What does Antonio Ferrari do? Maybe his motivation is the cheap labor. A hundred dollars a day, a hundred dollars a day, he gets the chief mechanic over from Dick Simon. The one thing we do know is he is sure not taking Michael Albrecht very seriously. He's treating Michael Albrecht as just another person who is upset and saying stuff he shouldn't be saying.

"I want her out of racing. I want something permanent to happen to her. I want this to happen, and what is Ferrari's response?

"Ferrari's response is to lead him on, yeah, don't worry about it, okay. I'll contact, uh… I've got mob connections." Findling told the jury that Ferrari's reason for saying that was "well, I just thought it would kind of go away."

They talked about mob connections "but does it follow through? No, because Michael Albrecht is not going to have his wife killed. Michael Albrecht is not going to kill his wife. He just talks a game.

"When Michael Albrecht is at his brother's house thinking about what happened, he's gotta be thinking about conversations with Antonio Ferrari, because he didn't kill her.

"Well, who would kill her? Well, he knows Ferrari's got mob connections. So then he thinks, hey, you know, this guy has a ton of financial problems. He gets served with more lawsuits than one can possibly conceive of, and Cynthia somehow messed him up."

Concerned about Ferrari's connections, Albrecht penned a letter to Lieutenant Jones and gave it to Mary Jo Albrecht. "Does he give the letter to Detective Jones right then and there?" Findling asked. "If he is trying, as Mr. Sells says, at that point, to send people down different roads, wouldn't he have just gone to Detective Jones, and said, you know I think Ferrari did it? He wasn't sending anybody down roads.

"He gives a letter to his sister-in-law to put away. That letter doesn't surface for two more years. He doesn't retrieve the letter from Mary Jo or give it to Detective Jones. That never happens.

"That letter is there if he winds up at the bottom of a lake or a river somewhere. He's thinking that's the letter that's gonna be turned over, and that's why it's given and that's why it's put away.

"So he's certainly not gonna turn on Antonio Ferrari and say, 'hey, Antonio, I think you did it.' That's not gonna happen."

In his vulnerable state, Albrecht also talked to his brother Randy, just talks the game with him, Findling related. But Mark testified that Randy said, "I told Michael I'll get somebody to take care of it."

Findling's voice raised as if he were declaring a civil war between the two brothers. Then he dropped to a more confidential tone. "Michael's response is, 'Hey, you're crazy.' Michael's a wimp. But this is the frame of mind that Randy has at that time.

"Now, there's another person that he talks to when he's in a vulnerable state of mind, just talks the game with him, and that's his brother, Randy Albrecht. Now, you know, Randy comes in here, and obviously, it's difficult for him to testify.

"But Randy draws out of Michael, during this emotional state when he is vulnerable, we already know he has said it to one brother, so while Michael is venting, obviously he is talking about this kind of thing. Man, I just want her permanently out of racing. I just want her out of there.

"Never does he tell anybody 'I want her killed.' 'I just want her roughed up.' That's what he says to him. Not permanently out of racing, 'I just want her roughed up.'

"But Randy admits everybody in the household is paranoid. Randy thinks there's parabolic microphones with the police scanning and listening to things. He thinks there's telephone taps.

"So everybody in the household is paranoid about phone conversations, but look how serious he has taken Michael, okay. Come, come with your daughter, and stay with us, all right.

"Noel flies down from Milwaukee, never flew before. He's going down in his car. He picks her up; they stay there, all right. Now are Randy and Mary Jo freaking out?

"They have a little boy that was, like, eight years old. There is no way that Mary Jo Albrecht is gonna let Michael stay in her house if she believes that he had anything to do with this, and Michael stays there after Cindy is found.

"And they are so overwhelmed and in fear of Michael Albrecht," Findling mocked how they sent Willie Hernandez to Indiana with him so Hernandez could help Michael pack up and come stay. "So then, Willie goes up there."

Hernandez and Michael took a ride to Milwaukee and he claimed that Michael pointed out the area where Cindy's body was found. Findling's response to that testimony was, "Willie says, well, Michael didn't want to watch TV. Well, Willie was not with Michael when Michael was being interrogated for hours upon end that first day.

"Look, Cindy's been found, here's where she's been found. Have you been there? Did you do it? Okay, the map that's in evidence, it's in the newspapers. So, Willie is saying, well, it's kind of unusual that Michael pointed in a direction, which, by the way, as you all know when he testified, we learned was the wrong direction anyway.

"Think about that. He pointed, wherever they were, to the... it was east and he pointed west; if it was west, he pointed east. He testified to the opposite direction, and irrespective of that, we already know it's in the newspapers with a map.

"And Michael's been in this interrogation for hours upon end when they're asking him what he did, where he did it, did you do this, did you do this there?"

Hernandez also related that Michael and Filter had a private talk in Milwaukee. Findling said that was quite reasonable. "And you can rest assured that they're calling one another!

"What would you do? If you knew you were in Milwaukee visiting family? If you knew that the police were only focusing on you? If you knew that everybody in the racing industry only cared about focusing on you, and didn't want to listen to one thing anybody else had to say?

"What would you do? Hey, man, have they called you? You know we were together that night. Yeah, man, we were watching movies, we did this, we ate, we watched football. You bet you're gonna be on the phone left and right! You are not a human being if you're not doing that!

"And to sit here and tell you that there's something wrong when your family is being called liars! When a little girl, who is eleven years old, is basically being called a liar! You know the sentiment of that family when they were talking to one another."

It was the tunnel vision of law enforcement that forced the family to circle the wagons. "Because nobody was focusing on anybody else. Also, there's some kind of reference by Randy that, at some point, Michael's on the phone and he says, I can't keep on sending money or something like that, to Filter.

"Well, we know from Filter that Michael has lent him two hundred dollars for an electrical bill. But what did he tell us? Michael did send him something from Florida, and we sat at the edge of our seats while he told us extension cords.

"You know, Randy didn't even tell the police this until, until a few months ago when Lieutenant Jones flew to Florida to tell him, hey, we got a court date. Anything else you remember?

"Here's what happened, your brother's been arrested, Filter's been arrested, you know, anything you remember?

"Yeah, I remember some kind of conversation where he mentioned Filter. Well, that conversation is now five years old.

"Now, we're left at a point where Michael has done nothing but just been a really hurt and upset husband. You know, and is he a jerk for being upset? I mean, you know, everybody, hopefully, in their lifetime, falls in love.

"And the pain, the pain of finding out that somebody that you love doesn't love you is excruciating. When the person that you share your deepest secrets with, the person that you're intimate with, rejects you, it is an unfathomable pain. But, according to Sandi and other friends, he's crabby about it. He's a jerk, I mean, what a jerk."

Michael found some letters. "He apparently goes in the apartment when he's taking care of the cats; it's right after the July nineteenth race, the Toronto race. He sees them then, but these are from early June when they're still living together.

"He sees these letters, and I've gotta tell ya, he's a crabby asshole that's a murderer. Because he finds a note. 'Keep your head up straight, proud and tall. Don't let, ever let anybody drag you down, because remember, everybody is somebody and you are a very special person. Don't let you ever forget that. When the time is right, we will both know it and the magic will happen. Thanks for the week in Portland. It was great.'

"You're an asshole, boy, what an asshole for getting upset about that! I mean, the despicable nature of anybody that would demean Michael Albrecht for having feelings, for thinking and being upset.

"So now he's upset and he talks to Ferrari and he talks to Randy, but he doesn't do anything about it." He did nothing but call Bill Filter. "You need to think about why he's talking to Bill."

Randy had told Michael to "just move on."

John Weland's response was "I don't talk about those things with men. I just didn't want anything to do with it."

Scott certainly needed no more problems and "Mark is honest as the day is long … looks right at Michael and says, 'We just weren't close.' That's it.

"He's not gonna call Kathleen, bless her heart. Kathleen, I want to talk to you, I know that I left you, and had an affair with Cindy when we were married, but can I cry on your shoulder?"

But Bill Filter had been Michael's friend for decades. "That's who he turns to, and he calls him, and he calls him incessantly," needing somebody to talk to. Filter had been through divorces. He was the one friends turned to for encouragement when tortured by rejection. The two friends spent time together in Indianapolis, doing things together when it wasn't crazy with hundreds and thousands of people jamming into events and going to the race.

"Albrecht and his friends are hanging out. They're going to Hooters. They're going to the Slippery Noodle. They're taking the bus tour… he arranges the bus tour for Bill, and Bill's just having a good time.

"So before Bill has any reason to start fabricating, he's out there just having a good time hanging out with his friend."

A couple of weeks later, Michael went to spend time with his family. "Whoa! He's setting up the murder now!" Findling taunted. "Because if these beautiful girls were my daughters, and I was living out of town, I'd be there every darn weekend seeing them. Those kids were as sweet as sugar. Those kids that the State wants you to believe are liars!

"You're liars! You have come to this court in front of this judge and this jury and committed perjury! That's what they want you to believe about these sweet, young ladies.

"Absolutely the most ridiculous thing in the world. He comes that weekend to be with his kids. He comes that weekend to be with his family, and that is the truth that wants to be ignored.

"Later on, he sees Filter. Now, remember, there's this dispute about did they go to Rodeo's on Saturday or did they not go to Rodeo's on Saturday? Well, nothing happened on Saturday."

They went to Rodeo's and then Michael went to visit his family. "And please remember this," Findling pleaded, "the unfairness, the inequity of interviewing these people repeatedly, while ignoring all other leads.

"Let me tell you folks, make your bet, you sit there and quiz one another about what you did three weeks ago, let it go… let alone six years and come back a week from now and do the same interview, and come back a week after and do the same interview, and come back afterwards and do the same interview.

"Things are gonna change. That's the way it works. That's law enforcement, and you know what, nobody begrudges it, because without law enforcement, we all sink. We just ask that you interview everybody and do your job. Don't take the easy way out."

The case did not hinge on the trip to Rodeo's. Over that weekend, "they want you to believe the whole time, he's plotting and planning. He's got the big murder plan, remember. He bought the saw you never heard about. He must have that saw; there must be a receipt somewhere. Well, I've waited all of two weeks for that receipt, nothing like that.

"What about the tarp or something to keep the blood away? What about the cleaning fluids that must have been involved in this sophisticated murder that was so planned out from Michael Albrecht?"

No, Findling insisted. Michael was busy with family. "He's a daddy. He does what a daddy does.

"Here's where it really gets tricky. He comes back to Kathleen's and at some point, he calls his answering machine. Was it one o'clock? Was it two? We're all gonna fight about Saturday night.

"Saturday night, that twenty-four hours before anything alleged to be happened. Let's fight about it. You know why we'll fight about it? 'Cause there's nothing else against him! There's no forensics. There's no evidence of spousal abuse. There's no DNA. There's none of any of these things. So let's fight about Saturday night.

"He called and checked his messages, like all of us do all the time. The next day, he wakes up and he has breakfast with his family. And you remember the little liars came, they testified… his daughters.

"The preposterous notion that they're fabricating just particularly offends me, and I'm sorry. But he had breakfast, Dad's special hash browns, and he's cutting his onions and his potatoes."

But the State says he's plotting murder even though there's no evidence to suggest he knew when Cindy was coming home. "It's not exactly like he and Cindy are getting along and she's sharing information with him. He's not taking care of the cats anymore. She doesn't have to come back for the divorce. All she needs to do is make a phone call.

"Later on, he goes and watches football with his parents. Now… which Filter theory do you believe in?

"We got A, we got B, we got C! One of 'em we just found out for the first time, first time. Now, Michael is in Indiana staking Cindy out. That was a new one, all right. There's nobody more shocked than them when that came out.

"But his mom talks about how they watched football. Well, if their big witness Bill Filter is telling the truth, we've got a new liar folks. It's Gwen Albrecht. That wonderful woman who came and testified to you about the significance of sitting around and watching football with her son, but we're gonna get into another big fight now.

"Here comes the other big fight, what time did he go to Kathleen's? Because there's a message... excuse me, there's, like, one of those one-minute calls from Kathleen's at three-thirty. Now... did he get back at four-thirty or five, or before three-thirty?"

The stories were confused because the family had "been interviewed nonstop by law enforcement? We got Indiana State Police, we got FBI, we got Speedway Police interviewing people over and over and over again.

"Okay, and boy, if you don't think that's gonna put a little tension in you. With due respect to Agent Craft. He's a pretty serious dude, staring you down and questioning you about your whereabouts— would be intimidating to any of us. Whether it's his intent or not. That's why he does what he does for a living.

"So let's talk for a second about the times that they think are involved. It's only well-planned out folks, if you're in Milwaukee at the time.

"It's only if you got to zip in, kill, remove, dispose of the body, get back so nobody can tell you did it. That's when it's got to be precision. When you're force feeding a theory of the case."

The family watched TV, cooked, and ate dinner. At seven, Noel and her boyfriend went to play darts. Then Michael and Dawn enjoyed father and daughter time.

"Well, you know, I wouldn't consider for a second that a seventeen-year-old girl is gonna come in here and lie. Number one, it didn't happen. Video or cable TV? The prosecution knew that video was available. You think they didn't check that?

"But who would think for a second, who would think for a second that this little girl is gonna come in here and stare you right in the eye and lie to you? Impossible, impossible.

"Dawn and her dad watch the movie and afterwards, Michael goes out and hangs out with Filter. And why not? His sixty days to the divorce are up. He goes out drinking with Filter from nine until two but Mr. Filter needs it to be a lie now.

"If Michael Albrecht had orchestrated a lie, because the prosecution wants you to believe that this group is all engulfed in this massive display of perjury, would he have chosen Bill Filter? Ridiculous.

"All he needed to do was just ask Kathleen, 'cover for me for the night, I didn't do anything wrong. Kathleen, not one thing wrong, I promise you, Kathleen. You know I love you, honey; we been sleeping together now the summer months while I had problems with Cindy. I love you. Just be my alibi witness, baby.'

"That's all he needed to do, but he didn't do that, because for over one half of a decade, he and Mr. Filter told the truth about what he did that evening. Mr. Filter told law enforcement repeatedly, 'I was with him that night,' okay. 'I was with him that night' and you know what, the most significant statement is December seventh. That is the key one.

"If he was a fake alibi, do you think for a second, he would have said... first of all, he says, he calls me all the time. So he's given on December seventh the telephone records.

"This is our fake alibi man, this is it. He's telling 'em, 'He calls me all the time about this divorce thing.' He was obsessed with it. He says to me back then before all this happened, 'She's a... excuse me, fucking bitch.'

"This is a great fake alibi you got here. This guy's really gonna work for you, Michael Albrecht. He's looking out for your best interest. Okay, and then he tells them that Michael Albrecht said, 'I wish she were dead sometimes.'"

Michael, Findling said, was just "a guy crazed with love, crazed with depression, but was just gonna move on. Who talked out of the side of his mouth, said things that he shouldn't have said.

"Eunice Beckendorf, in the deposition that was read, said it wasn't unusual for them to go out drinking. Everybody says it's not unusual for them to go out drinking, and so that's what they do that night."

Bill Filter can't say that because "when he's on the stand, he can't tell you what really happened because he's got a deal. He is locked in as of September 3, 1997." Filter had repeated his new story on the stand.

"But see, then he gets cross-examined. And then we learn that… well, I didn't go away at all that night. I never left that night, well, I may have left for a little while. I may have taken a walk to the gas station.

"Took a walk to the gas station? Well… you've testified previously… saying you didn't leave, that well, maybe, I went out for a drive, and maybe the drive lasted from ten to twelve o'clock, and maybe I got some gasoline at the Super America.

"So now it's a two-hour fill-in the gaps, and then he acknowledges that he's previously said, 'I may have gone to Filter's and had some drinks, but I don't really remember, I may have.' Oh, we've got new possibilities here."

Then there were the telephone records, the 1-900 numbers. "Whenever Eunice is not home, Mr. Filter's calling these numbers all the time. He's on the phone with a Houston telephone number thirty times; 8:02 a.m., 8:53 a.m. October thirteenth, October fifteenth 8:04 a.m., 8:19 a.m. Um… he's just on the phone nonstop, and the reason why I asked you to look at that is it's just one more thing that he didn't do during that weekend.

"So we know that he was with Michael Albrecht that night. That was the truth."

Filter changed his story and took the immunity agreement because "he has learned that if you stick with Michael, you're gonna get charged. It is, as he said, 'every man for himself.' And then when I cross-examined him and said, look, you know, you're acknowledging all these other things you did that evening, and you've given different testimony before suggesting you were out that evening... what's the problem, Mr. Filter?

"It's... I've spent the last five years convincing myself I was out drinking that night.' No, you didn't; what you did, Mr. Filter, is go out with Michael Albrecht that night, and right now, you are selling him out. You are selling the truth out! So that you can cover your own butt, and I don't care what Pat Knight says.

"A hundred thousand dollar bond, lock 'em up and take 'em away, and he's looking at eight years. And he also acknowledged when it first happened, he's thinking he may be looking at the death penalty or life sentences. So, he learns, hey, Michael's got problems, I am no longer becoming part of those problems."

The new story, the immunity story, is that "Michael has chosen him to be an assassin. Yes, this is Bill Filter, the man that is at the VA Hospital, probably there more than Eunice, who works at the VA Hospital. But Michael's picking Bill to be his murderer.

"He's got nothing in his background to indicate that he even knows how to use a gun, or inflict any type of pain, or use some kind of, you know, choke hold, or maybe he was a big wrestling fan himself. We don't know about that, okay. All we know is now Michael's chosen Bill to be his assassin.

"That's what Bill says when he's telling his story. The story that's gonna get him freedom." That story, Findling declared, came straight from the affidavit that Filter read with his lawyer. Filter's story conveniently matched the existing evidence.

"When Filter arrived in Indianapolis to give his statement, he was met in the parking lot and taken for coffee. He's part of the team."

"Well, things changed. 'Cause guess what, he's got Michael sitting around staking out Cindy in Indianapolis now. Bill's just gonna sell whatever he can so Bill can walk on out of here.

"Willie Hernandez said that Mike and Filter were talking very hush, and at one point, Filter and Mike left the bar and went outside while Hernandez stayed inside the bar. That's what the affidavit said.

"What did Filter say September third as he told you on his cross-examination? 'Mike and I were at the bar. It was kind of noisy too. I think there was live music that night, so it was kind of hard, you almost had to put your mouth in the guy's ear to hear him. We went outside even.'

"Now, he even mentions Pete Twiddy. Um… the affidavit, um… let's see. It says in there Sandi mentioned Cindy's boyfriend, Pete Twiddy. Filter says, 'Yeah, Twiddy, I know that name and I know it's a P and it ends with a T, but I can't remember the letter that went in between.'

"If that's not a guy that just studied a script, then what is it?

"Body found in remote area. The affidavit said, 'Albrecht contended that he would dump the body up north in a place where nobody would find her. Statement, he said… this is what he said September third, 'He said he had to find a remote area by a field, or something to hide it so nobody would find it for a while.'

"Cross-exam about the bedspread. Affidavit that he studied: 'It was later learned that a bedspread was missing from Cindy's bed.' What did he say on September third? 'He even talked about wrapping her up in a bedspread.' Direct quotation, you're on a roll, Bill, you're gonna get yourself freedom.

"And then he talks about Antonio Ferrari and of course, Ferrari's mentioned in the statement, and then he brings Ferrari up again, okay. Yeah, he talked about Ferrari with the mob connections. It's in the affidavit, and then he brings that up.

"The dental work, okay. Affidavit: Mike related that Cindy had undergone extensive jaw surgery during the time that they lived in Milwaukee, Wisconsin, and had several screws in her jaw from surgery.

"Now, he of course knows that she is beheaded, decapitated.

"So what does he say? 'He also stated that if it was gonna happen, her head had to be cut off, because she had all that dental work done. They couldn't find a body with a head on it, because of all the major dental work.'

"Well, she had the dental work when she lived in Milwaukee with Michael. And we also know from Mr. Filter that he was friends with Michael when Michael was married to Cindy in Milwaukee. Obviously, he knows about titanium or any of those that were involved from when they all lived there."

And then there was the insurance, Filter said. "If Michael Albrecht has done this for the insurance, because remember, the only reason he's paying that premium, as he told the police, and as you heard. When you have property before a divorce, you cover the equity until it is quitclaimed to one party or the other. You cover the equity.

"For fifteen dollars or whatever it is a month, you cover the equity, but, if he wanted the money, then why remove a source of identification? Why do you behead her, decapitate Cindy, so they can't figure out her identity? 'Cause if you do that, guess what you don't collect? The life insurance."

Findling pointed out that if Bill Filter's information came from the affidavit, it would also follow that he'd be aware that twenty-five hundred dollars was missing. But, the defense attorney asserted, if the wrong question was asked, then Filter became "a little confused, he's a little off the script." Did Michael supposedly tell him about twenty-five thousand dollars in life insurance? It could have been twenty-five hundred dollars that was missing.

"And of course, most significantly, Michael did not kill Cindy Albrecht. And if he did, I'm sure, in this great confession he makes to Bill standing by the paint job, he would have told him, but he didn't. So, guess what Bill can't say? 'Uh… he never told me how he did it.'

"Of course, guess what also was in the affidavit? There was no mention in there of how it was possibly done. So Bill specifically says, 'I can't tell if she was shot, stabbed, or strangled, I can't say anything.'

"Because there's nothing in the script that says that, so he passes that by as well. Now, just remember this folks, this new Indiana story. This generates doubt from Lieutenant Jones. Her Honor is gonna talk to you about reasonable doubt. The State must show you beyond a reasonable doubt that the alibi does not exist.

"If Lieutenant Jones acknowledges doubts about the witness who refutes Michael's alibi, then how can the jury believe anything Bill Filter says?"

Also, Cindy's initial airline ticket, found in her bag, was dated November first. "Which is exactly, on October twenty-eighth of 1992, what Michael told the police. 'I thought she was coming home October thirty-first or November first.' There is nothing to suggest that he knew otherwise.

"At that time, he was on the outs. But he's keeping up with her travel plans? He didn't know when she was coming back. And if he was going to be staking her out, why would he let her walk inside her apartment and then go and get her? Why not just abduct her beforehand? The whole theory is ludicrous.

"Michael gets subjected to interview after interview. As we said, Matt Kernel, a suspect, told to continue looking at, they never look at again, until we get a chance to examine him here in front of you.

"You know about everything that was done with Michael's family. What about Mrs. Kernel? Mrs. Kernel comes in here, and the only thing that they can tell you is that in December, she had an apartment somewhere else. They never refute the fact that she was living with this man and taking care of him.

They never refute the fact that she didn't spend a couple of years away from Matt.

"None of these things are resolved, except one thing: that Matt's alibi was never scrutinized. That Matt's family wasn't subjected to interview, upon interview, upon interview.

"Telephone records are destroyed after eighteen months. They had eighteen months to look at Matt Kernel's telephone records. They had the opportunity to search his residence. We know they found nothing on Michael Albrecht! We know they didn't find one stitch of forensic scientific evidence to say this man had anything to do with his wife's demise!

"They looked in the car, 'cause she had to have been decapitated before she got there, because there's not enough rain to saturate it, there's not a lot of blood there, so clearly, she's decapitated somewhere else.

"So they look in the Weland trunk, they do the Luminol test, there's no evidence of any blood! There's no bedspread in the world that's not gonna let saturated blood get through it. There's no evidence at all of these bloody things, no saws or anything.

"Why not make the effort? Why not try? What was wrong with Lieutenant Jones if he couldn't do it? Calling up Krueger, calling up Craft, and saying, you know what, let's do our job. Let's investigate, let's get a search warrant. Let's look at this guy. My God, he's got saws galore, this guy's got nothing! No evidence at all! Let's look at this guy! Let's see if he did it!

"Now they want you to sit here and reward laziness, and this man's life rests on incompetence and this is about comfort levels! It's about how comfortable you are removing his freedom based on zero effort!

"Nobody pulled anybody else's phone records. Nobody did anything, and those records are gone because they sat on this anemic prosecution for years, and now you're asked to look at it when they don't do anything!

"Do we know Matt did it? We have no way of knowing, but at least we tried. At least we brought you Mrs. Kernel! They never even talked to her. One telephone conversation and he gives up on her, and then they want to call these people liars!

"These despicable O.J. Simpson comparisons. Yeah, well, we're not talking about factious drug lords. We have somebody that they were told to investigate! And now you're gonna consider Michael Albrecht's future based on no effort! Oh, there is something wrong folks. There is something deeply wrong."

With five minutes left to summarize his arguments, Findling unfurled a passionate plea to the jury on behalf of his client, listing in quick succession arguments he hoped they would not be able to refute.

"Maybe she just had the big secret! Remember, Sandi, I've got a big secret, you can't tell anybody, you can't tell your husband. Becky, I've got a big secret. Pete… I'm gonna go home, you're gonna love me no matter what.

"Now what do you think it was? I don't know; they didn't care. It wasn't 'I'm going home, and Michael and I are gonna be divorced, the lawyer's gonna walk the papers across the street, and the case is gonna be over.'

"Do you think in your heart of hearts that was the big secret? It was something we will never know.

"And they want you to look at insurance records, 'cause the guy's doing what he's supposed to be doing in a divorce and taking care of the premiums, so that equity gets taken care of. So a guy goes ahead and collects on insurance because his lawyer says to do it, his lawyer takes the money, and oohhh, he's a murderer!

"But, as his lawyer said, you're damned if you do, you're damned if ya don't! And you bet they're on the phone left and right! I would and you would!"

"And if they felt so good about the evidence, we wouldn't be sitting here in 1998, trying this case. They want you to convict Michael Albrecht for petty reasons.

"And don't forget he knows the neck muscle test that he does with his kids. He's so bad! He plays games with his kids, but hey, let's play the neck muscle test and while we're at it, let's bring in Crabby, and maybe he got fired and maybe he didn't. Who cares?

"What we know is Mrs. Delaney came in and said when Cindy was missing, he was upset, he was terrified. That's what we know. We know that he felt the pain, but he wasn't allowed to mourn the loss because he was excluded. He was shut out. His name wasn't even on the obituary that announced the memorial service.

"Kathleen said Mike was pretty upset because nobody told him about it.

"But that's just another thing, nobody even told him about it, because from day one those people and the police wouldn't consider anybody else.

"Now, folks, there's nothing we can do about Cindy. We can only mourn her loss and no matter what I say, it's been six years now, but I'm a parent also with two kids, and to these folks... I sincerely... I don't know what to say.

"I don't want it to be me, folks, ever, and I'm sorry for you. But right now, six years later, this man has his Father's Day tomorrow and I want you to give him his Father's Day with those girls! These girls that are lovely young ladies. These girls that are not liars!

"These girls want their daddy, and I ask you to disregard the incompetence you have been subjected to and acknowledge the truth!

"Michael Albrecht is innocent.

"I ask you to deliver him to his family and I ask you to do it and feel good about doing so. Thank you."

CHAPTER 48

John Commons had a mere eighteen minutes to quench the fiery arrows of Findling's allegations that investigators did not adequately investigate the murder and that the Albrecht family was being judged unfairly. He said, "I trust that you are not gonna make your decision based on who shouts the loudest or points the finger the most.

"Fairness and impartiality are the guidelines of being a juror. I have confidence that you will be fair and impartial and I realize that you cannot be swayed by a lot of shouting and accusations, and prancing around and pointing at individuals in the gallery, because you can analyze the evidence.

"The defense certainly threw that word perjury around a lot, didn't he? But I never heard Mr. Sells accuse those people of lying. Those are good folks. That's a nice family. They didn't deserve to have any of this come down on them. Nobody said any of them lied.

"He threw up the word perjury over and over and over again, saying that we would accuse them of perjury. Perjury: a person who makes a false, material statement under oath or affirmation, knowing the statement to be false or not believing it to be true. That's a perjurer. I am convinced that they believed every word they said. How could they be perjurers if they believe it?

"It doesn't mean it's true, it doesn't mean it's a fact; that's for you to decide. I'm not gonna make any accusations that those folks are perjurers." John Commons paused to make eye contact with each juror and then continued calmly. "A lot was made of this probable cause affidavit, which was marked as Defendant's Exhibit L, but they never bothered to put it in evidence so you could see it, did they? You've never seen that affidavit.

"It was marked, it was waved around, it was talked about, but they never put it in evidence, their exhibit. While Mr. Findling is making his accusations about incompetence, and bias, and inappropriate motives, ask yourself about his. If he wanted you to know what was in that affidavit wouldn't he have put it into evidence?

"Credibility of the witnesses. Well, no way I can talk about the sixty-three witnesses called over the course of the last two weeks. So, what I'm gonna try to do, and I hope this will be helpful to you, I'm going to discuss the law on the issue of credibility.

"In considering the testimony of any witness, you may take into account his or her ability and opportunity to observe, the manner and conduct of the witness while testifying, any interests, bias, or prejudice the witness may have, any relationship with other witnesses or interested parties, and the reasonableness of the testimony of the witness considered in light of all the evidence in the case.

"I'm going to speak to you very particularly about two people and that's Bill Filter and Kathleen Albrecht. Because let's face it, it is the conflict in their testimony where the real rub is in this case, the two o'clock in the morning.

"Now, I'm not even gonna call Kathleen Albrecht a liar. I think that she's convinced herself that he came home at two o'clock in the morning, but I don't believe that she knew that to be true back in the beginning of all this."

What about Bill Filter? Was he biased and prejudiced? The defense claimed he was "locked into his statement" as of September third. "Well, consider his testimony in light of his situation, because that is part of all the evidence. These folks cannot believe that their husband, brother, father, son could be a murderer, and I understand that, and I'm sure you do too.

"They want to believe every possible positive inference that would indicate that he's not; they want to believe it. In the terms of the law, that's an interest, a bias, a relationship. You must weigh that in evaluating Kathleen Albrecht's testimony, along with all the rest of them.

"Bill Filter, on the other hand, is charged with assisting a criminal. Specifically, assisting Michael Albrecht by providing a false alibi. There's two ways in the law you can become culpable for somebody else's act. One is being an accessory before the fact; one is being an accessory after the fact.

"You've all heard, somewhere along the line I'm sure, that the act of one is the act of all. If you're in a group, if you're a participant, and one of 'em does something and you're doing it together, you're all responsible for it. All right, that's an accessory before the fact. Accessory before the fact is chargeable with the same offense as the person who commits the crime.

"A person by law who is an accessory after the fact is chargeable with assisting a criminal and that's what Bill Filter did by providing a false alibi. Now, there's a very, very important thing about the charge of assisting a criminal."

Commons referred to a 1995 Indiana Supreme Court decision. The case involved a fellow who was convicted of assisting a criminal. "The guy he was alleged to have assisted, however, was acquitted, found not guilty. If the principal is found not guilty, the guy that's charged with assisting cannot, by law, be found guilty. So what does Bill Filter have at stake by coming to Indianapolis, after having provided a false alibi, and initially telling his lawyer that he had given an alibi, and then changing his story?

"What's the smart thing for him to do? Stick with the alibi. If the alibi is to be believed, then Michael Albrecht should be acquitted. You can't be in a different place and commit a crime somewhere else at the same time. We know that's impossible.

"If Michael Albrecht is acquitted, there's no case against Bill Filter. So what is the smart thing for Filter to do? Stick with the alibi. He went to a lawyer and talked to him about that. His lawyer has testified that they analyzed the case, that he told him that he had defenses available to him.

"And in spite of that, he comes down here and says that he lied about the alibi. Now what does he have to gain by that?

"He's just… he's just confirmed that the charge of assisting a guilty… the charge of assisting a criminal against him is in fact the right charge. He's just confirmed it. Now, I grant you that the statement can't be used against him because he was given immunity as to the use of that statement.

"Let me make that clear, I think it's clear already, but let me emphasize it one more time, that the immunity doesn't mean that he's not being prosecuted, can't be prosecuted, can't be convicted. It just means that that testimony can't be used against him. All the rest of the stuff can be. All the rest of it can be."

Larry wanted to applaud his partner for offering such a great argument. He tried to read the faces of the jurors. Were they convinced by Commons' logic?

"So he has just confirmed that he's guilty of that charge," Commons reiterated.

"Now, when someone comes before you and makes an admission to something that makes them guilty of a crime, and still is willing to come forward and say that, that's pretty persuasive it seems to me as to whether they're telling the truth or not. When the easier and smarter thing may have been to stick with the alibi.

"I do not ask you nor expect you to find that Kathleen Albrecht is a liar. I believe under the totality of the circumstances, you do have to find, however, that she is mistaken. That she has convinced herself. That she has been persuaded in part by the discussions that they had, and she wanted to believe that it is true, that he could not have done it.

"The father of her children. She's still part of the extended family. She still cares for him. She wants to believe that it's not true, but it is.

"We're here because this woman was murdered. I made a duplicate of that picture. I'm going to make some marks on it and I can't mark the exhibit, so I have a duplicate here.

"And I look at the totality of the evidence and let me suggest to you as well, that the testimony of Bill Filter alone is sufficient to convict Michael Albrecht of the murder of Cindy... Cynthia Albrecht. His testimony alone is sufficient, but you don't have to rely on only his testimony."

Commons had torn a copy of a crime scene photograph into pieces. "There's all the other testimony. All the other considerations." He posted a piece of the picture on the whiteboard. "You've got Randy Albrecht." He added another piece. Continuing to add pieces of the picture as he described his evidence. "You've got Filter and you've got these phone records. You've got Hernandez; you've got Ferrari, insurance issues. You've got his own statements, which are contradictory.

"There was not an eye witness to this murder, so there are other possibilities. In the instruction on reasonable doubt, there is a sentence that says, 'There are very few things in the world that we can know of absolute certainty, and in criminal cases, the law does not require proof that overcomes every possible doubt.' A reasonable doubt has to be a fair, logical, common sense doubt, based on the evidence."

The picture pieces when put together created an almost complete photo of Cindy's body. Though a few small pieces were missing, it was clear that the photograph depicted Cindy's murdered body.

Commons continued. "Now, what we have here are all these different factors. Obviously, this is not the whole testimony, but all together, collectively, when you put this piece with that piece, in this piece, and this piece, put them together as I know you will, when you analyze all the evidence, you have the picture of Cynthia Albrecht. You have the solution to the case.

"You don't have every answer to every question, but you know who it is, and you know what the evidence is. And this other?" He held up a missing piece. "Does that really add anything? Does that add anything to the answers to this case?

"No. Mr. Findling in the very opening sentence said apparently no one had confidence in this case. Well, I stand before you with confidence, complete confidence, that a fair and impartial analysis of the evidence in this case leads to one conclusion and one conclusion only: Michael Albrecht is guilty of murdering Cynthia Albrecht."

On that Saturday, June 20, 1998, with the conclusion of Commons' argument, everything that could be done to either convict or release Michael Albrecht had been done. Larry Sells and John Commons were as weary as dust. They could not gauge whether they had won or not. All their hopes rested with the group of strangers in the jury box.

CHAPTER 49

After a brutal two week trial that began on Monday, June 8, 1998, on Saturday, June 20, the Marion Superior Court jury went into final deliberations. The waiting was intense, but Becky and Sandi refused to leave the courthouse. They finally ordered a pizza. Just before it was delivered, word came that the jury had ended eight hours of deliberation and was returning to the courtroom.

The women paid for the pizza and asked the deputy at the door to eat it. Appetites forgotten, they dashed back to the courtroom. When the guilty verdict was announced at nine p.m., friends and family of Cindy Albrecht hugged each other and sobbed for joy. Justice at last.

Michael sat pale and stone-faced; his family was silent and shocked. Richard Kammen announced that he too was shocked at the guilty verdict. Mike's other defense attorney, Drew Findling, complained that the case languished for years and then "they focused on the easy guy to look at."

Cindy's father, Louis Woodward, announced to the media, "It's the most wonderful Father's Day present I could ever have." He added, "I feel sorry for Mike's family."

Sentencing was set for ten a.m. on July twenty-fourth.

At Michael's sentencing hearing, Findling asked his family to speak to the Court. Each in turn was brought to the witness stand and sworn in. The first spokesperson was Denise Albrecht, Michael's current wife. She had met Michael at the BMW dealership where they both worked, in February 1993. They married in September of 1995. Findling asked her if there was anything she wanted to address to Judge Mangus-Stinson, "understanding that this is a sentencing?"

"I am an intelligent woman," Denise replied. "If I had any doubt in my mind, if I were afraid, I wouldn't have married him. It's a horrible thing to have somebody killed and decapitated. There are other men. I didn't have to marry him, but I fell in love with him, and I stuck by what I thought was right. I love him with all my heart.

"I will stand by you for the rest of my life. I know that you didn't do this." Denise said that she was sorry for the pain endured by those who had lost Cindy, but she insisted that anyone who knew Michael, his friends and family, knew he could not have committed the crime.

Michael's sister, April Hafemann was the next speaker. "I am Mike's little sister, and I grew up knowing that this man was my protector. I have four brothers. I had one that was cruel to me and that was my youngest brother. I had two that were just off into their own things and kind of ignored me until I got older, but this man, he took me for walks, he talked to me, he took care of my child when I didn't have the money after my divorce. Never asked me for a dime."

April told the Court that she loved Michael, that he was not capable of this murder, and that the accusations sickened her. She said, "Something has to be done to fix this, because what's happening today is not right. This man should have been set free, and I promise everyone in this room that I will work for the rest of my life to make sure that that happens."

"Mr. Albrecht would like to make a statement, Your Honor," said Findling. But Michael wanted to wait until the other speakers were done.

Rebecca Miller, Sandra Fink, and Pete Twiddy read victim's impact statements. The two women stood as those who had a close personal relationship with the victim. Twiddy stood as appointed speaker on behalf of Cindy's family. Kammen tried to object, but the judge said, "Well, the victim representative by statute is a person who has had a close personal relationship with the victim of a felony who is deceased. So they fit under the statute."

Becky Miller took the stand and Larry asked her, "And you realize that we're here today for the Court to determine what the appropriate sentence or punishment is for Michael Albrecht within the parameters of the law, what the law allows. You understand that?"

Becky did understand that Michael could be sentenced to a term of thirty to sixty years. She had worked long hours to craft her letter, agonizing over the specific words she wanted to say in the face of the man convicted of slaughtering her close friend and ripping away a piece of her soul.

"The reason we are here today is there are victims and there are volunteers," Becky began. "There's a vast difference between the two. Cindy is the victim here, and not Michael Albrecht. He is the only volunteer in this room.

"Because this coward felt it was his job to end Cindy's life, we have all been robbed of her goodness. From this point forward, Michael Albrecht should be entitled to nothing, no choices. He has had his fair trial, he has had his day in court, and he has had five and a half years of freedom. His time is up.

"It's time for him to take what's left of his life and be locked away from society. I know I would never trust him to walk among any of us again. He should not have any opportunity or choice except to live or die in prison.

"Mike, you remember us calling you from Cindy's apartment that morning even before we called the police. We knew then that you had done something to her. We just hoped in our naïve minds that you were holding her at your house and tormenting her like you used to love to do. We truly hoped that we could save her from you.

"Well, we're not naïve anymore, and we can't save Cindy, but since you didn't get away with this, you'll be locked up, you'll never hurt or kill anybody again.

"Because of Michael Albrecht's actions, all of our lives have changed forever, but besides knowing that evil walks among us, we've also made great friends and found many people that care and truly try to find justice for victims like Cindy.

"She was more loved than anyone you can imagine. Cindy was a wonderful person, and Mike will never destroy that memory each of us keeps of her. She still lives in many of our hearts.

"We'll never know if Cindy would have had children or opened that little restaurant she dreamed of someday, but we do know there was some sense of justice in this court for Cindy. There was nothing else that we could possibly do for her. Please, Your Honor, make sure this amoral creature never has another opportunity or another choice. Show Michael Albrecht the same mercy that he showed Cindy.

"Thank you to everyone, especially the jury, who showed the strength of character to do the correct and honorable thing for Cindy and all victims like her."

Becky's letter appeared to have moved everyone in the courtroom; everyone but Michael, that is. He sat looking detached, as if waiting for a long commercial break to end.

Sandi Fink took the stand next, knowing that this would be the last time she would ever see Michael Albrecht. She could not get him out of her life fast enough, but she was going to have one final say. Larry said to her, "You understand you have a right now to express your feelings and opinions about what the appropriate sentence should be in this case and what you would like the Court to do."

"Yes," Sandi replied.

"So feel free to do so now." He stepped back, not realizing he had just released a hurricane.

"I honestly don't know how to tell you exactly what Cindy Albrecht meant to me. She was my dearest friend." Sandi struggled to keep her voice steady, appropriate for court. She had waited years for this day and was determined not to mess up. She read, "She was supportive, never judgmental, and thoughtful beyond belief.

"She was really too nice. Becky and I used to tell her that all the time. We called her Ellie Mae. She tried to encourage and help people.

"Now she's just another statistic. Murdered, dumped in the woods with no head, bared naked for the entire world to see on October twenty-fifth. That's a real special day. That's my birthday, my birthday. Happy birthday to me. Now every year instead of celebrating life, I remember the horror of death. Thank you.

"I have children that knew Cindy and I have young twin boys that will never know Cindy. These kids have been robbed of their innocence at such a young, impressionable age. It's quite impossible to explain how you can cut someone's head off and then go to Florida on vacation for five years. Explain that to young children.

"If he had been in jail back then," Sandi continued, "he wouldn't have had the opportunity to victimize another unknowing woman, the latest Mrs. Albrecht. Lord only knows what would have happened to her had she ever tried to escape his clutches. Mike did a great job keeping all his women thinking they could do no better than him. After all, he got the ex-Mrs. Albrecht to sleep with him a whole month before the dead Mrs. Albrecht even moved out of their marital home.

"And regarding the statement that Cindy broke up Mike's first marriage, well, Cindy was not the one that was married, Mike was. Mike's the one that broke his marital vows, Mike's the one that broke his promises to his children.

"We heard Mike described in here as a wonderful father. Well, let me tell you, wonderful fathers do not go visit their children with their dead wife in the trunk. And friends? Your only friend now, Mike, is denial. As long as you have denial, and you can live and sleep with denial, then you can keep your sanity.

"None of us were ever quite sure how Crabby went from slot car champion to IndyCar mechanic in two years, but we were certainly never impressed. He called teammates nasty names, which I can't say in court, on a daily basis."

Michael Albrecht sat unmoving, ignoring Sandi as if she were a fly on the other side of the room. He was possibly aware, though, of her husband, Mike Fink, who glared at him from the railing.

Sandi continued reading. "I think he really thought he was Spock from *Star Trek* when he administered his neck muscle test. But you never tried that on the big boys like my husband, did you? Because he'd have knocked your block off, Lurch. You always thought you were so intimidating, but you're the biggest coward I've ever had the horror of knowing.

"You couldn't stand the thought of Cindy doing anything superior to you, so you killed her because you couldn't stand the fact that you're a failure. I mean, really, working for Dick Simon in the IndyCar business is the bottom of the barrel. Everybody knows what a liar and cheat Dick Simon is, unlike Mr. Ferrari, who came in here and told this Court the truth.

"That's all we ever wanted. That is all any of us ever wanted, was the truth. Cindy did not have a secret life. She had no thing with Matt Kernel. He was a pawn used by the defense to divert the attention away from Mr. Albrecht, the murderer.

"Obviously, I'm mad. I am really mad. I'm furious. I can barely control myself, let's put it that way. Looking at you makes me sick. You know the-the motions you made while I was testifying about your wife, like I was making you sick?

You remember. Your attorneys had a little discussion with you about it, not to do that.

"We didn't sign up to be part of this, Mike. You did this to us. You never counted on Cindy having friends like Becky and I. You know, we showed her how to wear cute clothes and fix her hair, and we actually made her laugh. Various accusations have been made regarding Becky and I, but we are the ones that have never rested over the last six years, all because we loved our friend so much.

"You deserve to die just like Cindy did, with big, strong hands wrapped around your neck, squeezing and squeezing and squeezing until you don't have another breath left."

Sandi's rage was palpable and when she snapped her fingers at Michael, someone whispered "Barbie doll gone mad" to Derrik Thomas, the ABC news reporter. He had to step out into the hall before his laughter erupted.

"There are no holds barred in a sentencing hearing," Larry explained.

Sandi nodded. Michael was dismissing her and she was livid.

"You can roll your eyes all you want. I think it's funny. You're in a pretty bad position right now, Mr. Albrecht. Maybe prison life will live up to its reputation. I certainly hope so. I hope you get everything there that you've ever dreamed of. I implore you, Judge, to give this evil man the maximum sentence. It's the very least he deserves."

Before Pete Twiddy took the stand, Larry questioned him about an event on Saturday morning. "Before court started that morning, before the judge entered the courtroom, or at least before the proceedings started, did you receive a communication from the defendant, Michael Albrecht?"

"Yes, I did," Pete replied.

Larry said, "Would you please tell the judge about that?"

"When I was sitting... I believe it was the second row there, I was sitting there, looked over at Mike," Pete related, "he positioned himself between the two lawyers and mouthed to me, 'you're next,' smiled, and winked. That's about it."

Having reported this incident, Pete was then invited to make his victim's impact statement. He said, "I don't have anything prepared today, Judge. This has been a long, long five and a half years of my life, the worst five and a half years of my life.

"But the one thing I've realized lately is the number of people that Cindy affected, and people that didn't even know her. When I went to the last two races ago in Cleveland, literally hundreds of people came up to me to express their condolences, people that couldn't say anything to me before this, that didn't know what to say, wanted to come up to me and-and-and express, you know, the feelings that they'd had over these periods of time, and tell me stories about how she'd affected them, how she had basically put some light in some of their lives. And to see the pain still on-on people's faces because she's gone...

"I went in to see Roger Penske, and he sat there and he just shook his head and looked at me and he-he said, 'thank you, you did a good job.' And he couldn't talk anymore. And I said, 'do you want to talk about it,' and he looked at me and said, 'I can't talk about it, it still hurts me so much that I can't even speak about it.'

"I walked out of the trailer and ran into Kathy Penske, and she sat there and she grabbed my hand and she looked at me and she welled up with tears and her mouth started—and I think she-she probably put it best. She looked at me and she said, 'That man killed an angel.'

"And he did. She was a magnificent person, she was a great worker, and then she became a great lover. She-she was the highlight of my life, and now we have many, many victims, as the family has spoken about, Mike's family has been talked about. All these victims over here, Cindy's family, they loved her very, very much.

"They've had to endure this, to go on through this, to live through this, and people tell me we're reaching justice here. It's not the justice that I know. I've grown up all my life believing an eye for an eye. But the law does not believe in that, and him living in jail is going to be justice.

"I don't know that I believe that, but the only thing that's kept me going is the hope and belief that justice would prevail and that we would come to the correct sentence here.

"And my belief is-is that if we send him to jail with the opportunity of getting out, that would enable him to continue on. I think he needs to understand the horrors and everything that he now faces in jail. And he's a real tough guy with a hundred-and-twenty-pound girl. It's too bad I don't have the opportunity to show him what a man's all about.

"So, I-I plead with you, and-and ask you to give him whatever the max is, because there's no sentence you can give him today that's going to make up for Cindy's loss. It is not going to make up for anybody's pain. It is not going to bring her back. And we all have to move on, and the only way we can move on is to know that the maximum has been given here."

CHAPTER 50

From his seat at the defense table, Michael Albrecht made a final statement to the Court. "Your Honor, first I'd like to express my sympathy to Cynthia's family for their loss. They were friends at one point," he said. "I've shed my share of tears over her loss, certainly, but I'd like to state for the record that I am not guilty of this crime, no matter what the jury has decided.

"Far as I was concerned, the trial was nothing more than a grave injustice. The prosecutor's case was built on deceit, using testimony from witnesses who benefit from their own lies. I've had to sit here and listen to people make personal remarks against me. Pete's ridiculous accusation that I made a comment to him that he's next is-is absolutely ludicrous.

"I sat here and conducted myself as professionally as I could, listened to people tell lies, and just sat and took it, and I'm not going to stoop as low as they have and point the finger back. We didn't do that during the trial, I'm not going to do it now.

"No direct evidence was ever presented, and I believe that reasonable doubt has existed through the entire trial. A wrongful conviction resulted, and I will tell you that I intend to fight this through all legal channels that are possible to me until justice is served. Thank you."

The courtroom fell to silence. Becky and Sandi seethed with the desire to shout Michael down but they maintained control. Had Michael's speech resonated with Judge Mangus-

Stinson? Earned him a lighter sentence? They could not read her face. *Please,* their hearts begged, *the maximum sentence. Make him pay for what he did to Cindy.*

There would be ample opportunity to celebrate once the steel doors slammed behind Michael. He was guilty. Proven guilty. But how guilty did the judge think he was?

Larry Sells signaled the judge. "One question," he said. "One."

Nodding his thanks to the judge, he stood at the end of the prosecution's table nearest to the defense, less than ten feet from Michael Albrecht. Larry stared directly into Michael's eyes, then hit the table with a startling **smack**!

His one question, his final question. "Where is Cindy's head?"

His voice reverberated through the windowless courtroom.

Newscaster Derrik Thomas said the silence was unreal, an actual pin drop moment.

"We obviously object." Kammen's voice squeaked a bit.

"I'll sustain the objection," replied the judge.

But Larry stood there, towering over Michael and his lawyers. The question hung like a deep, underwater breath for a solid two minutes.

Finally, Michael spoke. "You're asking the wrong man, sir."

With Larry's question still quivering the air, it became Kammen's task to plead for a softer sentence for his client. Kammen said to the judge, "I know that the law places upon you the responsibility to sentence Michael, and it's difficult in this situation, because we're not dealing with the typical situation.

"We're dealing with the situation where I believe that Michael was innocent, but the jury has convicted him, and we all have to live with that."

Larry found the defense attorney's argument neither novel nor interesting. Sure. His client was innocent and the rest of the world was wrong. Tell that to Cindy!

Sitting quietly, he took careful note of the arguments Kammen tossed to the judge. He and Commons had just won a very hard case and they were not about to let Michael's lawyers persuade the Court to give him a padded sentence. It still galled him that because he could not produce a murder weapon or an eyewitness, he'd been unable to seek the death penalty.

Kammen said of the State's case that "this crime did not happen the way they said it did." He claimed that the timeframe for the drive from Milwaukee to Indianapolis was impossible even if Kathleen was wrong about the time Michael returned.

How did the crime happen? Kammen reflected that "the truth of the matter is that we do not know, and the jury has accepted a theory that makes no sense."

While others had said that their faith in the system would be shaken if Michael did not receive the maximum sentence, "I have to tell you my faith in the system is shaken because of the verdict," Kammen said.

Filter, Kammen claimed, had benefited from "the practice of exchanging leniency for testimony." The Tenth Court of Appeals had exposed the practice as "nothing more than a legal bribe." Filter had been given a bond he could not make and an opportunity to free himself from it. It was a tragedy that Filter had benefited from the system, Kammen told the Court.

"The lawyer in me says, well, you know, the presumptive sentence is forty years, and if we look at this coldly and critically, any other murder, I mean murder is a horrible thing, and I don't know that we can distinguish between one horror and another," Kammen said.

He added that he understood Cindy's family's need to believe that justice had been done, "but we all know, as we look inside our souls, that whatever happened that night did not happen the way the State suggested."

Kammen acknowledged that the judge, knowing the pros and cons, the aggravators and mitigators, and the law, must make a decision about Michael's fate, "and it would be disingenuous of me for me to sit here and-and try to say more than-than what I've said, Your Honor."

It was now Findling's turn to convince the judge that Michael was worthy of leniency. He began by expressing his sorrow to the Albrecht family "for what they're experiencing in the loss of Michael for so many years." He also acknowledged the grief of Cindy's family, saying he was sincerely sorry for their pain.

Nevertheless, his concerns, he told the judge, were, "I look at the issue of residual doubt," and "I believe in my client's innocence."

He did not mention Cindy's innocence.

"There are issues that Your Honor was privy to," Findling said, adding that they were "forced to stay away from certain issues," including the lie detector test and Matt Kernel's current legal issues. "But what Your Honor knows is that at the end of 1992 through the end of 1996, Newton County prosecutors had this case. Two administrations of Newton County prosecutors investigated this case."

Those prosecutors of Newton County had "invested money in flying to Florida to be part of an investigation of Cindy's death and whether or not specifically Michael Albrecht had anything to do with her death."

With all the evidence they had, "they made the decision not to prosecute Michael Albrecht," Findling said. Yet Marion County prosecutors had come to court with the same weak evidence, but "the prosecutors in Marion County made a decision to approach Bill Filter." Again, Kammen said, they acted within the law, so there is no slamming them and saying they did something illegal.

"But I can't help but say had the defense done what they did, as Your Honor knows, that would have been obstruction of justice. Had we gone to a State's witness and said, this is what we can offer you for your testimony, that would be obstruction of justice, which is one of the reasons now in half a dozen states in the United States of America, as the law stands right now, the prosecution of Michael Albrecht would have been impossible."

His residual doubt then focused on Filter's bought testimony. "What shocked me most of all… is that Lieutenant Jones, in one of the more shocking re-direct examinations of my career, if not the most shocking, turns to the jury on questions of the prosecution and says, I even believe that Mr. Filter's testimony is not right and that he— perhaps even he had something to do with it. Even Lieutenant Jones believes that perjury was perpetrated on this jury.

"And I think when you look at all these things, to me, it's that residual doubt that a Court should take into consideration when it hands out its sentence in this case," Findling concluded.

CHAPTER 51

Called upon to state his case, Larry Sells reminded the Court, "The case has been tried, verdict has been rendered, a verdict based upon the law and the evidence. I take exception to the fact that getting someone to finally tell the truth, however long it may take, amounts to obstruction of justice.

"And even though Lieutenant Jones may have had the impression, based upon everything that he knew, that perhaps William Filter was more involved than he was willing to acknowledge, that does not mean that, in fact, he was, and I-I would not present to this Court what I consider to be perjured testimony for any reason.

"I don't know what information the Newton County prosecutor's office through two terms of prosecutors reviewed in deciding whether or not to file charges in this case, and it's really not relevant to these proceedings.

"I know what evidence I reviewed, and it left no questions in my mind about the guilt of Michael Albrecht, and I stand here today with not one single doubt in my mind of his guilt, no doubt whatsoever.

"Even if they want to call Randy Albrecht a liar, and to call Antonio Ferrari a liar, but even if they wish to do that, the evidence just does not lie.

"Besides the phone records, those insurance premium checks that were made out by the defendant do not lie. Those are there. There's no question about it. The only possible reason that he would make those premiums is either because he's a psychic and knows something is going to happen to her so he makes those payments, or he intends to do something to her himself and he wants to profit from that, in addition to getting even with her.

"I stood here and said I wasn't going to argue guilt or innocence, and I'll stop there. Just some things I wanted to get off my chest, Judge.

"We ask the Court to consider the character of the defendant. Anyone who, after sitting through two weeks of testimony, condemning testimony as to his actions, could sit there and look across the room at a person and make the comment *you're next* is completely devoid of character, and that is something we ask the Court to consider.

"Let's get to the circumstances themselves, Judge, a little bit more particularly. We don't know the shock, pain, and horror that Cynthia Albrecht experienced when she was killed. We would hope that it happened quickly. Dr. Pless testified that it happened quickly.

"But nonetheless, there had to be some agonizing seconds or moments for Cynthia Albrecht. And certainly, her soul had to agonize over what happened to her afterwards, being left naked in the woods, her head severed.

"And certainly, her family and friends have agonized for nearly six years since this occurred, and that's something that the Court should consider in imposing a sentence in this case.

"Mr. Twiddy indicated that his beliefs have always been that a person should receive an eye for an eye when they commit a wrong. Well, we can't do that. The law does say that the punishment should fit the crime, but it does not provide for an eye for an eye.

"We can't creep around like a coward in the night and spring upon him and choke the life out of him, crush his windpipe, break his neck. We can't stuff him like a spare tire in the trunk of the car and carry him around for hours. We can't drag him into the woods, demonically sever his head, leave his naked, headless body on the ground like road kill for buzzards and maggots and rats to feed on.

"We can't carry the head away like a trophy and dispose of it so it would never, ever be found. We cannot subject him, Your Honor, to the same indignities that he subjected Cynthia Albrecht to and that he caused her family and friends to have to relive on a daily basis and will for the rest of their lives.

"We can't do that, Judge. We are too civilized to do that. But we can put him away in a place where he can spend the majority of the rest of his life thinking about what he has done to Cynthia Albrecht, to her friends and family, and to his own family.

"I can understand, and I respect the feelings that the Albrecht family has for their beloved son and husband and father and brother. I don't share those feelings. And I think it's time, Your Honor, it's finally time for Michael Albrecht to pay the price for the depraved acts that he's committed, and the only fitting punishment is the maximum punishment which the law provides, which everybody who knows the punishment system in this State knows is only half of what this Court gives him, and, without question, it is probably not sufficient for these acts. But we would ask for the maximum sentence and urge the Court to impose it."

Judge Mangus-Stinson explained to those present the factors that she, as the Court, would have to consider in sentencing Michael. First, she said, was the risk that Michael would commit another crime. She noted that a defendant with minimal or any prior criminal history "but who commits a very serious crime" makes it "difficult for me to assess" the risk.

"Under the facts as found by the jury," she continued, "the crime is that upset by his wife's desire to leave the marriage, her success, her finding happiness, he found a way to get his revenge and stop that happiness. I suppose the risk that he'll commit another crime might be dependent upon him getting involved in circumstances like that, which he'll be unable to do in the Department of Corrections. But, in any event, I can't eliminate that risk because the fact is, the jury has found that he committed this crime.

"Turning to the nature and circumstances of the crime committed, the facts, I think, were summarized well with respect to those circumstances that you pointed out, Mr. Sells; that is, the substantial planning that was involved in the crime, the desire for profit, and the dismemberment of the victim following the crime."

As for the character of the defendant, the judge said, "I think that the evidence supported a finding that he was domineering, if not controlling, of Cindy until she got a little bit more self-esteem, found herself with some confidence in the world, and didn't like the fact that he lost control as she moved on in her life.

"On the other hand," Judge Mangus-Stinson added, "you can't look at Michael Albrecht's three daughters and not give him a little credit. Mind you, he was absent a lot of their life, but they were beautiful girls who I believe, based on the evidence, their stepmother loved very much.

"Another thing that sticks in my mind was pretrial testimony, but there was testimony at one of the races... prior to this happening... between the defendant and Cindy Albrecht was to try to impose guilt on her for how the girls would be reacting to the divorce and the separation, and using those girls in that way is troubling to me because those girls love their father."

The judge said of Michael Albrecht's daughters, "I believe they're nice girls who came in and told the truth, and so there's a side to the defendant's character that has to be accounted for to his favor with respect to them."

Other significant facts the judge said needed to be considered were Michael left town following Cindy's disappearance and continued to pay insurance premiums when he knew they were separated.

The Court also needed to analyze mitigators, facts in favor of the defendant, and aggravators. The judge said, "The defense has argued the mitigator of residual doubt. The Court rejects that mitigator for this reason. For two weeks of their lives, twelve people plus three… listened to the evidence in this case thoughtfully, thoroughly, asked good questions, paid careful, careful attention to what went on in this courtroom, and they reached a decision that I am not about to in any way diminish or disagree with.

"I think that the most important point about Mr. Filter and the circumstance of his statement and his testimony is that every fact that went into his statement giving and testimony was disclosed.

"He was cross-examined at length. The jury was well aware of the circumstances of his statement. That was for them to weigh.

"I think the girls will miss their dad and they love their dad. But their loss is minimal compared to the loss of Ms. Albrecht's family and friends and the terror and horror that they have had to relive.

"For aggravating circumstances, the Court finds dismemberment to be an aggravator. Dismemberment is considered an aggravating circumstance sufficient to warrant the death penalty in Indiana," the judge said.

"I also find that substantial planning went into the crime. I find that as an aggravator. That it was for profit. I find that as an aggravator. And then it's my responsibility to weigh those aggravators against the mitigators in the case."

Besides these issues, the judge went on record regarding the delay in prosecution. "I certainly don't know what went into that decision… but there may well have been an issue of resources," she said of the Newton County prosecutor's decision.

"So, the Court does find that the aggravators outweigh the mitigators. That is, the Court finds that the defendant's plan to kill his wife, to stop her happiness, to stop her leaving him, the timing of the killing immediately prior to the finalization of the divorce, the dismemberment of her body, and the collection of proceeds from her insurance policy after that far outweighs the fact that he doesn't have much of a prior criminal history or the loss to his children, who can still visit him where he'll be staying."

With all this said, Larry and Cindy's loved ones listened anxiously for the final pronouncement. "And so, the Court does believe in this case that the maximum sentence is appropriate and will impose a sentence of sixty years…" Her words were cool water on a painful burn. "…sixty years executed, to be served in the Department of Corrections."

She began to explain to Michael his rights to appeal. She asked about his financial situation. He and his wife did own a home but he owed debts for attorney's fees and had no money in the bank to speak of.

Kammen said, "Your Honor, he is indigent personally. His family may or may not employ counsel."

The judge responded, "Well, just because we have a thirty-day deadline, and because of the length of the sentence—is all the money from the insurance gone?"

It was. The Court would need to hire him a pauper attorney.

Judge Mangus-Stinson ended the hearing by addressing Cindy's loved ones. "I want to express my condolences to the family. While this process is over, I know your loss is not, and I think Ms. Miller mentioned that at least there has been some good come out of this, to know that people will support you and stand by you and work with you, and I can only tell you that the comments about your daughter, your sister, your friend, your loved one are universally positive. She was obviously very special and I know your loss is, therefore, all the more great. But I would remind you that you have each other, and the system has done the best that it can. Thank you."

CHAPTER 52

Larry, Pete, Sandi, and Becky met at Union Jack's to celebrate the verdict. Most of the IndyCar people who had helped in the search and attended the memorial service were back home or at jobs, but about twenty other people arrived to help celebrate. The manager brought them Dom Perignon. Sandi says she still has the cork. "It's in the box."

She still carries the hurt. "I think that a lot of people who are against the death penalty or against this or against that never had a personal tragedy such as this that affects them. Passing judgment on something they know nothing about. But it changed our lives. It changed us forever." Before 1992, she had believed the death penalty was right "but not with the same passion. They better never call me for jury duty because he's guilty."

Pete Twiddy's wound is eternally deep. Hey says, "If it weren't for Larry, I wouldn't be here. I'd be in prison or I'd be dead." In the years since the trial, he has married and found happiness. That does not mean he has lost his desire to mangle Michael.

Becky says, "He thought he was home free." The celebration of justice for Cindy also carried a wave of relief. "All the time we were going through this there was a little bit of that in the back of your head: What's he going to do to us if he gets loose? Because we were the main ones and he knew it.

"Sandi made her husband come to the sentencing just for that intimidation factor, and I remember him standing at the rail just glaring at Mike Albrecht." This makes her smile.

All through the trial, Larry nibbled through the wires of the defense's panoramic show of Matt Kernel as the killer. A druggie with a fractured eye socket could never plan and pull off such a tidy killing. Why, when he was in too much pain to get off the sofa, would he drive the body one-hundred-ten miles when he had a lake on his own property?

Larry countered the defense on each punch, knowing that he knew the case better than they did. He allowed the defense to tear down his witnesses, confident that he would build them back up. He had run a great race and says he owes a huge debt to the chief mechanic in his own legal garage.

"I give a lot of credit to Scott Wyatt," Larry says. "Without him, the case could not have been won." Wyatt was working behind the scenes, gathering court decisions that supported Larry Sells' and John Commons' objections. Larry described Wyatt as "the smartest kid in law school." He did research, brief writing, addressed legal issues, and prepared for Michael's extradition.

Wyatt took care of the paperwork, getting everything in order for the extradition, and called Larry when they were ready to get on the plane.

Larry wanted to go for the death penalty, but the call was made by County Prosecutor Scott Newman. Their decision was to walk away from the death penalty because the evidence was mainly circumstantial. Larry opted to fight for the longest prison sentence allowed: sixty years.

Larry notes that on the night he killed Cindy, Michael carried her body out the back door and very carefully closed the patio door to her apartment. This was done to keep the cats inside and safe. Michael killed his wife but he loved the cats.

Judge Jane Mangus-Stinson gave birth to a seven-pound baby girl on August 6, 1998. On June 9, 2010, Judge Magnus-Stinson became a judge of the United States District Court for the Southern District of Indiana. She is now Chief Judge of that court.

Becky Miller and Sandi Fink have enjoyed long and happy marriages. They have sons in college who love racing.

On June 4, 2023, Michael G. Albrecht will
be eligible for release from prison.
In accordance with Indiana State law, he will have,
at that time, paid the full price
for Cindy's life.

Larry's Notes:

The jury was advised by Detective Lieutenant Bill Jones of the entire law enforcement investigative efforts, thanks in large part to the defense "opening the door." Otherwise inadmissible evidence was permitted by the Court to rebut the constant defense assertions that law enforcement did not do its job. After Jones testified, it was obvious to all, except the defense, that no stone was left unturned. That every potential witness or suspect was questioned, often more than once. That all available forensic evidence was gathered and tested. That voluminous records were obtained. The evidence pointed to one inescapable conclusion, that Michael Albrecht killed Cindy.

His lawyer knew nothing about the insurance Albrecht had on Cindy's life until Albrecht told him about it. Albrecht told him because he needed legal help to get it, and the lawyer happily accommodated him for a substantial fee.

PHOTOS

Al and Shelley Unser in the Winner's Circle with "mini"
Al and daughter, Cody after the 1992 Indianapolis 500.

Al Unser Jr. won the Championship of CART (Championship Auto Racing Teams) driving for Penske in 1994.

Larry Sells in 1998. He still has a reputation as a fierce and tireless prosecutor.

ALBRECHT, MICHAEL G

Michael Albrecht.

George Harrison of Beatles' fame with his lovely wife, Olivia, standing on top of the Penske trailer.

Filming the "Racing Justice" episode for Investigation Discovery. (l-r) Sandi Fink, Bill Jones, Paula Zahn, Becky Miller, and Larry Sells.

Bill Jones with Pete Twiddy behind him. They both stood as champions for Cindy Albrecht.

Becky Miller and Sandi Fink still toast Cindy each October 25th, the day of her death and also Sandi's birthday.

Judge Jane Mangus-Stinson is now Chief Judge of the United States District Court for the Southern District of Indiana.

In the Penske kitchen, Cindy Albrecht, Sandi Fink, and Rebecca Miller often cooked up more fun than food.

One exciting breath before the 1992 Indianapolis 500, Cindy Albrecht, Sandi Fink, and Rebecca Miller gather at the Wild West Themed Marlboro party.

Laguna Seca California race, Oct. 1992. End of race, end of season. (l-r) Sandi Fink, Cindy Albrecht, Mike Fink, Rebecca Miller, and Debbie Stringer. This was their last photo. The girls would never see each other again.

Laguna Seca, California, 1992. Rebecca Miller and Cindy Albrecht. Last race of the season and last hug.

May 1992. Fun during break time at the kitchen trailer. Cindy pranked the photo by making herself "headless." (clockwise from top left) Cindy Albrecht, Rebecca Miller, Bob Lawes, and Sandi Fink.

"Pretty, kind-hearted Cindy." This photo, demonstrating Cindy Albrecht's "Ellie Mae" personality was displayed during the murder trial.

*Moments before the accident that knocked
out her teeth, Cindy Albrecht prepares to ride
the waves at Skeleton Lake, Canada.*

Cindy Albrecht could drive the wheels off a pace car.

In 1992 Indy 500, Al Unser Jr. Wins over Scott Goodyear by .043 seconds. It was the closest race in the history of the Indianapolis 500.

Investigators believe Cindy's body was carried out of the apartment and through a path in the woods.

For More News About Larry Sells and Margie Porter, Signup For Our Newsletter:

http://wbp.bz/newsletter

Word-of-mouth is critical to an author's long-term success. If you appreciated this book please leave a review on the Amazon sales page:

http://wbp.bz/rtja

CHAPTER ONE

TURNABOUT

Green Bay's television stations led off their newscasts with a chilling mystery on Thursday night, November 3, 2005.

A fiercely independent, happy-go-lucky young woman from the heart of dairy country was gone. No one had seen or heard from her during the past four days. Television anchors painted a grim outlook as photos of Teresa Halbach flashed across the screen. Viewers were left uneasy and fearful of a worst-case scenario. Surely someone watching the distressing news would remember encountering Teresa over the past few days. At least, that's what the small-town Calumet County Sheriff's Office in Chilton, Wisconsin hoped.

But it was not Teresa's face displayed on the television screen that drew a red flag with one of the Manitowoc County residents. It was the image of her missing sports utility vehicle, a Toyota RAV 4.

During that time frame, Kevin Rahmlow lived around Mishicot, a small but proud Wisconsin town of 1,400, people of German, Swiss, and Bohemian heritage. Back in the day, Mishicot had six hotels, three general stores, a movie theater, a grist mill, and a brewery. By 2005, the community's three original churches still stood the test of time but Mishicot looked different. The town's gas station, owned by Cenex, was one of the local hangouts. People came there for fuel, a cup of coffee, and to buy their cigarettes. The popular business was at the corner of State Highway 147 and State Street.

Kevin Rahmlow vividly remembers when he pulled into the Cenex. It was Friday, November 4. Inside the convenience store, the missing person's poster caught his eye. Teresa Marie Halbach, the flier noted, was 5-foot-6, 135 pounds. Brown eyes and light brown hair.

"I remember that the poster had a picture of Teresa Halbach and written descriptions of Teresa Halbach and the car she was driving," Rahmlow said.

As it turned out, Cenex was one of many small-town businesses, bars, and cafes where Teresa's concerned friends and family slapped up posters. They were desperate for answers, hoping somebody, anybody, remembered a sighting. And if the locals didn't see Teresa, perhaps they saw her Toyota RAV4. It had a large Lemieux Toyota sign on the back of her vehicle where the spare tire hung.

When Rahmlow saw the poster, he remembered something.

"On November 3 and 4, 2005, I was in Mishicot. I saw Teresa Halbach's vehicle by the East Twin River dam in Mishicot at the turnabout by the bridge as I drove west of Highway 147. I recognized that the written description of the vehicle on the poster matched the car I saw at the turnaround by the dam."

That Friday afternoon, Rahmlow happened to spot a man in a brown uniform. The man was sporting a badge. "While I was in the Cenex station, a Manitowoc County Sheriff's Department officer came into the station. I immediately told the officer that I had seen a car that matched the description of the car on Teresa Halbach's missing person poster at the turnaround by the dam."

After speaking with the uniformed deputy, Rahmlow went on with his life.

He had no idea whatever became of the matter. He later moved to another Midwest state. He even missed the initial Making a Murderer craze on Netflix that captured world-wide attention.

**

In December 2015, a true crime documentary about the Steven Avery murder case was released on Netflix, but Rahmlow didn't get swept up in the media frenzy. An entire year passed before he finally turned on Netflix to watch it. And as he watched Making a Murderer, the Minnesota man had a flashback. He remembered his encounter at the gas station in Mishicot from more than a decade ago. And besides being familiar with Manitowoc County, Rahmlow knew some of the key people who worked hand in hand with special prosecutor Ken Kratz to cement the guilt of Steven

Avery. Avery, as the world now knows, was a previously wrongfully convicted man who lost eighteen years due to a barbaric daytime rape along the Lake Michigan shoreline during the summer of 1985. This was the crime that allowed dangerous sexual predator Gregory Allen to get away by the forces who ran the Manitowoc County Sheriff's Office, notably Sheriff Tom Kocourek, who was about forty years old at the time.

Fast-forward to 2007. Avery stood trial in Chilton for Teresa's murder even though the prosecution's evidence was like a piece of Swiss cheese. And yet despite his side's many holes, Ken Kratz overcame his murder case's numerous physical evidence shortcomings thanks to the unbelievable eyewitness testimonies from a number of unscrupulous people who very much had a stake, a big stake, in the desired outcome of an Avery guilty verdict.

December 12, 2016

Two weeks before Christmas, Rahmlow sent a text message to someone he recognized from Making a Murderer. By then, Scott Tadych was happily married to Steven Avery's younger sister, Barb. At the time of Teresa's disappearance, Barb Janda lived in one of the trailers at the Avery Salvage Yard compound, a forty-acre tract out in the middle of nowhere surrounded by large gravel pits. At the time of Teresa's disappearance, Barb and Scott Tadych were steady lovers and she was in the process of getting another divorce, this time from Tom Janda.

After watching Making a Murderer, Rahmlow informed his old acquaintance how "I need to get in touch with one of their lawyers."

Rahmlow explained in his text message to Scott Tadych how he recognized Teresa's vehicle as the one he saw by the old dam, either November 3 or 4. He also remembered having a conversation with a man whose face regularly appeared during the Making a Murderer episodes.

Scott Tadych did not respond.

Rahmlow reached out again, ninety minutes later. The second time, he texted his phone number to Tadych. He wanted to discuss the matter over the phone.

"OK, I will I am really sick now can hardly talk so I will call tomorrow," Tadych texted back.

But Tadych never did call back.

"I did not hear from Mr. Tadych the next day or any other day responsive to my request for attorney contact information for Steven Avery or Brendan Dassey," Rahmlow said. "I received another message from Mr. Tadych on December 19 (2016) at 6:10 p.m., which was not responsive to my request."

There is no doubt in his mind that Rahmlow saw Teresa's RAV4 along the rural stretch of two-lane State Highway 147 near the East Twin River Dam. The turnaround on the highway was barely a mile from Avery Salvage.

A licensed private investigator in Illinois and Wisconsin, James R. Kirby was hired by Kathleen T. Zellner & Associates to investigate Teresa's murder case.

"I requested abandoned and towed vehicle reports for the time period of October 31, 2005 through November 5, 2005, from the following agencies: Mishicot Police Department, Two Rivers Police Department, and the Manitowoc County Sheriff's Department," Kirby said.

This, of course, was the period when Teresa was last seen in Manitowoc County, near Mishicot. On a Saturday morning six days later, under highly suspicious circumstances, her Toyota RAV4 turned up, double parked, on the far back ridge of Avery Salvage, near a row of junked vehicles. The spot of the find bordered the massive sand and gravel pit operated by Joshua Radandt.

The question lingered. Who moved Teresa's SUV to the far outer edge of Avery Salvage? Was it the killer working alone? Was it the killer working in tandem with an accomplice? Or was it somebody affiliated with the volunteer search party? Or was it one of the Manitowoc County Sheriff's deputies?

Incidentally, at the time of her disappearance, Teresa's RAV4 had no front-end damage. This small but critical detail is substantiated by the fact that the missing person fliers made no mention of any broken auto parts or wreckage. But when her sports utility vehicle surfaced on the Avery property, it showed heavy front-end damage. Weirdly, the broken blinker light from the driver's side was neatly tucked away into the rear cargo area of the murdered woman's auto. Why would the killer do something so strange? Of course, the logical scenario was that the killer had nothing to do with moving the vehicle to Avery's property, and that the mishap occurred, late at night, during the clandestine efforts to sneak the vehicle onto the Avery property without Avery or his family members catching on.

In any event, private eye Kirby's inquiry into the RAV4 spotted by Rahmlow on Friday afternoon, November 4, 2005, revealed the "Mishicot Police Department had no responsive records. Based upon the response of Two Rivers Police Department and Manitowoc County Sheriff's Office pursuant to my request, none of these agencies logged an abandoned vehicle on Highway 147 near the East Twin River Bridge."

Obviously, one of the most plausible scenarios for why the police did not log the abandoned vehicle spotted near the Old Dam on Highway 147 in rural Manitowoc County, which was Manitowoc County Sheriff's territory, was because the auto belonged to Teresa, and it got moved as a direct result of Manitowoc County's intercession.

http://wbp.bz/wca

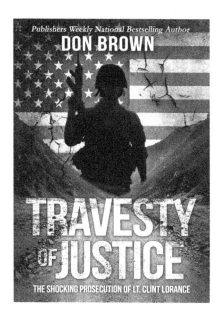
Introduction

.

Landmines,
Suicide Bikers
and the Bloody War in Afghanistan

On July 2, 2012, two days before Independence Day in America, a young Army lieutenant, a decorated member of the elite 82nd Airborne Division, took charge of his platoon in Kandahar Province, Afghanistan. First Lieutenant Clint Lorance was one of the most decorated junior officers in the United States Army.

With an impressive seven Army Achievement Medals on his chest, most of them earned as an enlisted man, Clint had served overseas on two separate tours before Afghanistan. First, he was assigned to the Eighth Army in Korea in Pusan, where he was often near the dangerous and volatile Demilitarized Zone on the border between North and South Korea. After that, he served in Iraq, during the Iraq War, at Forward Operating Base Kalsu, 20 miles south of Baghdad. During his tour in Iraq, Clint's post came under heavy rocket and mortar fire from the enemy on a daily basis. He often led dangerous convoys outside of the post while in Iraq, frequently drawing rocket fire, mortar fire, and gunfire.

Clint put his life on the line for his country. Many soldiers, coming under the type of constant fire that Clint had endured in Iraq, elected to do their time and get out. That is understandable. Combat is a living hell that most Americans will never be forced to witness up close and personal. For those who served and then got out, their service is no less diminished, and should be greatly appreciated by all Americans.

At the end of his dangerous tour in Iraq, Clint could have left the Army. A number of his buddies did. But Clint elected to stay. Service to his country was in his bloodstream and ran through his veins. Clint Lorance wanted to continue to serve, even if it meant giving his life for America.

The Army recognized his hard work, dedication, and service to his country, and offered him the opportunity to earn a commission as an officer. He responded to the challenge, and entered the Army's Green-to-Gold program, competing to become an officer in the United States Army.

Clint excelled in the officer candidate program, soon earned his commission as a second lieutenant in the infantry, and then became a paratrooper in the elite 82nd Airborne Division.

Now, as a young officer, he had been called to serve his country in a third dangerous overseas tour, this time in Afghanistan.

On the morning of July 2nd, Clint had been on the job as platoon leader for only three days when he called his men together at 5:55 a.m. to brief them on the day's mission.

Lorance had been called in to take command of First Platoon, Charlie Company, when the platoon's previous commander, First Lieutenant Dom Latino, was wounded by an exploding improvised exploding device (IED), which blew the hell up when another American soldier stepped on it, a couple of weeks before Clint Lorance would take command. Shrapnel had torn through Latino's face and abdomen, and they rushed him off the battlefield to try and save his life. Like Latino, many of the soldiers in First Platoon had taken a beating from the IEDs. Some were injured, some maimed, others killed.

An IED is a deadly, homemade bomb built by the Taliban, and then hidden in the ground, for the purpose of killing and maiming American soldiers. Between 2008 and 2010, nearly 60 percent of American soldiers who died in Afghanistan were killed by IEDs. Sometimes, these devices were set off remotely, triggered via radio transmitters in the hands of Taliban operatives hiding well out of sight.

Sometimes, a single step on a routine patrol triggered the explosion, as these "pressure plate IEDs" were set off by pressure alone. But whether the IEDs were pressure detonated, or radio triggered, the results proved deadly for American GIs.

In southeastern Afghanistan, where Clint and his men had been deployed, the environment was exceptionally dangerous.

Here's what 4th Brigade Deputy Brigade Commander Col. Scott Halstead, who later testified in the court-martial of Lieutenant Lorance, said, under oath, at trial, about the battlefield conditions in which these paratroopers were operating:

"Zhari/Maiwand (the district in Kandahar province where the platoon operated) is almost entirely—I mean it's a gigantic minefield ... Our paratroopers were, justifiably so, very cautious. They'd seen many of their Ranger buddies killed and maimed."

In addition to mine-ridden battlefields, the Taliban had been employing another terror tactic to kill Americans. A tactic that was impossible to defend against.

Motorcycles.

The Taliban had begun strapping explosives to their bodies, mounting motorcycles, and then charging toward American troops, blowing themselves up at close range. This became known as a "VBIED attack" for Vehicle Borne Improvised Explosive Device. This tactic gave attackers the dual advantage of 1) engaging in Islamic martyrdom, while 2) murdering Americans and anyone who sympathized with Americans. The tactic of mass-murder-by-motorcycle had increased in recent months, and under suicidal rules of engagement employed by the American military in 2012, self-defense against suicide bikers became an impossible choice.

American troops were hand-strapped from firing, unless they could first determine "hostile intent," which normally meant identifying a weapon on the attacker. Then, after determining the presence of "hostile intent," our soldiers had to analyze the enemy for a potential "hostile act."

The American soldier in 2012 was relegated to the role of battlefield lawyer, forced into a series of mental gymnastics to reach a legal conclusion about whether to fire in self-defense. All this in a war-torn battle zone, in a historically war-torn country, in the ancestral home of the Taliban.

But the Americans could not always identify bombs on fast-approaching motorcycles. Nor could they see bombs under the insurgent's shirt, or hidden within the motorcycle. Motorcycles moved too quickly for positive identification of anything, and life or death often hung upon split-second decisions.

Soldiers were trained to fight, not to play lawyer on the battlefield.

A split-second too long of playing lawyer in a barbaric war zone, then deciding at the last second to refrain from firing against a fast-charging motorcycle, could lead to instant carnage, perhaps multiple deaths for American troops in the motorcycle's path.

But as an American soldier, if you opened fire to defend yourself against what looked like an aggressive motorcycle charge coming at your troops at 40 mph, you had better make damn sure the Taliban was armed. Because if you tried to defend yourself and your troops, and those bodies on the ground after an attempt at self-defense in a war zone are not armed, you had better be ready to face the music with your high command.

By 2012, the same question had grown pervasive throughout American forces in Afghanistan. Would the American chain of command have your back?

Would politically correct rules of engagement, designed to appease the ever-complaining Afghan government of Hamid Karzai, be used to keep Americans from protecting themselves? These questions haunted our troops, and they were questions wrought with life-or-death consequences.

This became the impossible dilemma faced by American ground forces in the 11th year of the Afghan war: defend yourself, and hope like hell that they were armed after you fire; or cross your fingers, and pray that they didn't pull guns and spray you with fire as they passed, toss grenades at you, or blow themselves to hell and back and take you and your buddies with them.

The choice was impossible. But this dilemma had come down from the American high command, which seemed to care more about enforcing politically correct rules of engagement than it cared about the lives of its men.

Even in the weeks before Lieutenant Lorance take over at First Platoon, the Taliban had carried out several high-profile suicide attacks by motorcycle in Afghanistan.

On April 12, 2012, seven American soldiers, members of the Ohio National Guard, had come off the battlefield and retreated into the city of Maimanah, the capital of Farayab Province. They needed respite from the savage war, and visited a park in a more peaceful area of northern Afghanistan.

But in Afghanistan, no place is off limits to the Taliban.

Striking with the surprise of a sudden lightning bolt, their Taliban attacker, mounted on a fast-moving motorcycle, struck out of the blue, a fast-moving human bomb. The explosion killed 10 people, including several of the principal targets, three American soldiers.

Master Sergeant Sgt. Hannon, who died that day, worked for the Department of Veterans Affairs back home as a lawyer serving veterans. With a heart for those who served, including the aging World War II vets, Shawn helped them with their legal needs, putting together wills and health care directives, and giving them advice. Though he could have made tons of money at a private firm, he gave his life to veterans. He was also a great soldier, had been wounded on previous deployment and received the Purple Heart. "If somebody in the world needed help, he'd be there," one of his co-workers told the *Military Times*. Shawn left behind a wife, Jamie, and a son, Evan, who was 9 months old.

Master Sgt. Jeffrey J. Rieck left behind a 15-year-old son, Joel. At a military funeral in Columbus 12 days after the fatal motorcycle attack, Joel accepted the American flag that had been draped on his father's casket from Maj. Gen.

Deborah Ashenhurst, the Ohio Guard's commanding officer, who knelt before the boy on one knee.

Capt. Nick Rozanzki, 36, had been married to Jennifer for five years. Their two young daughters are Emma Kathryn and Anna Elizabeth. Nick had been a marathon runner, and an avid soccer player and coach. Volunteering large amounts of time to young people, Nick coached for 15 years for Eagles Soccer Club.

In that one motorcycle attack, two wives lost their husbands, and four children lost their fathers.

The Army calls the weapon that killed these men a "suicide vehicle-borne improvised explosive device." Translated from military-ese to English, it means "motorcycle with a bomb, and impossible to detect before it blows the hell up."

On June 6, 2012, three weeks before Lt. Lorance took over First Platoon, the Taliban carried out another motorcycle attack, this time outside the Kandahar Air Field used by the U.S. Air Force to keep logistics, supplies and reinforcements supplied to the U.S. Army. The suicide motorcyclist charged into a populated area often frequented by American troops.

The massive explosion killed 22 people, and wounded 50. Fortunately, no Americans were in the crowd at the time of the attack, and the "talibiker" killed mostly civilians. But the bloody carnage sent a clear message to all: "If you are an American soldier, or if you work with or near American servicemen, you are a target."

The increase in suicide-bomb-by-motorcycle had sent shock waves throughout U.S. forces in Afghanistan. Against this backdrop, Clint Lorance took command of his platoon on June 29, 2012, determined that none of his boys would be shipped home in body bags. In that noble cause, the lieutenant would succeed.

But it would cost him his freedom.

Chapter 1

"All rise!"

The military judge, Col. Kirsten V.C. Brunson, U.S. Army, Judge Advocate General's Corps, cloaked in a black robe, stepped into the courtroom and surveyed the scene before her. It had been a long trial, and now, the military jury was about to render its verdict.

Under the soft-white glow of four massive globe lights hanging from the ceiling, the courtroom was packed with a small army of military officers, civilian court personnel, and civilian onlookers. Every face was tense, every eye glued on the judge. The silence, broken only by the solitary cry of the bailiff, was deafening.

Stately dark mahogany desks and barrister rails set against the red burgundy carpet provided a stark contrast to the red-hot tension that now filled the room.

To Judge Brunson's left, when facing the front of the courtroom and the large dark paneled "bench" where the judge is seated, the military jury, or "members" as they are called in the military justice system, had taken their places. Some glanced at the accused. Others looked away, to deliberately avoid eye contact.

"Please be seated."

Col. Brunson was one of the Army's best trial judges. Prior to taking the bench, she had served as the Army JAG Corps' regional defense counsel, managing dozens of junior defense counsel over a large swath of the United States.

She had been in this very courtroom many times, but never had the suspense matched this moment. Never had the drama boiled over into the hot anticipation that the next few moments would bring.

Fort Bragg, home of the Army's elite 82nd Airborne Division, the U.S Army Special Operations Command, and the U.S. Army Special Forces Command, was considered its most strategically important military installation. From here, American Green Berets had launched some of the most important clandestine missions in the nation's history. From here, the famed 82nd Airborne Division had deployed many times in defense of the nation—to Normandy, Market Garden in Holland, the Battle of the Bulge, Vietnam, Grenada, Iraq, and Afghanistan.

From Fort Bragg, legendary Delta Force commanders including Col. Charlie Beckwith, Lt. Gen. Jerry Boykin, and Maj. Gen. Bill Garrison had launched clandestine missions all over the world, supporting American interests, from Southeast Asia to Colombia, from Saudi Arabia to Somalia, or any other spot on the globe requiring rapid-response counter-insurgency.

But Fort Bragg was also noted for another, less heroic reason, one the Army would rather blot from the public's memory.

Several of the most publicized military crimes in American history happened on this post. Forty-three years previously, in the most notorious murder case in Fort Bragg history, Green Beret Capt. Jeffrey MacDonald, an Army doctor, was accused of stabbing his wife, Colette, and two young daughters, Kimberly and Kristen, with an ice pick. Their bodies were found in officer housing on Castle Drive. MacDonald had been stabbed, too, in the ribcage, and blamed the crime on drug-crazed hippies. MacDonald's wounds were determined to be self-inflicted, and a federal jury convicted him of triple homicide, of killing his wife and two daughters.

Then came the notorious domestic-murder spree of the summer of 2002, when four Fort Bragg soldiers killed their wives in a period of six weeks. Two were murder-suicides with a gun. A third soldier stabbed his wife 50 times. The fourth strangled his wife to death. These crimes were carried out by some of the Army's most elite, Special Forces soldiers. Three of the four had just returned from Afghanistan at the time of the murders.

By August of 2013, the memories of these gruesome acts had faded. The MacDonald quarters, preserved many years as a crime scene, was destroyed to make room for a more modern post housing development. Three of the four soldiers from the "Summer of 2002" murder spree were dead. The fourth was imprisoned and incarcerated for his crimes.

Now, all these years later, as Judge Brunson looked out over her courtroom, another soldier in a high-profile case was about to face the verdict of the military justice system. The charges: attempted murder and murder.

First Lt. Clint Lorance, 28 years old, a decorated officer in the elite 82nd Airborne Division, sat at counsel table in his Army service dress blue uniform, moments from his fate. If he felt any fear about what the jury was about to say, his face didn't show it.

While the Lorance case was another in a historical string of high-profile murder prosecutions at Fort Bragg, the facts underlying Clint Lorance's prosecution were different from the others. Very different.

Capt. MacDonald was convicted of stabbing his wife and daughters with an ice pick. The soldiers in the 2002 murder sprees used pistols, knives, and physical strangulation by hand. In contrast, Lt. Clint Lorance never touched a murder weapon, never pulled a trigger, never laid a finger on the men he was accused of killing, and never even saw an alleged victim. Still, the Army had charged him with attempted murder and double murder.

Lorance, the prosecutors claimed, ordered men in his platoon to fire on a motorcycle in a Taliban-invested battle zone in southeastern Afghanistan. At the time of the order, the motorcycle had charged his platoon at a high rate of speed, on a rural dirt road that had been controlled by Taliban forces. Both sides of the road had coiled barbed wire to prevent anyone from entering it.

Signs were placed, in English and Afghan, restricting the roads in the area to only police and military. But coming down a road controlled by the Taliban, the motorcycle kept speeding toward the point where lead elements of the American platoon crossed the road. And, there was not one rider on the motorcycle. There were not two riders on it. But rather, there were three riders on the single red motorcycle.

Lorance knew that the Taliban had used motorcycles as a weapon in suicide missions to blow up Americans in blood-strewn carnages. The prior incidents at Kandahar Airfield and the "talibiker" attack in Farayab Provence provided evidence of the Taliban's suicide-by-motorcycle tactics.

In addition, the month before Lorance arrived, in June of 2012, First Platoon had been battered by the enemy. Four of its 40 men were killed or seriously wounded by land mines, IEDs, or rifle fire. Unidentified and unseen Taliban snipers had fired on the platoon every day. The casualties were so bad, and the landmines so thick, that at the end of June, the Army had pulled First Platoon back off the battlefield for five days for emotional counseling and therapy away from the fighting, and to spend time with "combat stress specialists."

Now, First Platoon had returned to the battlefront, with Lt. Lorance as its new leader. Under the most difficult, dangerous and bloody circumstances imaginable, Clint Lorance's main goal was to keep his men out of body bags, and to keep them from losing limbs and becoming bloody human stumps. American soldiers had suffered enough carnage.

The morning of July 2 promised more burning heat. The searing temperatures, which had eclipsed 100 degrees for 26 out of the last 30 days, had reached 100 degrees by 6 a.m., nearly an hour before they pushed off on their patrol.

After Lt. Lorance conducted his pre-mission briefing around 6:30 a.m., at 6:55 a.m., the platoon left its post on an armed patrol through rows of grape fields and into a Taliban-infested village.

Because the landmines were thick, they were forced to move out from their post in a tight single file, one man behind the other, with mine sweepers out front to detect for lethal bombs in the ground. A step too far to the left or to the right could set off IEDs powerful enough to take out multiple men in a single blast. The plan called for them to move out from their forward operating base, to the west, first through heavily vegetated grape fields, where visibility proved difficult.

They would move through the grape berms for several hundred yards, then turn north, cutting across the grape rows into the small village, known as Sarenzai, where they would move through the back of mud-hut building and then turn and move along the single dirt road through the village. There, they would sweep the village for Taliban operatives, before turning right on the dirt road to head back to their post. Their march pattern resembled a giant fishhook, out into the fields, then looping up into the village, then the spear of the platoon hooking back to the right, down the main road, back toward base.

That was the plan, anyway.

On the route planned for the morning of July 2, the men of First Platoon would cross over much of the same ground that had gotten so many Americans killed or mutilated in recent days. Even after five days of respite and counseling for combat fatigue, that thought loomed at the forefront of their minds as they prepared to return to Taliban country.

Trouble did not procrastinate.

About 10 minutes into their hot patrol, as lead elements of the platoon reached the main road of the village, an emergency call came to Lt. Lorance by radio. Military-aged males with motorcycles were gathering on the far side of the village.

Then, a fast-moving motorcycle appeared. It approached in-bound on the restricted road controlled by the Taliban, closing on their position along the road where his platoon was emerging from the grape fields, and visible to only the Afghans in the lead and the few forward American soldiers.

Lt. Lorance could not see the motorcycle, but one of his paratroopers called out to warn him.

There was no time for debate. No time for introspection or battlefield lawyering. No time to conduct a legal balancing test on whether to use force.

Lorance had to make a split-second decision. Delay could mean death.

Either protect his troops, or cross his fingers and hope that the insurgents on the motorcycle were Santa's helpers from the North Pole, bearing lollypops and candy canes for an early-morning snack for his soldiers as a midsummer's treat. Unable to see the motorcycle himself, his view obstructed by grape berm, and with a split-second of time available to him, in the most Taliban-infested place in the world, Clint ordered his men to open fire. The Afghan National Forces, who were with the American platoon on patrol that morning, also opened fire on the motorcycle.

A shower of bullets rained down on the insurgents, killing two of the three riders. The third rider escaped off into the village, and was never captured.

But when the military found no weapons on the dead riders, Army officials decided to prosecute Clint Lorance for murder, arguing that he had violated the rules of engagement.

It's possible that the bike was strapped with explosives. We will never know. The locals took the bike off the street before the Army could secure it. The Army never recovered the motorcycle.

And now, his court-martial having been completed, First Lt. Lorance would meet his fate.

Inside the new courthouse facility, with Georgian red-brick façade and four towering stark-white columns out front, all eyes were riveted upon the military judge and jury.

Military Judge: "The court is called to order. All parties are again present as before to include the court members. Col. Gabel, has the court reached findings?"

President of the Court Martial (Col. Gabel): "We have, Your Honor."

Military Judge: "And are those reflected on the Findings Worksheet?"

President of the Court Martial (Col. Gabel): "They are, Your Honor."

Military Judge: "Would you please fold that in half and hand it to the bailiff so I can examine it?"

The bailiff retrieved the document from Col. Gabel and handed it to the military judge.

Military Judge: "Please return that to the president."

The bailiff did as directed and returned the document to the president of the court-martial, the military's equivalent to the foreman of the jury.

Military Judge: "The findings appear to be in the proper form. Accused and defense counsel, please rise."

Lorance stood. And as he did, his silver paratroopers' wings, set off against the dark navy blue of his uniform jacket, glistened under the courtroom lights. Below his jump wings were impressive rows of green, orange, red and yellow medals telling the history of his service to his country.

The boyish look on Clint's face contrasted against the erect military bearing that he bore. With four gold buttons lined in a vertical row down the front of his dark-blue jacket, Clint Lorance could have made the cover of an Army recruiting poster. He looked the part, bore the part, and wore the part.

The sharp military appearance was not all that set Lorance apart. For a young officer, who began his career as an enlisted man, Lorance's achievements to date had been spectacular. A quick perusal of his "salad row" showed that he had earned an impressive seven green-and-blue Army Achievement medals, all accumulated in fewer than five years of service.

On top of that, he had been awarded two of the more prestigious dark green-and-white Army Commendation Medals for meritorious service. Perhaps in a dose of unexplainable irony, the most recent Army Commendation Medal had been awarded for the period of time in which Lt. Lorance was charged with attempted murder and double murder.

The medals on his Lorance's chest proclaimed one truth: this officer was a star among his peers. But none of that mattered now. Not if the Army, and not if his country turned on him in this momentous hour.

Military Judge: "Col. Gabel, please announce the findings of the court."

President of the Court Martial: "First Lt. Clint A. Lorance, United States Army, this court-martial finds you— on the charge of attempted murder—guilty. On the charge of double murder—guilty."

http://wbp.bz/toja

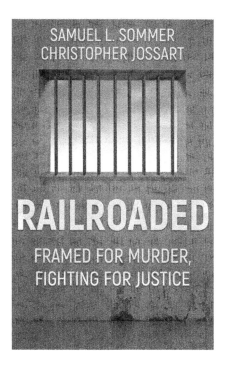

Within moments after pulling into a donut shop parking lot to meet, Sam is kidnapped by detectives with the engine still running. While held in custody, he is beaten and allegedly confesses to the murder.

Court proceedings amount to do-overs, appellate victories and overturns, and mysterious documents. Sam is found guilty of murder in 1971. Within short order, his case is highlighted in college law courses.

After surviving years of power-hungry guards and moving often from prison to prison for good behavior, Sam is released on parole in 1991. Justice continued to railroad him until 2015 when he finds an eerie document in the police archives that proves his innocence. That discovery triggered the re-opening of his case and free legal assistance. What will a momentous turn of events bring next?

http://wbp.bz/railroadeda

See even more at:
http://wbp.bz/tc

More True Crime You'll Love From WildBlue Press

A MURDER IN MY HOMETOWN by Rebecca Morris
Nearly 50 years after the murder of seventeen year old Dick Kitchel, Rebecca Morris returned to her hometown to write about how the murder changed a town, a school, and the lives of his friends.

wbp.bz/hometowna

THE BEAST I LOVED by Robert Davidson
Robert Davidson again demonstrates that he is a master of psychological horror in this riveting and hypnotic story ... I was so enthralled that I finished the book in a single sitting. "—James Byron Huggins, International Bestselling Author of The Reckoning
wbp.bz/tbila

BULLIED TO DEATH by Judith A. Yates
On September 5, 2015, in a public park in LaVergne, Tennessee, fourteen-year-old Sherokee Harriman drove a kitchen knife into her stomach as other teens watched in horror. Despite attempts to save her, the girl died, and the coroner ruled it a "suicide." But was it? Or was it a crime perpetuated by other teens who had bullied her?
wbp.bz/btda

SUMMARY EXECUTION by Michael Withey
"An incredible true story that reads like an international crime thriller peopled with assassins, political activists, shady FBI informants, murdered witnesses, a tenacious attorney, and a murderous foreign dictator."—Steve Jackson, New York Times bestselling author of NO STONE UNTURNED
wbp.bz/sea

Made in the USA
Monee, IL
01 May 2020

28196341R00213